IMAGES
of America

THE CHEROKEE NATION AND TAHLEQUAH

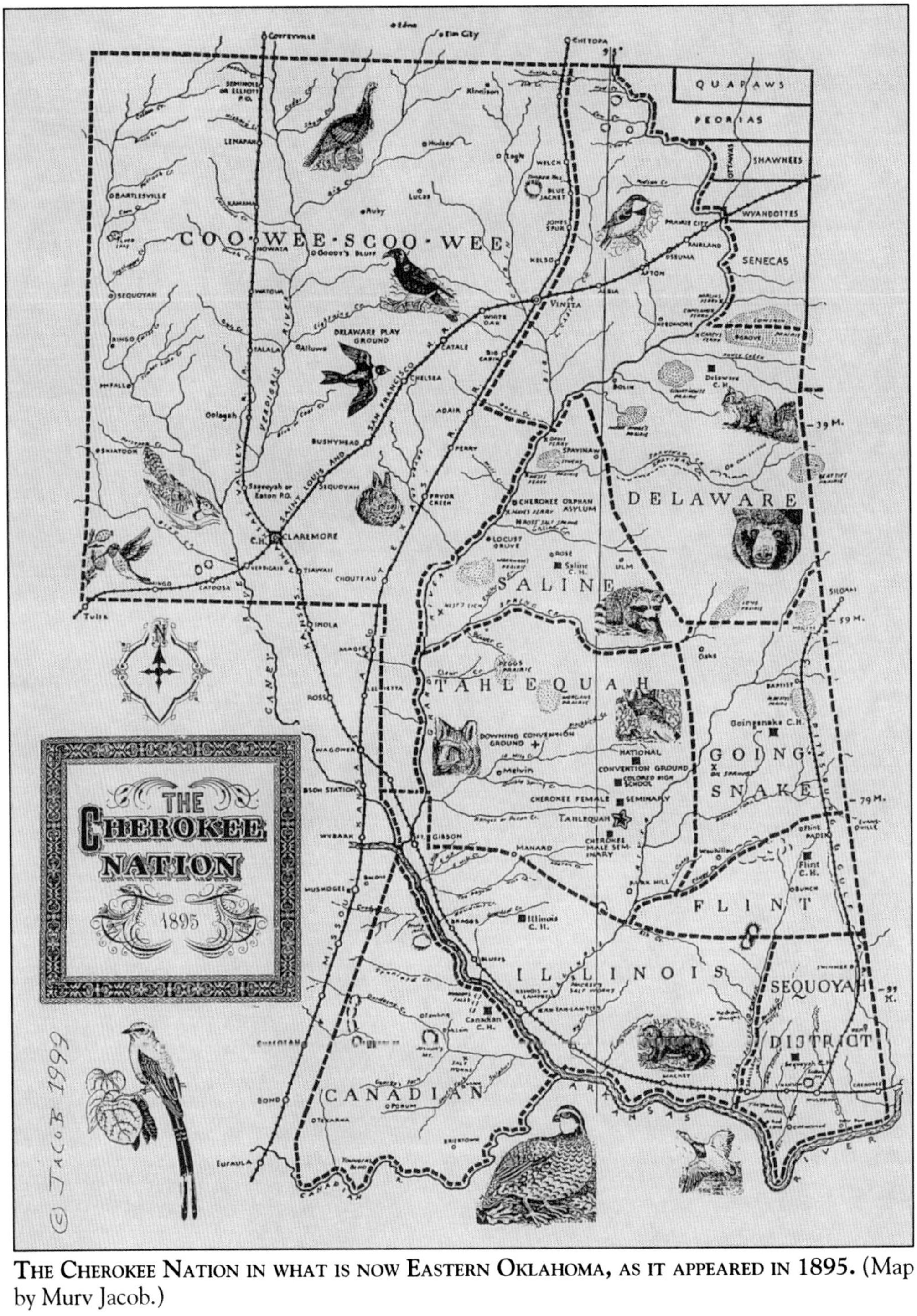

THE CHEROKEE NATION IN WHAT IS NOW EASTERN OKLAHOMA, AS IT APPEARED IN 1895. (Map by Murv Jacob.)

IMAGES
of America

The Cherokee Nation and Tahlequah

Deborah L. Duvall

ARCADIA
PUBLISHING

ISBN 978-0-7385-0289-2

Published by Arcadia Publishing
Charleston, South Carolina

Printed in the United States of America

For all general information contact Arcadia Publishing at:
Telephone 843-853-2070
Fax 843-853-0044
E-mail sales@arcadiapublishing.com
For customer service and orders:
Toll-Free 1-888-313-2665

Visit us on the Internet at www.arcadiapublishing.com

This book is dedicated to Oklahoma's "Red Dirt" songwriters.

Contents

Acknowledgments

For their generous contributions to this collection, special thanks go out to the Cherokee National Museum and Archives, Sioux and Raymond Vann, Lisa LaRue Tennison, the Sequoyah County Historical Society and its director Earl Strebeck, Brenda Carpenter, Ralph and Loretta Dunham, the Will Rogers Memorial and its archivist-librarian Pat Lowe, Rogers State College, Lena Fourkiller, Duane and Tammy Canada, Betty Holcomb, Roy Hamilton and the Christie family, Robert and Evelyn Conley, Lena Fourkiller, the Cherokee Honor Society, photographers Sammy Still and Bobby Watkins, the Cherokee Studies Institute and Jean Gilmore, Denyce Dunham and Joel Mayes Finch, Sally Sanders Finch and the Mayes descendants, Gayle Ross, the Murrell Home's director Shirley Pettengill, Hank Baker, Charles Banks Wilson, and historical researchers Murv Jacob and Knokovtee Scott. Resource materials include *Among the Cherokees* by Dub West, *The Cherokee Nation of Indians* by Charles C. Royce, *John Ross Cherokee Chief* by Gary E. Moulton, *The Cherokees* by Grace Steele Woodward, *Tahlequah, NSU, and the Cherokees* by Odie B. Faulk and Billy Mac Jones, *Will Rogers Official Genealogy and Bibliography* by Pat Lowe, *The Old Home Ranch: Birthplace of Will Rogers* by Ellsworth Collins, *Will Rogers—Oklahoma's Gift to America* by Dub West, *Roadside History of Oklahoma* by Francis and Roberta Fugate, and *A Brief History of the Cherokees, 1540–1906* by Mary Evelyn Rogers. Wa-do!

INTRODUCTION

According to legend, the Real People, or Cherokees, came from the sky vault to live on the Earth after Buzzard had prepared the land for their habitation. Here they lived in peace with the birds and animals for many years. Then the people began to use weapons to kill the animals for their meat and hides, until at last the animals sought a method of defense against them. Together the animals made diseases that would strike down the people and lead to their destruction. But the plants of the Earth took pity on the Real People. They vowed to provide a cure for every disease brought on by the animals. Wise medicine men and women studied the plants and herbs and have passed down those cures through generations of their descendants.

Some historians believe the Cherokees branched off from the Iroquois Indians about 2,000 years ago. In pre-Columbian times, the Cherokees were a fierce and war-like race whose villages could be found from the buffalo prairies of Kentucky to the savannahs of Georgia, and from the mountains of Virginia to the hills of Alabama. The central village was located in western North Carolina and was called Keetoowah.

Within the tribe, the people were divided into seven clans. It was forbidden for two people from the same clan to marry. A child was taken into the clan to which the mother belonged. Strict adherence to the clan structure insured children who were mentally and physically strong. The clans date to the days of legend, when it is said that there were originally eight clans, but one broke away from the tribe and went off to the woods to become the Bear people. The seven remaining clans still exist today. Their names are Wolf, Deer, Bird, Paint, Blue, Wild Potato, and Long Hair. At ceremonial grounds, seven arbors, one for each clan, surround the sacred fire. Those who have clan affiliation through their mothers are allowed to sit beneath the respective arbors.

Wars were fought with European invaders and neighboring tribes whose villages were interspersed with those of the Cherokees. Villages were positioned along an ancient trail that ran from Georgia to Kentucky and was used by the woods bison as a migratory route. When an attack on a settlement occurred, runners would follow this trail to warn and prepare the other Cherokee villages for battle. The phrase "on the war path" has as its origin references to this trail.

Only those Cherokees who chose to be warriors were called on to fight in wars. Often disputes between Indians resulted from warriors stealing women from another tribe. This practice was used to alter the gene pool, thereby strengthening the tribe. Even so, those caught in the act faced certain death by torture at the hands of the other women of the village.

As colonial interests grew along the eastern coast, the Cherokees were forced farther inland. Smaller coastal tribes came to the Cherokees for sanctuary and were adopted into the tribe, the men into the Wolf Clan and the women into the Bird Clan. The powerful Wolf Clan guarded the passes and for 150 years held the lands safe from invaders.

The British maintained penal colonies in Georgia and the Carolinas. Young soldiers, some officers from noble Scottish and Irish families sent to guard the prisoners, were among the first whites to marry into the Cherokee tribe. The ships carrying prisoners also carried smallpox to the Cherokee villages. Over half their number was lost to this disease. The Cherokees had treaties with the British. They did not recognize the authority of the newly formed states that sprang from the British criminal tribes who rebelled against the English crown. The states drew their boundaries right around the Cherokee settlements and began to claim tribal lands.

This onslaught of land-hungry whites caused numerous Cherokees to move west as early as 1800. The Old Settlers, as they came to be called, first moved to Arkansas, an area where hunting parties had often traveled. The great Shawnee leader Tecumseh located the Old Settlers, along with other southeastern Indians who were migrating westward, and attempted to unite them to fight the whites for their homelands. Tecumseh's brother "the prophet" warned that unless they joined in the fight, Tecumseh would "stamp his foot." Soon after, a frightful earthquake struck the area and many moved still farther west. Facing continual pressure from whites, the Old Settlers pushed on into western Arkansas and the Indian Territory of what is now Oklahoma. They began to build homes and work the land.

The constant struggle with the whites for Cherokee land led to a division in tribal leadership in the southeast. A small group formed the Treaty party and favored moving the Cherokees west and out of the way of the United States. But the vast majority sided with Principal Chief John Ross and refused to back down to the demands of the states.

In 1835, a dozen members of the Treaty party secretly signed a treaty that agreed to the removal of the Cherokee people from their homes. In December of that year, barely 100 persons from the Treaty party signed the Treaty of New Echota. The treaty relinquished to the United States all the land owned by the Cherokee Nation east of the Mississippi River. For this the Cherokees were to receive $5 million and a large tract of the western lands already partially occupied by the Old Settlers. By signing the treaty, the party invoked the ancient "blood law" of the Cherokees, which named death the consequence for selling Cherokee lands. This faction moved as agreed to Indian Territory.

The idea of removal of the southeastern Indians to the West was first introduced by Thomas Jefferson. The final removal was carried out by President VanBuren, but his predecessor Andrew Jackson initiated, orchestrated, and insisted on it. Jackson was called "Old Hickory" by the whites but was known as "Chicken Snake" to the Cherokees. Jackson's promise to the southeastern Indians was that their new lands in the West would belong to them "as long as the grass grows and the water flows."

The southeastern Cherokees continued to fight for ownership of their homeland. But after a bitter and trying three years of negotiation, Gen. Winfield Scott and the Army of the Potomac were ordered to round up the Cherokee people and drive them from their homes. Afterward Scott referred to the removal as "the worst bit of work I'd ever been forced to do."

Although some wealthy Cherokees traveled in comfort to the West, most of the people were confined in stockades and then driven over a miserable trek that will forever be known as the Trail of Tears. Some followed various routes across land, while others took the treacherous journey up the Arkansas River. Many died along the way, including Quatie Ross, the wife of Principal Chief John Ross.

The infamous removal of the Five Civilized Tribes from their southeastern homelands was abhorred by many prominent citizens of the United States. The famed author Henry David Thoreau, in protest, refused to pay income taxes to the federal government and was imprisoned. A visiting friend reportedly asked of him, "What are you doing in here?" Thoreau replied, "The question should be, what are you doing out there?"

Reunited with the Old Settlers and the Treaty party in Indian Territory, the Cherokees remained divided into factions. Three signers of the Treaty of New Echota, Major Ridge, John Ridge, and Elias Boudinot, met with death as the directive of the blood law was carried out. Sequoyah, inventor of the Cherokee syllabary who had moved west ahead of his brethren, helped to work through the tensions of that turbulent time. What followed was a period of growth as towns sprang up and life resumed.

The Civil War brought with it more strife and division for the Cherokees. Wealthy ranchers and plantation owners considered themselves as Southerners and were reluctant to lose their slaves. Agents of the Confederacy offered them a good deal if they would help to fight the Union. The Nighthawk Society of traditionalists formed, and its followers sided with the North. A main concern of the Nighthawk Keetoowahs was the abolition of slavery. Chief John Ross and his party chose to remain neutral and let the whites fight their own battles. In many families, the war pitted brother against brother. Cherokee Brig. Gen. Stand Watie was the last Confederate general to surrender, months after the Civil War finally ended.

War left the Cherokee people with widespread devastation and continued division. Still more white settlers and entrepreneurs wanted access to the land, and federal laws prohibited any real control by the Cherokees. Eventually the confusion this caused throughout Indian Territory led to the formation of the Dawes Commission, a federal plan to manipulate and remove control of the lands of the Five Civilized Tribes—Cherokee, Choctaw, Chickasaw, Creek, and Seminole. It was several years before plans were finalized. At first the people as a whole rebelled against the idea of dividing the land. But as the years passed, some leaders began to feel that there was no choice but to work with the federal agencies.

Thus it was that, in 1906, the final roll of the Dawes Commission Act was taken. Cherokee people whose names appeared on that roll were living within the boundaries of the Cherokee Nation in Indian Territory at that time. Each eligible person could receive an acreage of allotted land, but there were many who distrusted the federal government and refused to sign the rolls. To some, this division of the common land evoked the Cherokee blood law. The great traditional leader Redbird Smith was taken in chains in a wagon and forced to sign the Dawes roll at gunpoint. People who had outstanding arrest warrants were jailed when they attempted to sign, and others fearing arrest would not come forward. Still others who were quarantined with illnesses were left out.

Seeing an opportunity to capitalize on the allotment, unscrupulous whites pretending to be of Indian blood applied to receive land designated for members of the Five Civilized Tribes. It is estimated that some 100,000 people in Indian Territory were eligible for land. Over 300,000 showed up at enrollment centers before the rolls of the Five Tribes were closed. Cherokees who had reported blood quantum of greater than one quarter were assigned a guardian to oversee their affairs, as they were deemed incapable of handling their own property. Following the land allotment, the busiest federal court in the nation was the court in Muskogee, handling lawsuits between Indians and the guardians of their lands.

The Dawes Commission Act of 1906 is considered by some as one of the biggest land swindles of all time. Ironically, the requirement for membership in the modern Cherokee Nation in Oklahoma is to have a direct ancestor who signed the Dawes Commission Roll.

In November 1907, Oklahoma became a state. The Cherokee Nation comprised 14 counties that lie in the far northeastern corner of Oklahoma. After statehood, the Cherokees turned their energies toward citizenship and building progressive communities within their nation. But even in modern times, tradition continues to thrive. Cherokees are committed to preserving their rich heritage. There are many speakers and teachers of the language, the ancient arts and crafts are still being produced, and traditional ceremonies and celebrations continue to be observed at sacred sites throughout the Cherokee Nation.

The images in this volume date from the late 1800s and portray the resilience, courage, and accomplishments of the great Cherokee Nation. Their history is a compelling chapter of the American saga. May we forever take its lessons to heart.

One

FAMILY

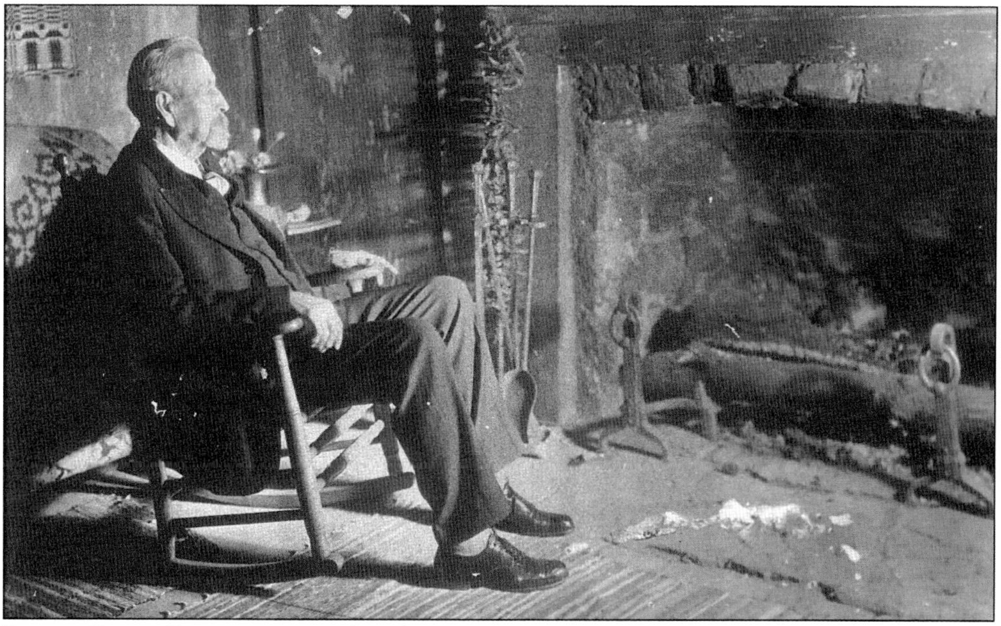

ROBERT BRUCE ROSS, C. 1930. This photograph was taken at the John Ross home in Rossville, Georgia, as Robert Bruce Ross, the chief's grandson, sat in reflection before the fireplace. Principal Chief John Ross lived here before the forced removal of the Cherokee Nation. Robert Bruce Ross traveled to Rossville to host the dedication ceremonies naming Ross Landing as an official historic site. Born August 13, 1845, Robert attended Tahlequah's first public school and the Cherokee Male Seminary. He served in the Third Regiment of the Union Army. Following the Civil War, Robert Ross became involved in Cherokee government. He served three terms as sheriff and as a member of council in 1875 from the Tahlequah District. He was a Cherokee Nation senator for three years and a delegate to Washington in 1882. He chaired the delegation that negotiated the terms of allotment with the Dawes Commission and was appointed postmaster by Theodore Roosevelt. He shares the Ross legacy with numerous relatives and descendants. (Courtesy of Cherokee National Archives.)

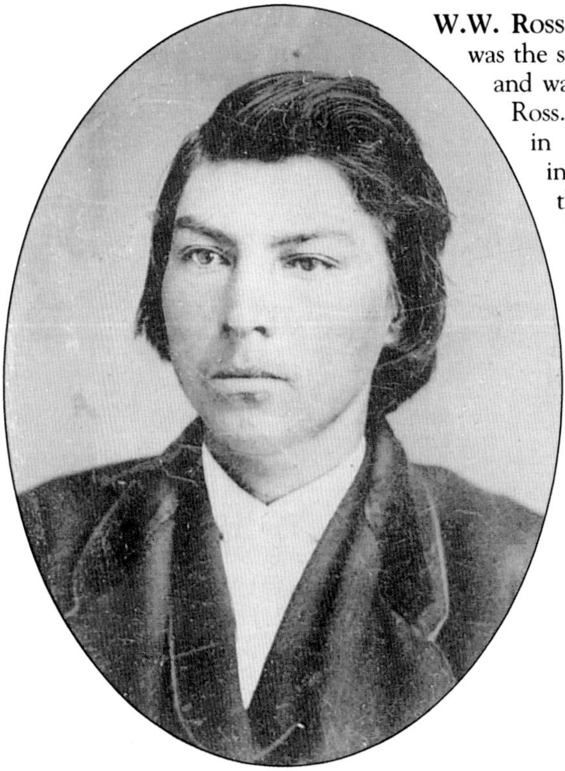

W.W. Ross, May 8, 1871. William Wallace Ross was the son of Allen Ross and Jennie Fields Ross and was the grandson of Principal Chief John Ross. The Ross family was almost like royalty in the Cherokee Nation and especially in Park Hill, the cultural center before the Civil War. (Courtesy of Cherokee National Archives.)

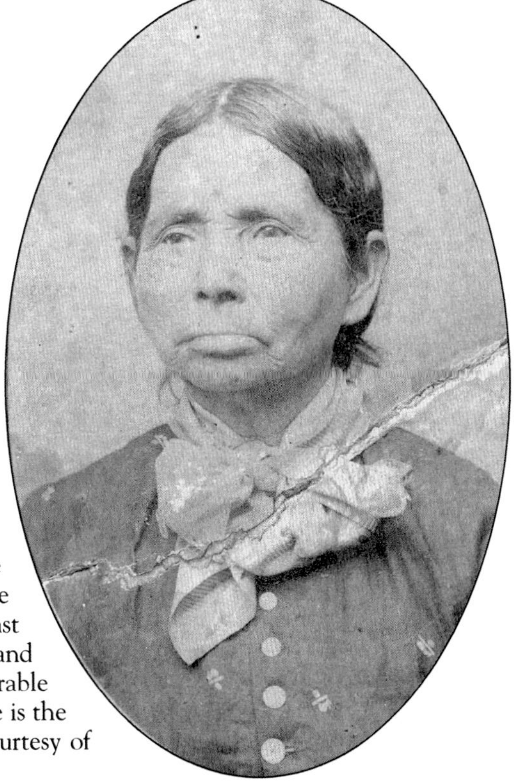

Annie Fields Ballard, c. 1860. The spirit and tenacity of the Cherokees appears on the face of Annie Fields Ballard, a survivor of the Trail of Tears. Many women in the southeast were taken at gunpoint from their homes and forced to walk hundreds of miles under miserable conditions to a new home in the West. Annie is the grandmother of Archable Leroy Ballard. (Courtesy of Cherokee National Archives.)

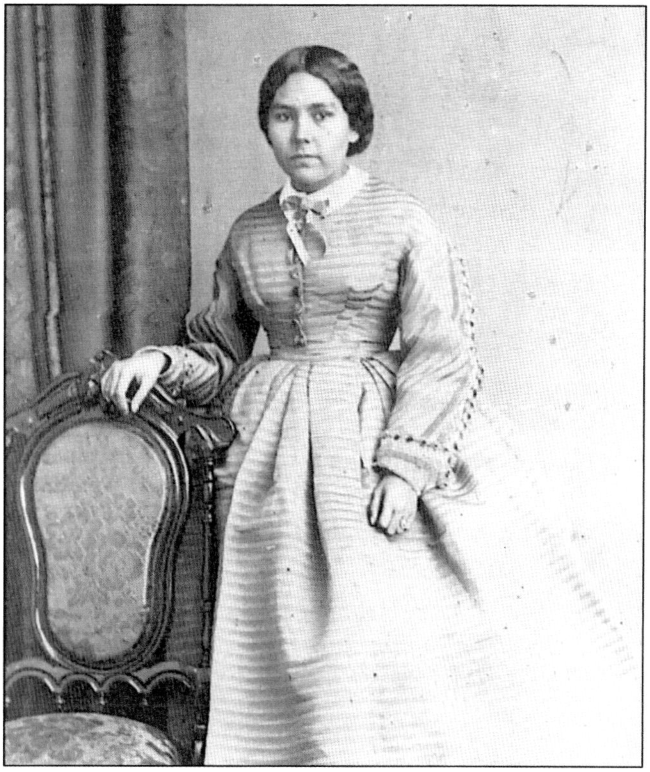

JENNIE MURRELL, C. 1860. Jennie Pocahontas Ross was born in 1833, the only daughter of Andrew and Susan Lowery Ross. Andrew was the nephew of Principal Chief John Ross. Jennie was raised and educated by the George Murrell family after her father's death. She attended the original female seminary at Park Hill and later was a teacher. Jennie married John Dobbins Murrell, George Murrell's nephew. (Courtesy of Cherokee National Archives.)

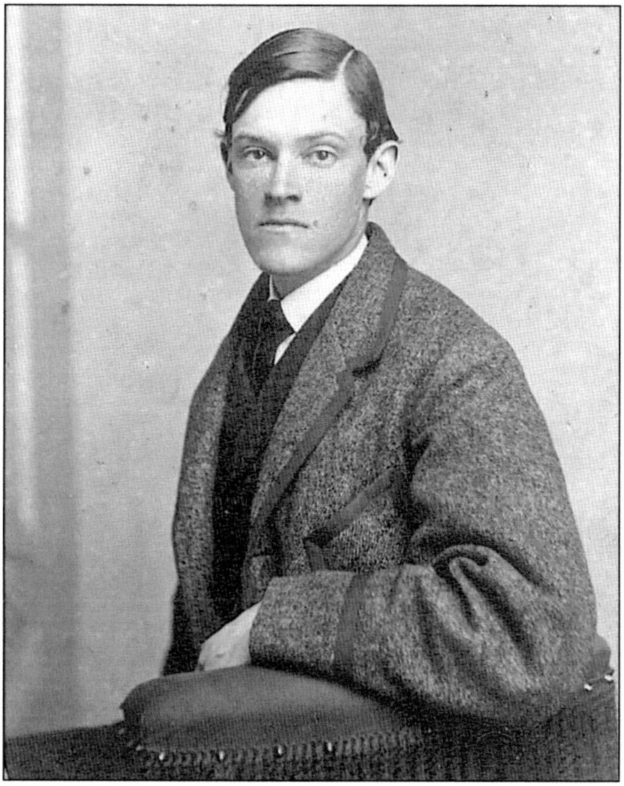

POPE FIELDING MEIGS, C. 1860. Meigs was an eastern relative of Jane Meigs Nave. During the Civil War, some of the Southern sympathizers who owned fine homes in the Cherokee Nation had no choice but to leave them and return to the safety of their families in the East. The Meigs family collected this photograph of their New York relative when Jane went there to stay. (Courtesy of Cherokee National Archives.)

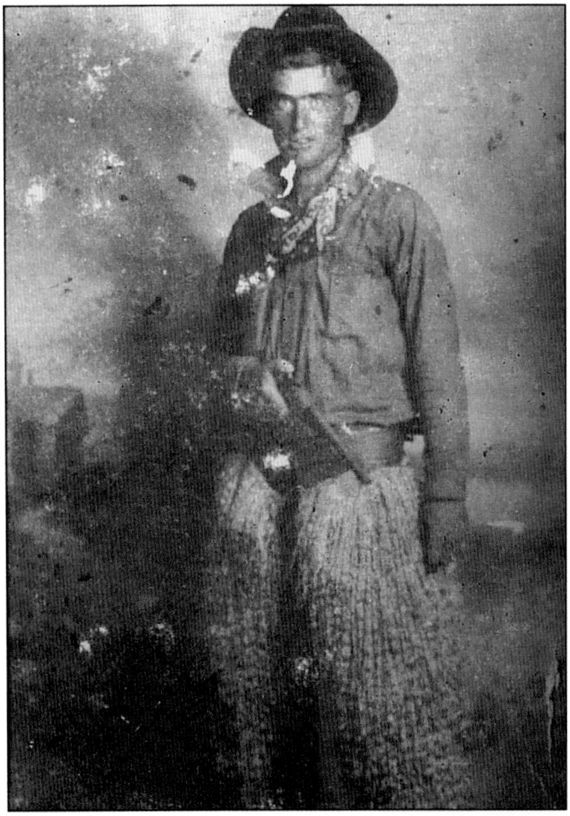

Julius Smith, Age 18, c. 1910. Julius proudly poses with his pistol in hand and wearing fine woolen chaps and cowboy attire. He was an original enrollee on the Dawes Commission Roll at number 428. In 1923, Julius married Emma Louise Rushing of Briar Town. The couple had 18 children, many of whom are current members of the Cherokee Nation. (Courtesy of daughters Dorothy June Smith-Nicholas and Sioux Nell Smith-Vann.)

The Smith Family Home, c. 1905. William S. Smith, a real Texas cowboy, built this home for his wife, Simmie Robbins Smith, on her allotted land. All but two of their 13 children were born in the home, located northeast of Porum, Oklahoma. William worked as a trail driver, herding cattle from Texas to Kansas. (Courtesy of Dorothy June Smith-Nicholas and Sioux Nell Smith-Vann.)

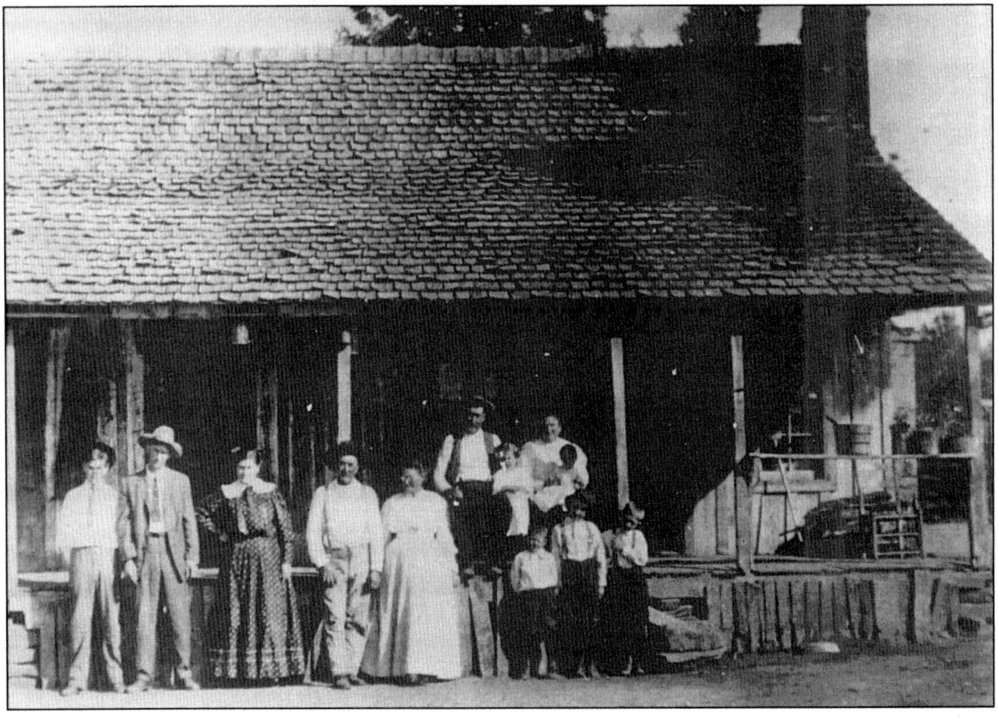

PEEKSABOVE WOLF, LATE 1800S. Pictured here in leg irons, Peeksabove Wolf was also known as Little Arch Christie. Wolf was a relative of Cherokee patriot Ned Christie. Family members today speak fondly of his memory. (Courtesy of Cherokee National Archives.)

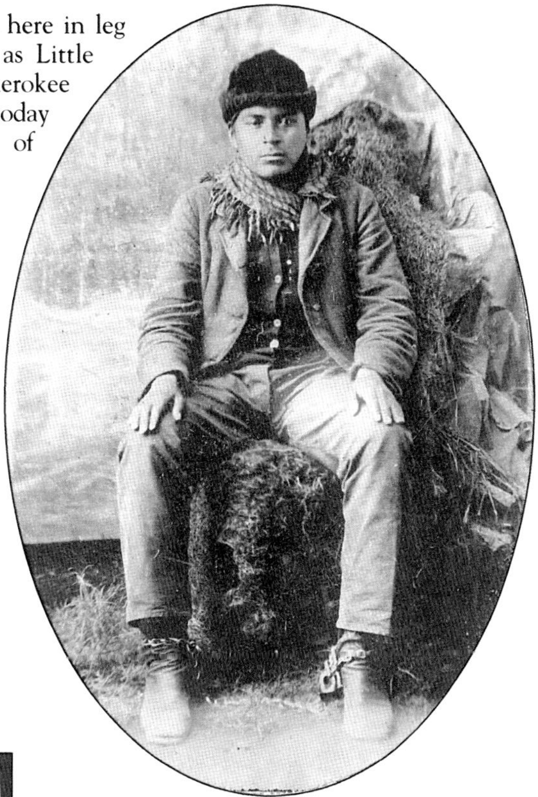

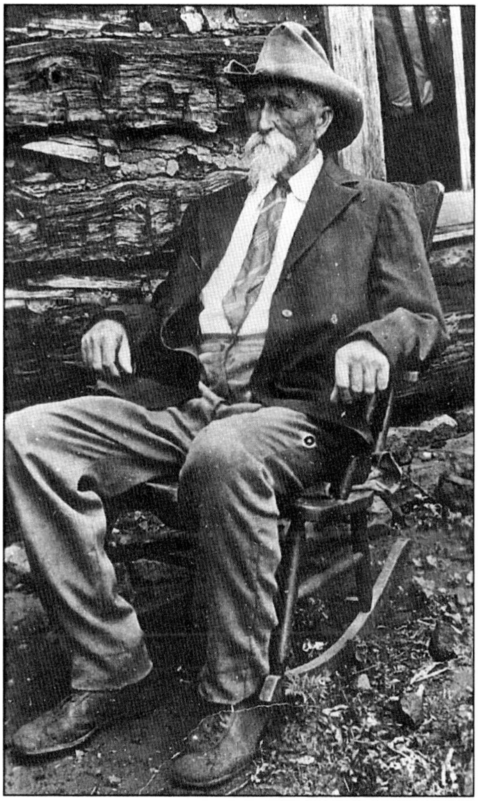

ALVIN ANDREWS, C. 1900. This photograph of Alvin Andrews outside his home in a rocking chair characterizes the elders living in the Cherokee Nation before statehood. Rough-hewn logs made sturdy homes for farmers and ranchers who populated the rural areas. Andrews's home would have been located in what is now Rogers County. (Courtesy of Rogers State College.)

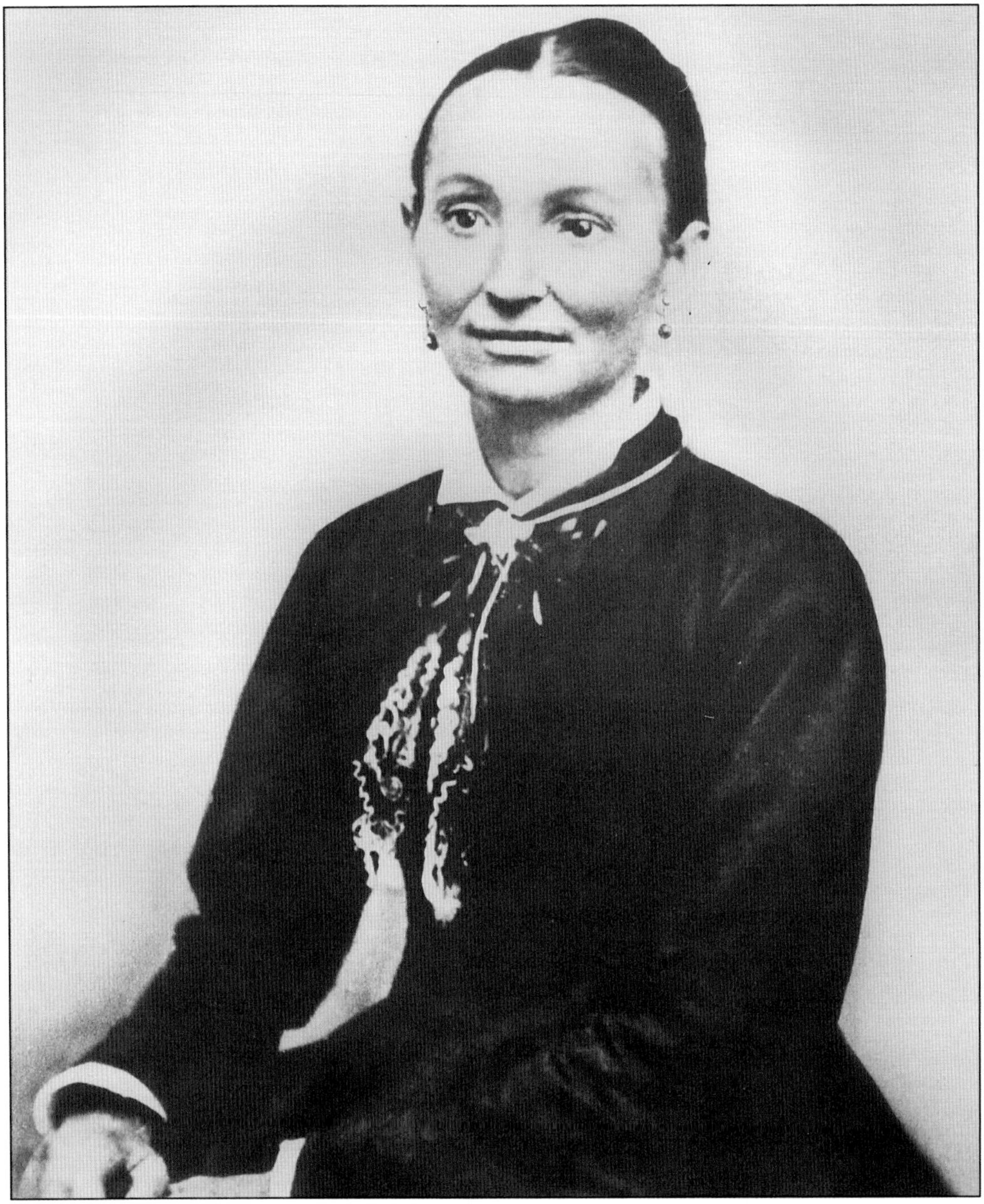

MARY AMERICA SCHRIMSHER ROGERS, C. 1860. Mary America, the daughter of Old Settlers of wealth and prominence, was born on her father's plantation in Tahlequah in 1839. She was afforded a fine Eastern education. Mary attended the Academy at Cane Hill, Alabama. Upon her return, she studied piano and voice at the Cherokee Female Seminary in Park Hill. Mary married Clement Vann Rogers, also from a family of landholders, and moved to their new ranch in the Cooweescoowee district, now Rogers County. While Clem served in the Civil War, Mary returned to her father's home in Tahlequah. When Union forces took control of the city, they asked if the women at the Schrimsher plantation were good Union loyalists. They were informed that the women were good Southern patriots. As a result, their plantation home was reduced to ashes. Mary gave birth to eight children. Her youngest was America's beloved Will Rogers. (Courtesy of Rogers State College.)

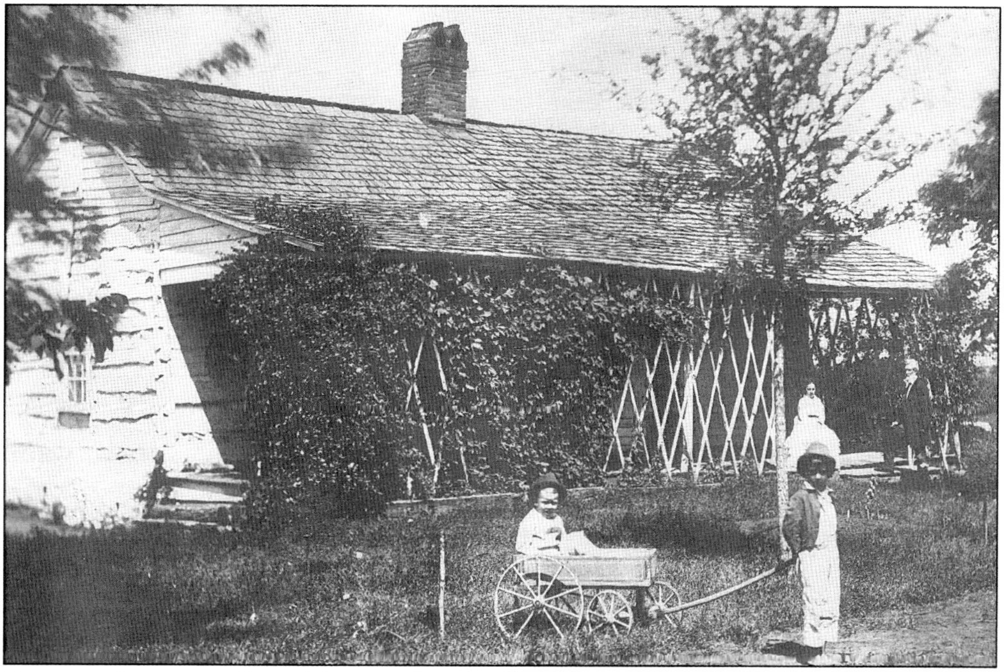

HOME OF PRINCIPAL CHIEF WILLIAM POTTER ROSS IN FORT GIBSON, C. 1870. Pictured on the porch step is Principal Chief William Potter Ross, elected to the post by the Cherokee council following the death of John Ross in 1866. In 1863, he was captured by Civil War general Stand Watie in Tahlequah. Watie spared Ross's life for the sake of his mother, a family friend. (Courtesy of Cherokee National Archives.)

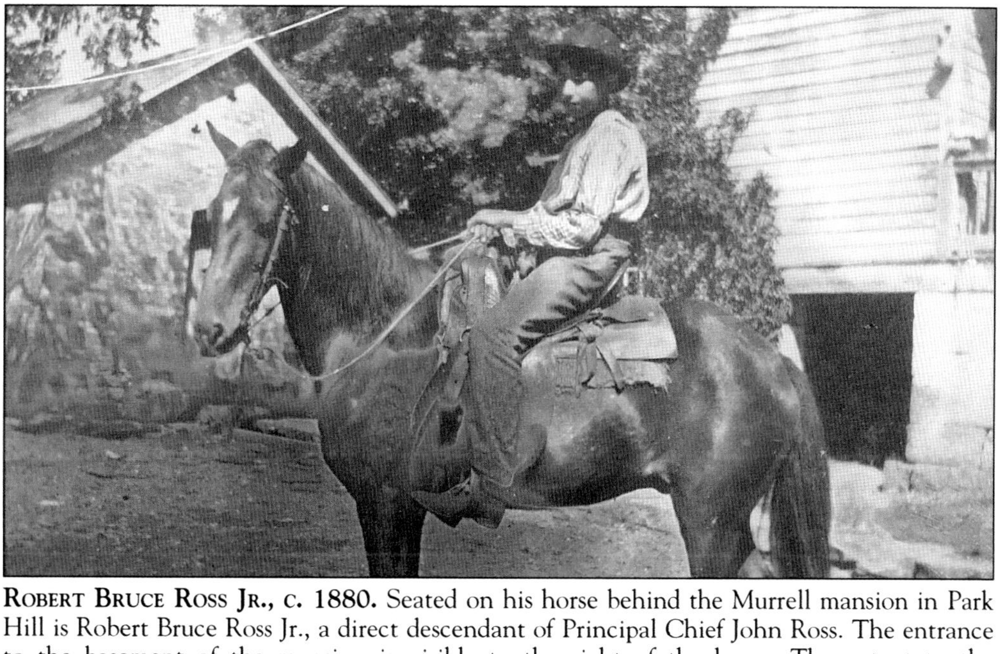

ROBERT BRUCE ROSS JR., C. 1880. Seated on his horse behind the Murrell mansion in Park Hill is Robert Bruce Ross Jr., a direct descendant of Principal Chief John Ross. The entrance to the basement of the mansion is visible to the right of the horse. The patent to the Cherokee Nation was hidden in this basement during the Civil War. (Courtesy of Cherokee National Archives.)

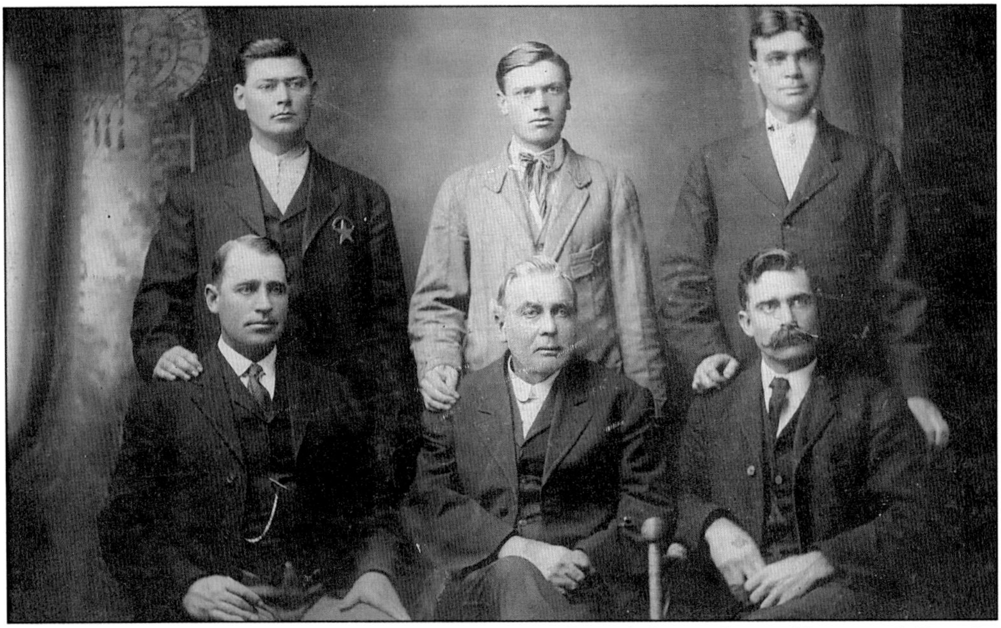

Dickenson Brothers with their Father, c. 1900. From left to right are (front row) Ott, the brothers' father, and Claude Dickenson; (back row) Oscar, Thad, and Frank. This Irish family came to Indian Territory from Virginia just prior to statehood. Brothers Ott and Oscar went on to become millionaires in the city of Tulsa. Frank worked in law enforcement and remained a resident of Tahlequah. (Courtesy of Ralph and Loretta Dunham.)

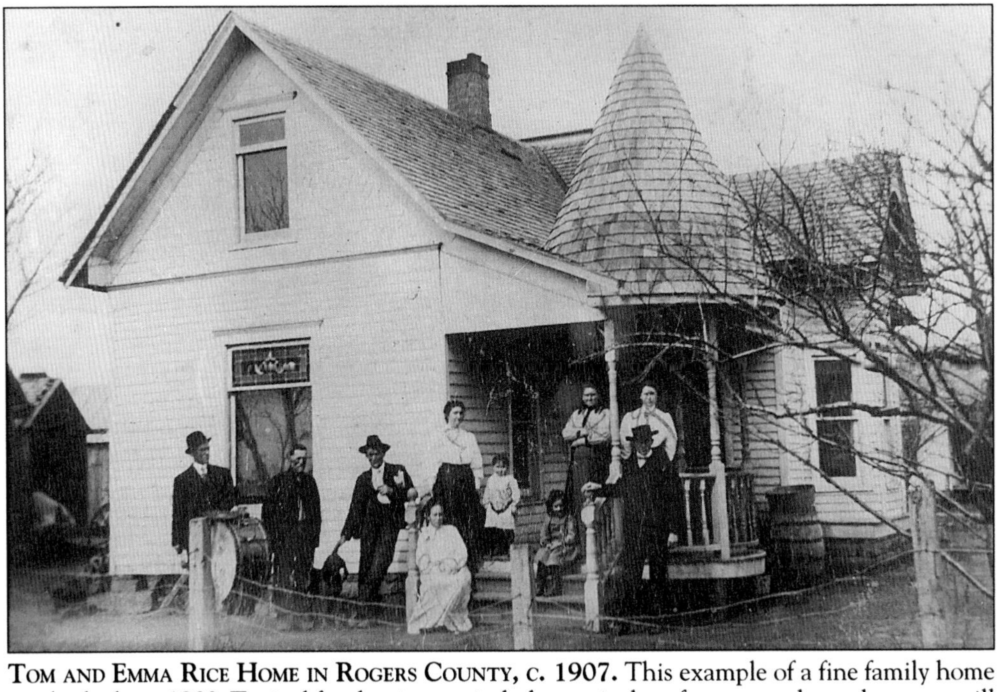

Tom and Emma Rice Home in Rogers County, c. 1907. This example of a fine family home was built about 1900. Typical for the time period, the conical roof structure shown here can still be seen on restored homes in the Cherokee Nation. The Rice family may have just enjoyed a performance by a drummer and guitarists. (Courtesy of Rogers State College.)

OLD RICE HOTEL IN INOLA, c. 1909. Pictured is the Alexander family, operators of the Old Rice Hotel. This fine structure had double fireplaces to serve the rooms. Barely visible are lightning rods on the roof. These were essential for protection from severe storms that frequent Oklahoma's "tornado alley." Notice the intricate lattice work and carved columns of the porches. (Courtesy of Rogers State College.)

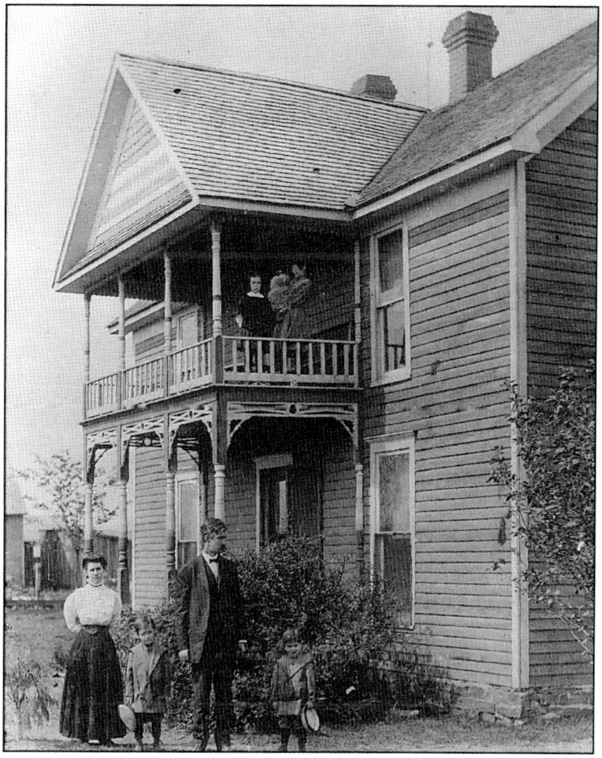

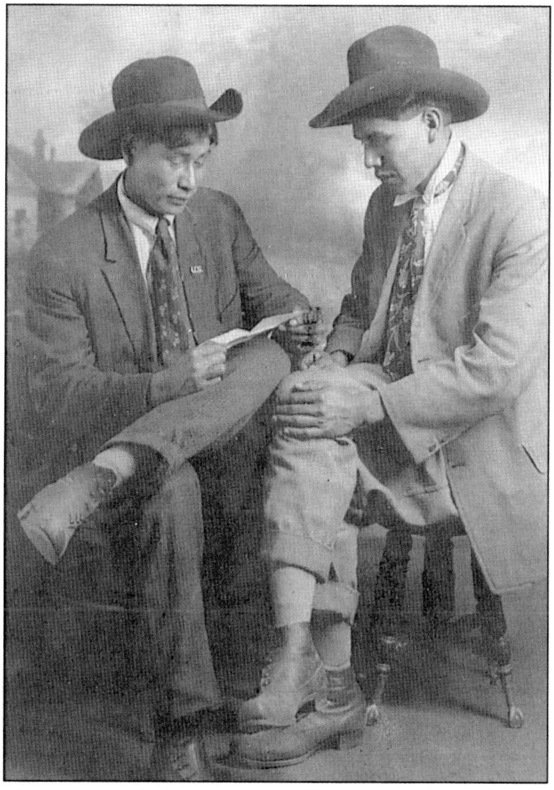

TOM STEELEY AND RUFUS PRITCHETT, c. 1890. Two finely dressed full-bloods pose for a picture postcard in Tahlequah. Steeley appears to be reading a letter to Pritchett. Both are from established families whose descendants and relatives are plentiful in the modern Cherokee Nation. (Courtesy of Cherokee National Archives.)

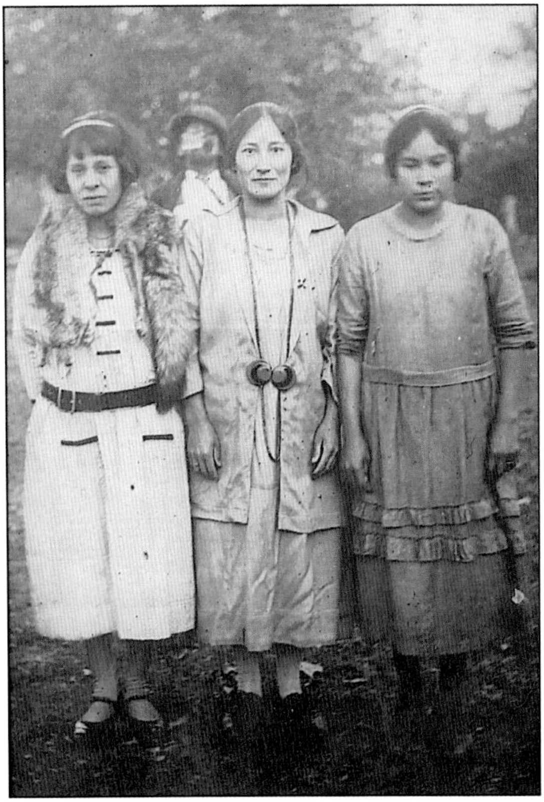

YOUNG WOMEN OF FASHION, C. 1925. Pictured, from left to right, are Annie Fox, Maud Scott, and Jennie Christie. Annie Fox wears the tanned hide of a fox, as some unknown person looks on from behind. Jennie Christie is a relative of the Cherokee patriot Ned Christie. (Courtesy of Lena Fourkiller.)

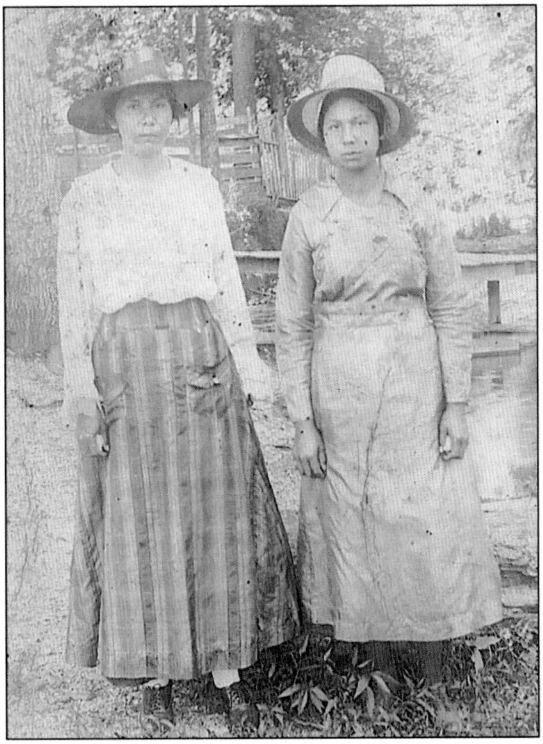

MEMBERS OF THE NOFIRE FAMILY, C. 1910. Sally Walker Nofire, left, stands with her daughter Mary Jane at Old Caney Creek in southeast Cherokee County. The Nofire family is deeply rooted in the Cherokee Nation. A community area, Nofire Hollow is named for them. Their descendants and relatives, including fluent speakers of the language, are plentiful within the Cherokee Nation today. (Courtesy of Lena Fourkiller.)

Ray Elmo Canada, c. 1912. Looking very much like a boy but wearing a girl's dress is Ray Elmo Canada of Oologah. In early statehood, small children were often seen wearing the clothing of older siblings, without regard to gender. Ray's middle name came from his great-great-grandfather Elmo Fish, a Cherokee patriarch. (Courtesy of Duane Canada.)

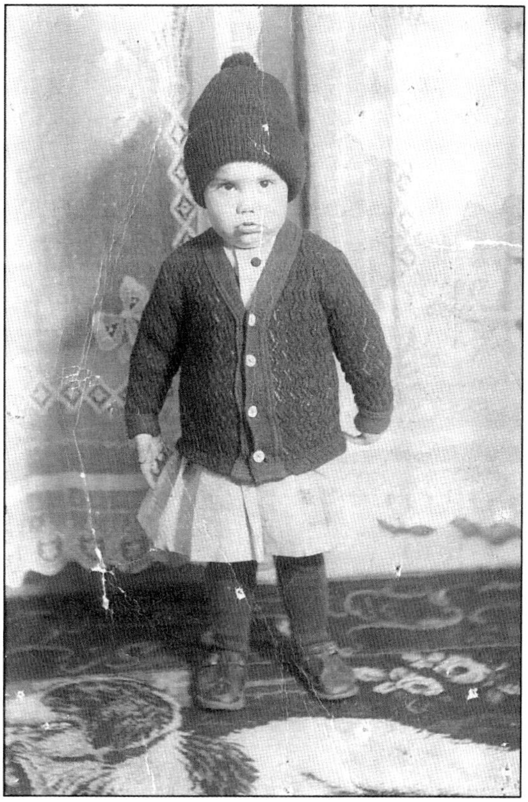

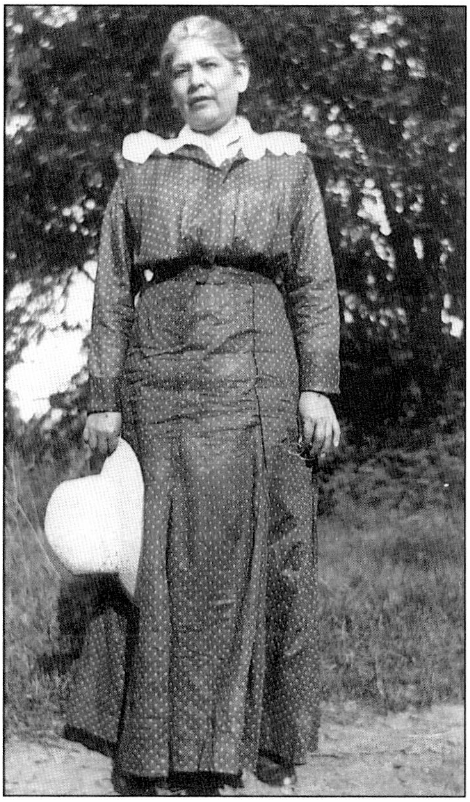

Mary Duvall, c. 1910. A census taken after the Civil War shows that one-third of the women were widowed and one-fourth of the children were orphaned as a result of the fighting. Mary Duvall, a full-blood Cherokee orphan, was taken in by Principal Chief William Potter Ross's family. She was given a home and a fine education. Mary remained with the family and never married. (Courtesy of Cherokee National Archives.)

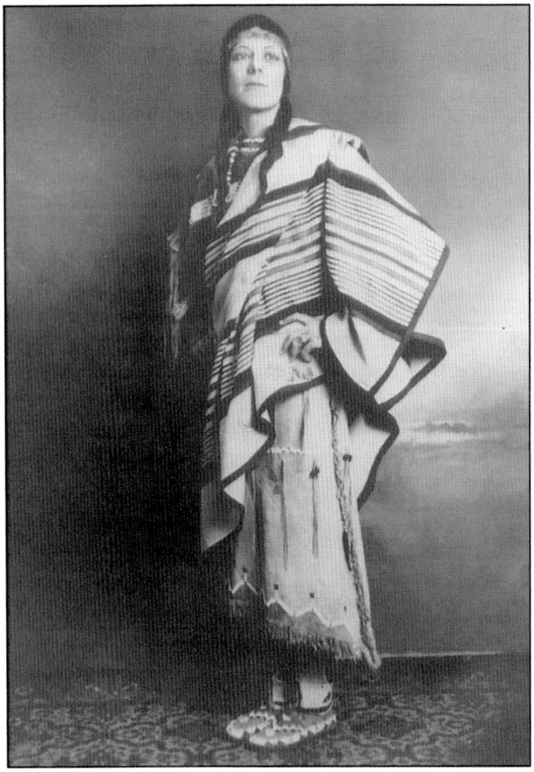

SARAH MAYES MCGILBRY, C. 1915. A direct descendant of Principal Chief Joel Bryan Mayes, Sarah is shown here dressed in western plains attire for the Queen of the Indian Convention competition. Sarah, having won the contest, was asked to travel on a tour of the United States. Her father did not approve of her leaving, and she respectfully declined. (Courtesy of Sally Sanders Finch.)

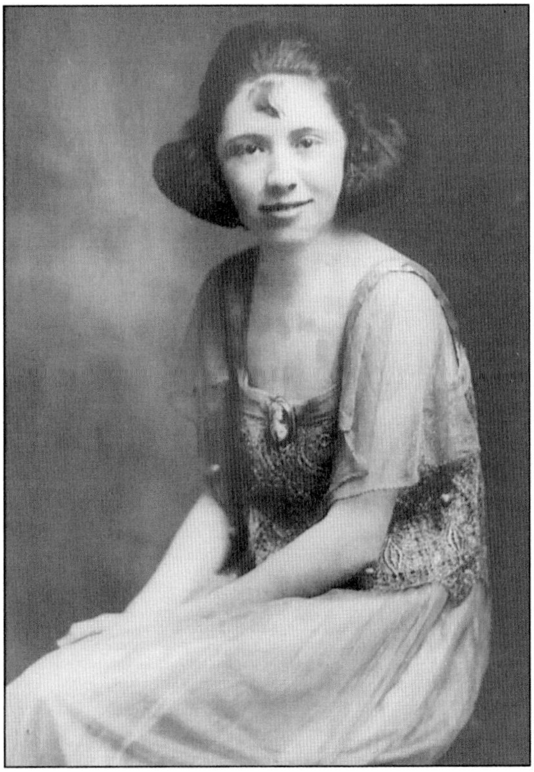

RUTH MAYES WESTLAKE, C. 1912. Ruth was born in what is now Mayes County. Like her sister Sarah, pictured above, Ruth received an allotment of land through the Dawes Commission. Both sisters sold their land and used the money to attend a private school in Mississippi. There the two girls, who had been practically raised on horseback, took riding lessons. (Courtesy of Sally Sanders Finch.)

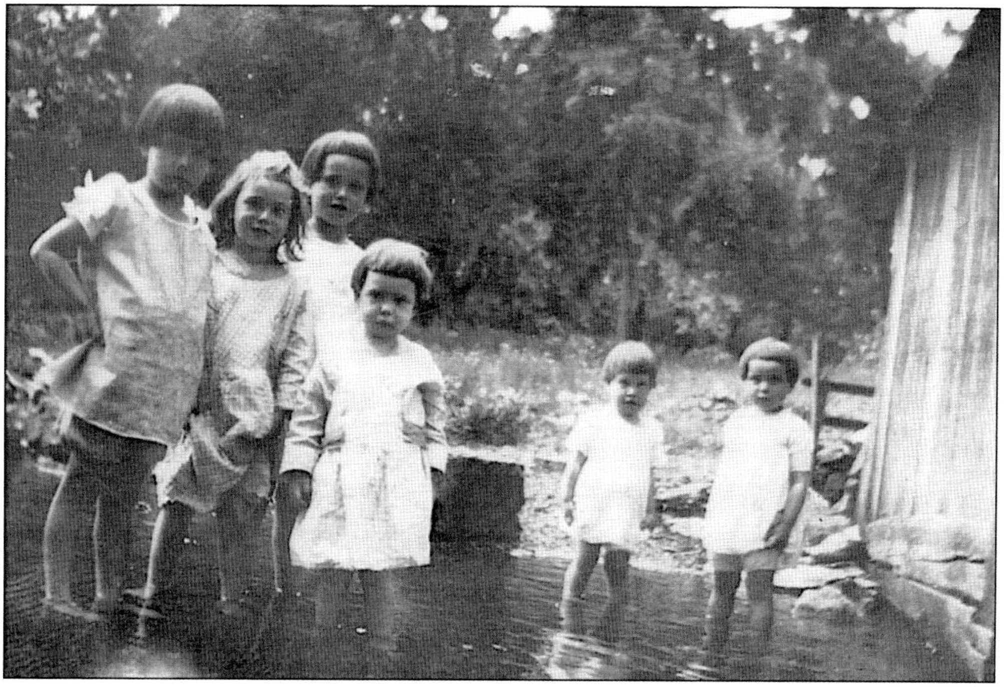

SANDERS COUSINS, C. 1925. Wading in the icy water of Old Wauhillau Springs are, from left to right, Theda V., Betty, Jewel, Pearl, Anawake, and Gladys. The Cherokee Nation abounds with fresh-water springs such as this. In rural Oklahoma, spring houses like the one shown here were often built above the spot where the springs emerge from the earth. (Courtesy of Sally Sanders Finch.)

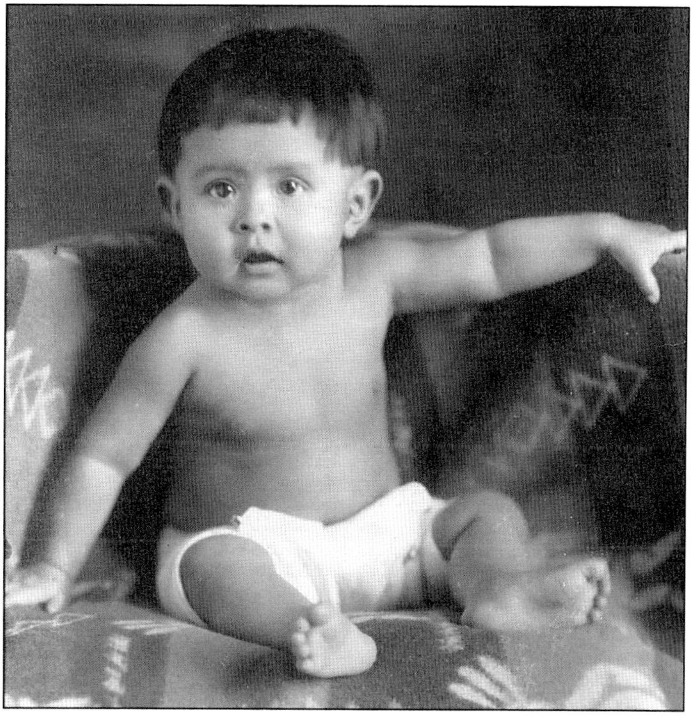

GEORGE COCHRAN, EARLY 1900S. This beautiful child will one day become noted for his artwork. George Cochran's familiar signature has his name inside an arrowhead. It can be seen on numerous paintings and prints of his work in businesses and homes throughout the Cherokee Nation. (Courtesy of Brenda Carpenter.)

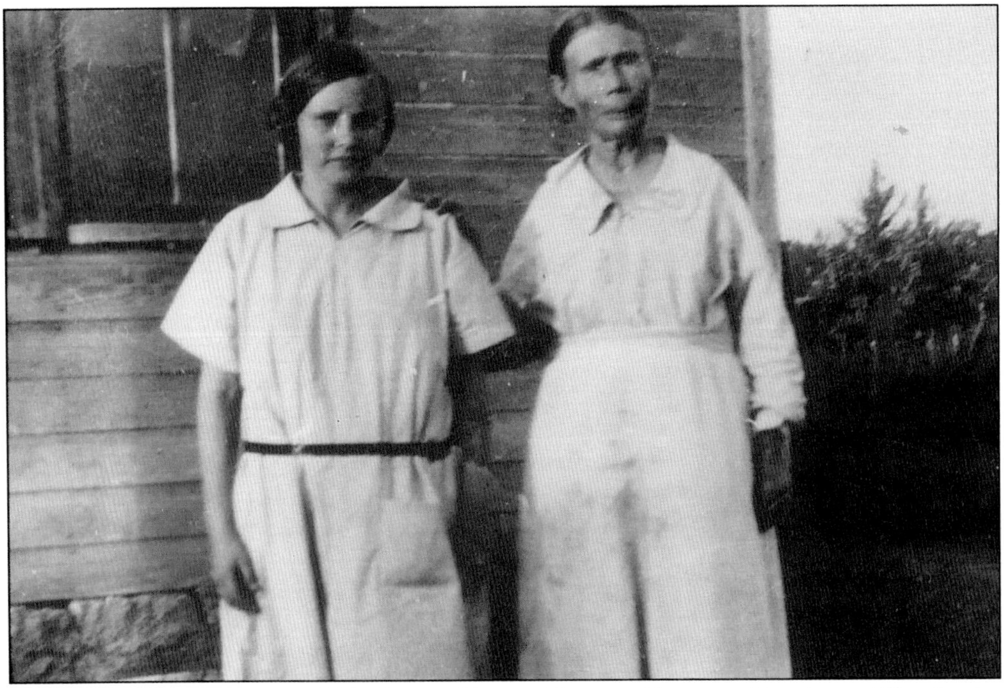

Ellen Louisa Dunham, c. 1920. Pictured here with one of her granddaughters, Ellen Louisa Dunham was born in Missouri in 1852. From there she moved to Indian Territory near Webbers Falls, where she gave birth to three children, Florence, Joseph, and Jesse. Her son Jesse moved to Hulbert and began the Dunham family of Cherokee County. (Courtesy of Ralph and Loretta Dunham.)

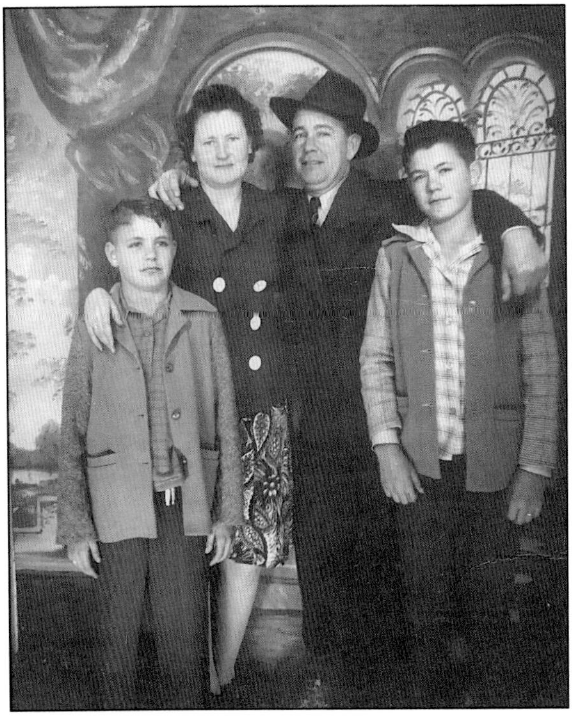

Charles Dunham Family, c. 1940. Charles and Josie Dunham are pictured here with their sons Don (left) and Hubert. The couple were active members of Tahlequah's First General Baptist Church, where Charlie sang in quartets and led the choir for decades. Both Charlie and Hubert served several terms as city council members in Tahlequah. (Courtesy of Ralph and Loretta Dunham.)

DICKENSON SIBLINGS, C. 1947. Pictured are four children of Frank and Martha Evans Dickenson, who were raised on Bear Creek in Tahlequah. Known in the community for their family good looks are Donna, Loretta, Thelma, and Ott. Loretta (Dunham) worked temporarily in California in the 1940s as a welder in the shipyards and picking fruit during hard times in Oklahoma. (Courtesy of Ralph and Loretta Dunham.)

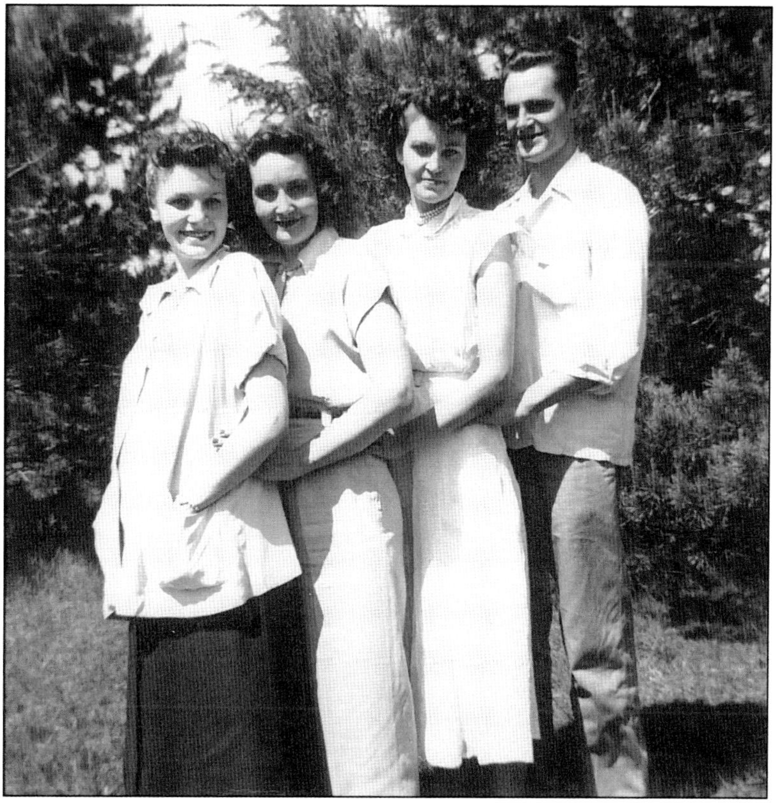

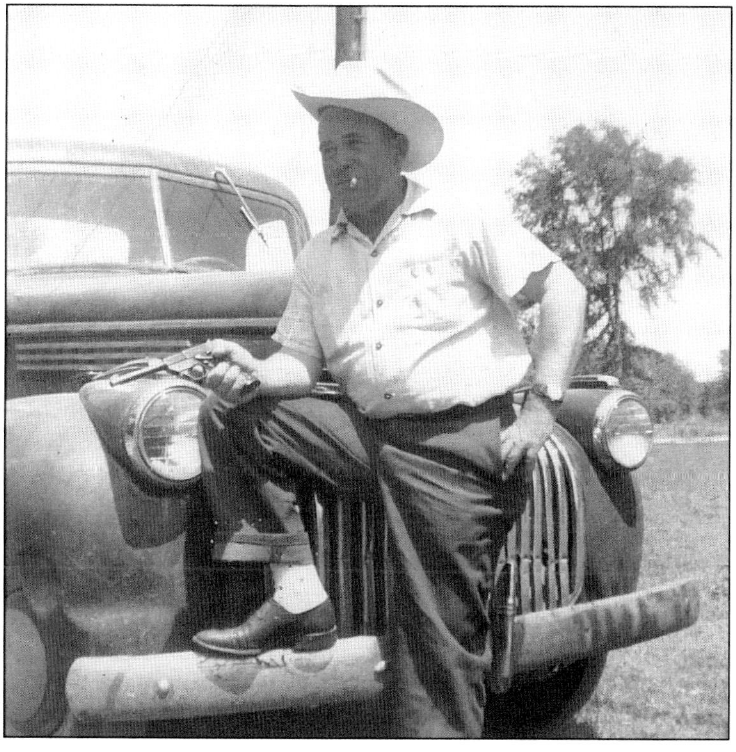

RALPH DUNHAM, C. 1950. Born in Hulbert, Oklahoma, in 1919, Ralph Dunham is the son of Jesse and Ida Bailey Dunham. A dead shot, Ralph has been an avid hunter and helped with the coon hunt scene in the movie about Tahlequah, *Where the Red Fern Grows*. A skilled equipment operator, Ralph worked on most every road project in eastern Oklahoma. (Courtesy of Ralph and Loretta Dunham.)

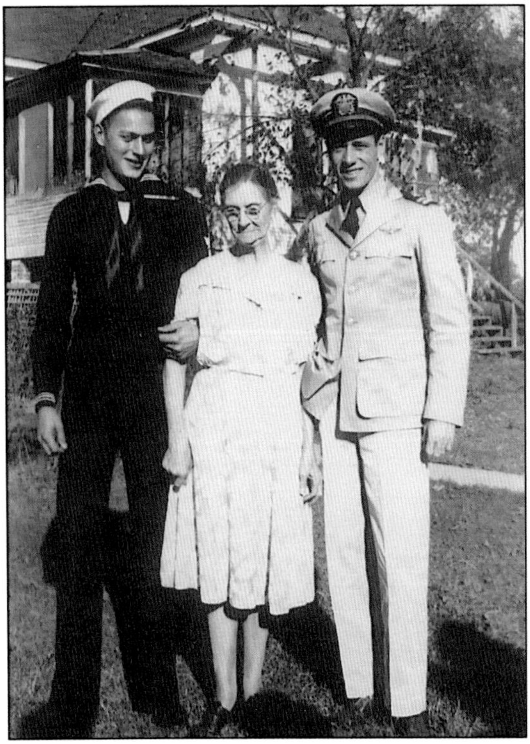

Soldiers Home on Leave, c. 1944. Sporting his Navy uniform, Samuel Sanders poses with his grandmother Florence Nicodemus Mayes and cousin Bobby Langston. Samuel is the son of Robert Lee and Charlotte Mayes Sanders and a direct descendant of Principal Chief Joel B. Mayes. (Courtesy of Sally Sanders Finch.)

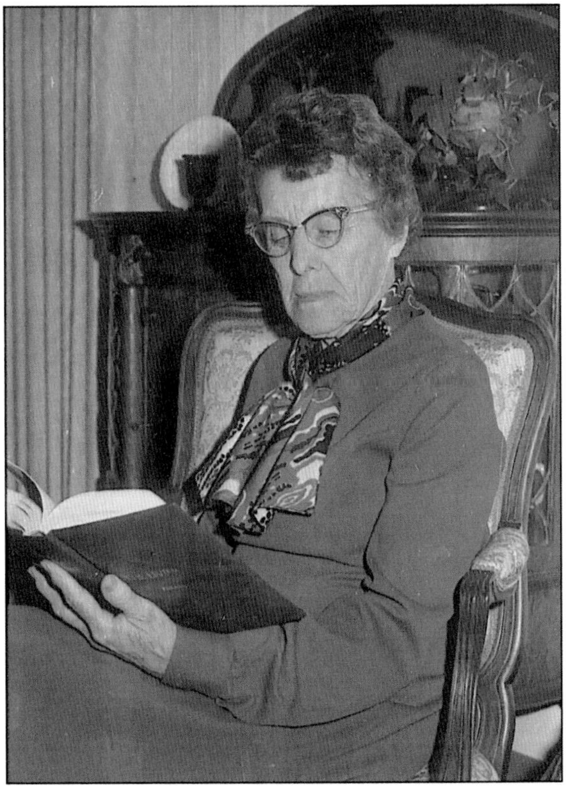

Charlotte Mayes Sanders. Charlotte attended the Cherokee Female Seminary from 1906 to 1909. Always an avid historian, she collected and saved for her family important historical documents and photographs. Her voice is preserved on wax recordings at the Smithsonian Institution. She appears here around 1980 seated in an heirloom chair holding the Mayes family Bible. (Courtesy of Sally Sanders Finch.)

Two

LIFESTYLE

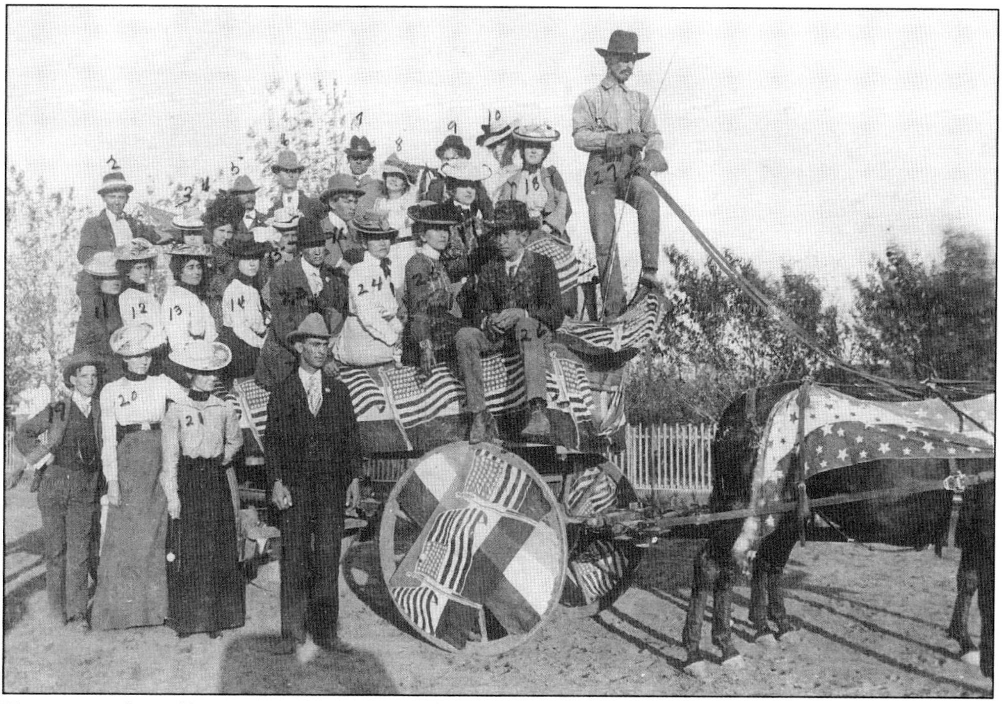

FOURTH OF JULY PARADE, C. 1901. Even before Oklahoma became a state, a spirit of patriotism was felt within the Cherokee Nation. The turn of the century was a time of rapid growth and excitement in the booming communities. New businesses were springing up everywhere, as lots were sold to entrepreneurs. The devastation of the Civil War was long past and the future held the promise of fortune. Gala celebrations took place throughout the Cherokee Nation in honor of the Independence Day of the United States. The Cherokee citizens shown here will not enjoy the benefits of American citizenship for many more years. In 1919, veterans who served in World War I were made citizens for their contribution to the war. In 1924, all Cherokees were made citizens, but some full-bloods remained as wards of the federal government in matters pertaining to land. (Courtesy of Rogers State College.)

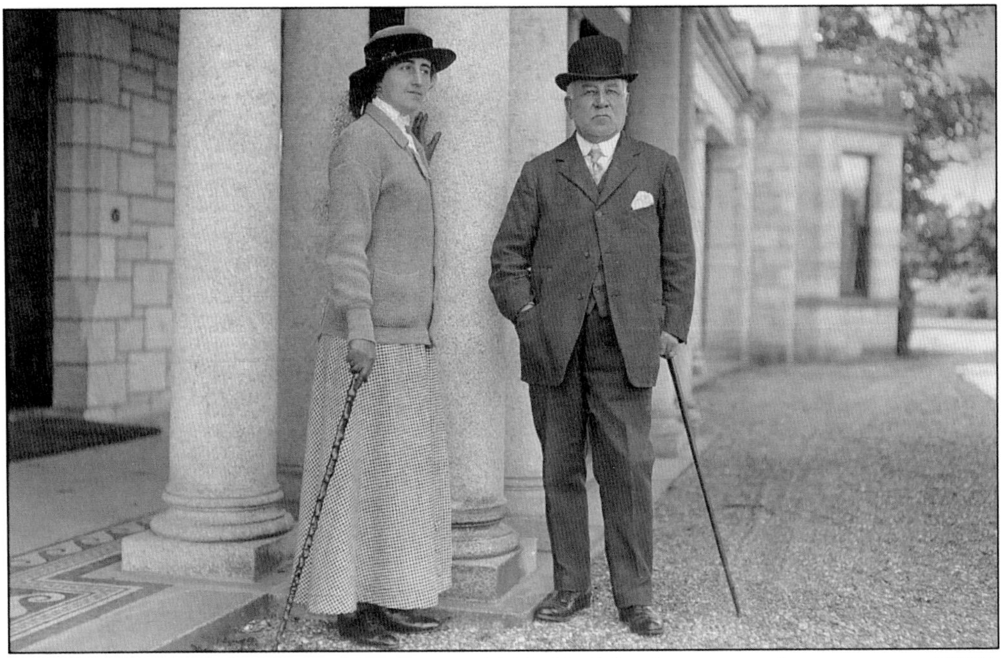

BEULAH BENTON EDMONDSON CROKER, C. 1900. Beulah, the niece of congressman W.W. Hastings, claimed to be a descendant of Sequoyah, inventor of the Cherokee syllabary. She worked as an educator in Indian Territory, where she taught at both the Cherokee Female Seminary and Bacone College. Beulah led, on horseback, the first women's suffrage parade down New York's Fifth Avenue. (Courtesy of Cherokee National Archives.)

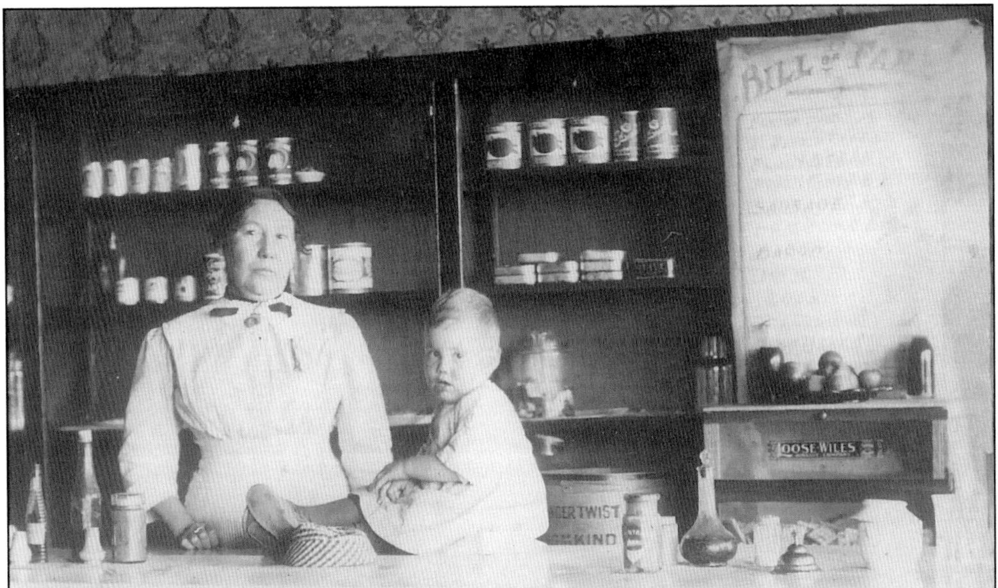

FANNIE E. CANADA AND SON, C. 1885. Fannie stands behind the counter of her combination grocery store and cafe in South Coffeyville, near the northern edge of the Cherokee Nation. To the far right hangs the "Bill of Fare," or menu of food items. Notice the condiment bottles and salt and pepper shakers on the counter. (Courtesy of Duane Canada.)

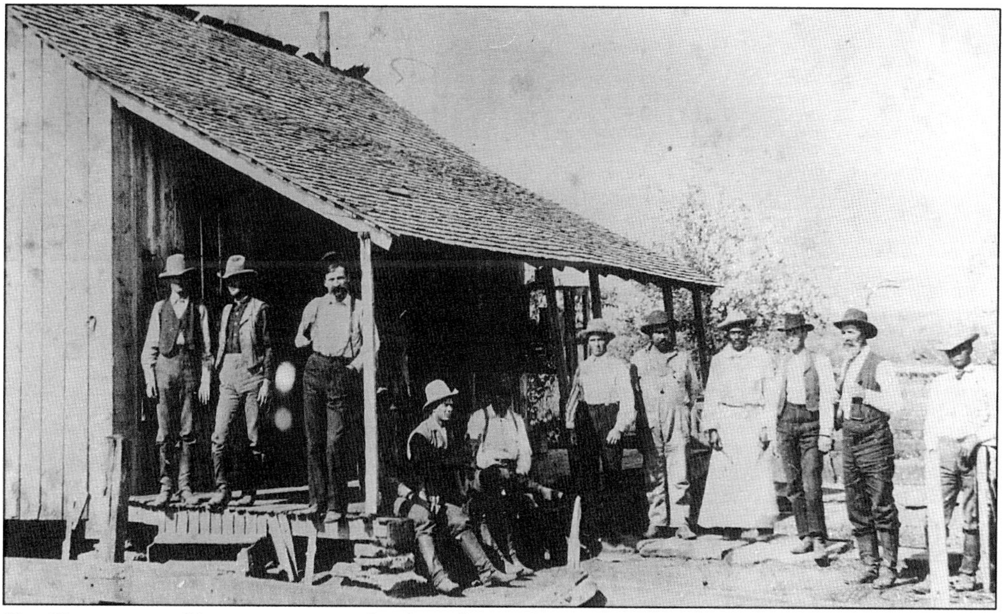

The Daugherty Ranch, c. 1892. Real cowboys relax around their bunkhouse on the Daugherty Ranch. Since the days of the Old Settlers, the western Cherokee lands boasted sprawling cattle ranches. In 1898, the Curtis Act, along with the coming of the railroad through grazing lands, marked the end of the big ranches. With allotment, the land was broken up into tiny family farms. (Courtesy of Rogers State College.)

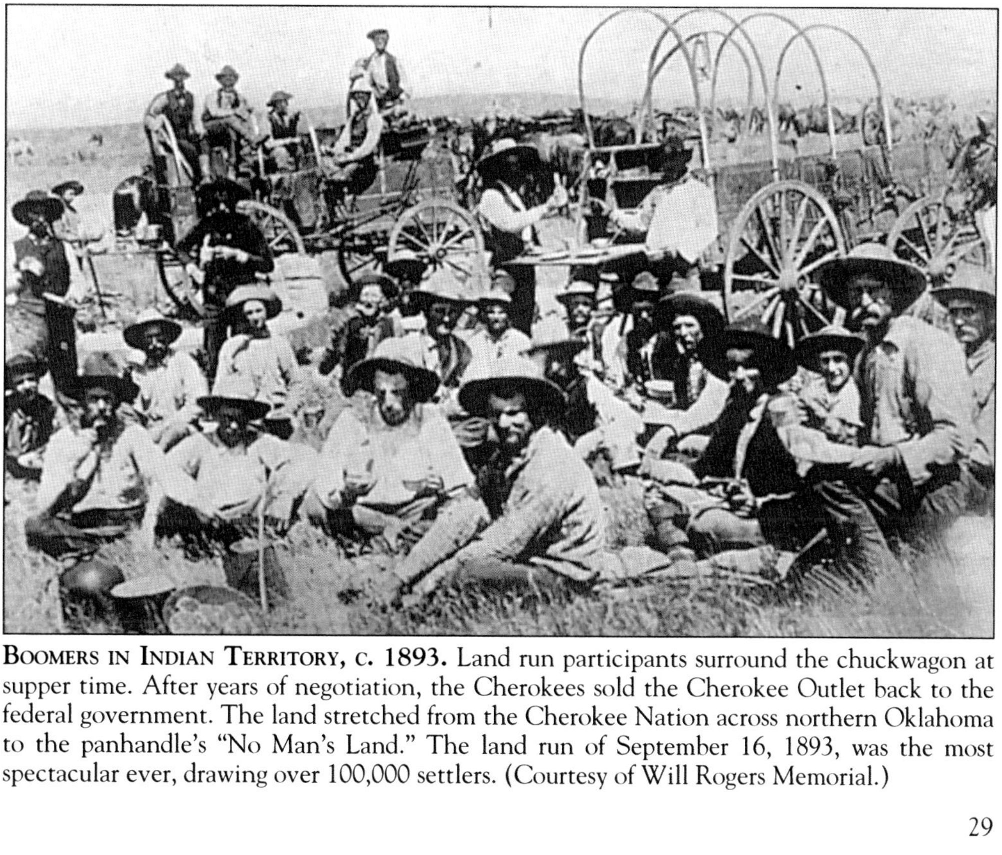

Boomers in Indian Territory, c. 1893. Land run participants surround the chuckwagon at supper time. After years of negotiation, the Cherokees sold the Cherokee Outlet back to the federal government. The land stretched from the Cherokee Nation across northern Oklahoma to the panhandle's "No Man's Land." The land run of September 16, 1893, was the most spectacular ever, drawing over 100,000 settlers. (Courtesy of Will Rogers Memorial.)

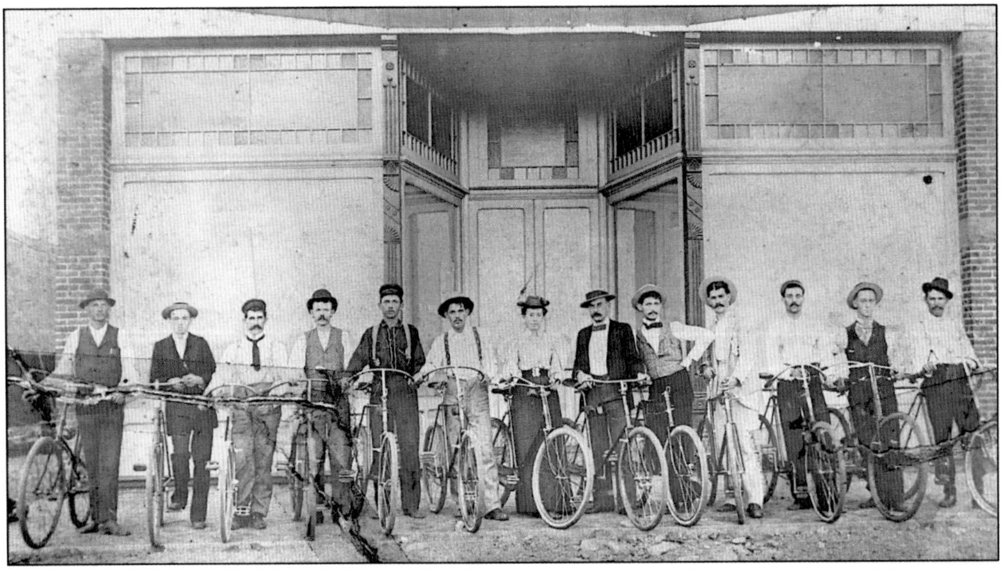

Claremore Bicycle Club, c. 1900. Thirteen members of the Claremore Bicycle Club appear outside Neilson's Store in the bustling city of Claremore, Indian Territory. In the very center of the group stands the only female member represented. Notice the delicately carved window trim and colored-glass sections of the storefront. (Courtesy of Will Rogers Memorial.)

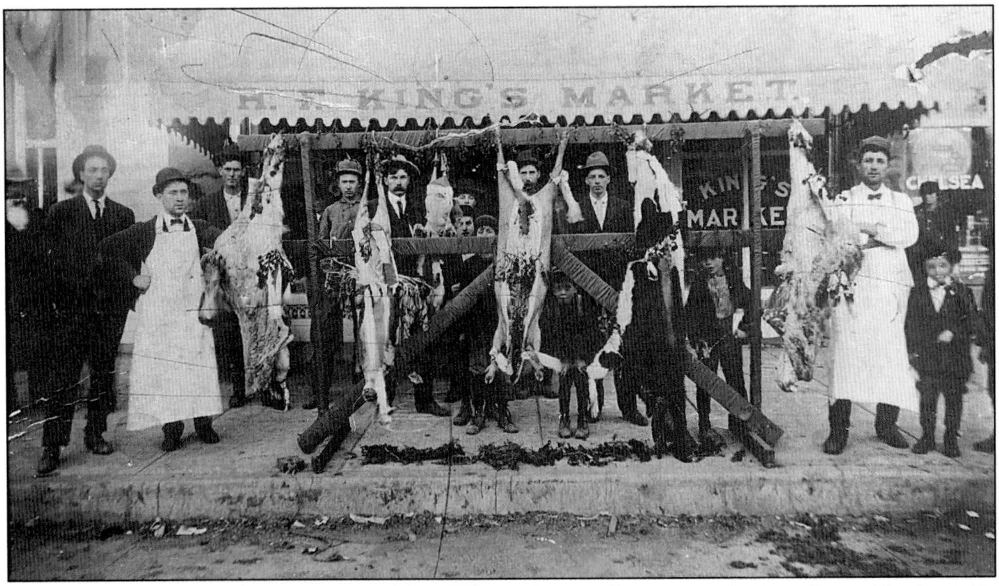

King Market in Chelsea, c. 1902. Dressed out deer and goats are displayed outside the H.F. King Market in Chelsea. Notice that there are no women in this picture, but there are several young boys gathered to view the spectacle. The concrete sidewalks attest to Indian Territory's building boom in the early 1900s. (Courtesy of Rogers State College.)

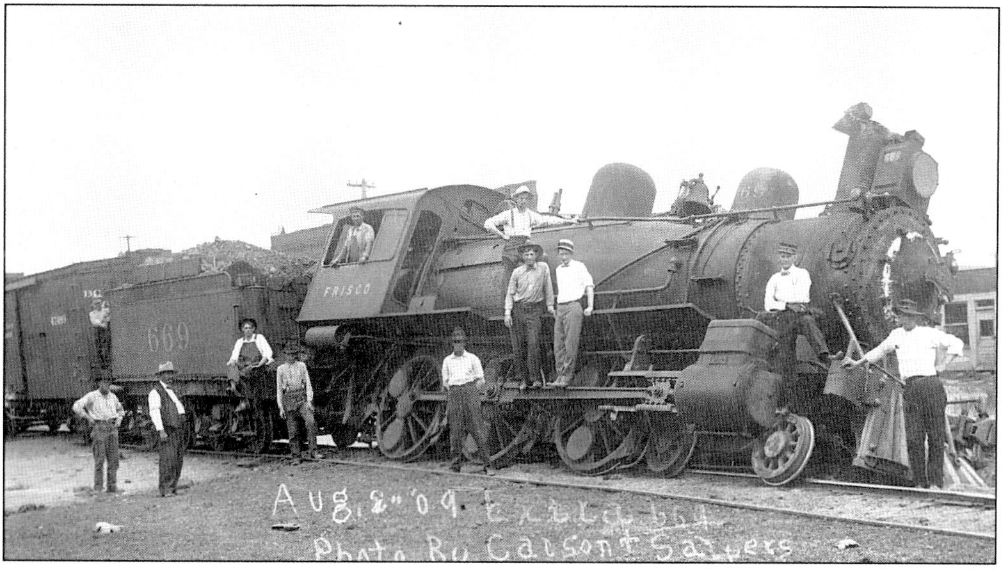

Derailed Train in Old Claremore, c. 1904. Onlookers inspect the engine of a derailed train on the Frisco Line. The railroad had a profound impact on life in the Cherokee Nation, being both sought after and despised. The Treaty of 1866 provided for the building of two rail lines through the Cherokee Nation. (Courtesy of Will Rogers Memorial.)

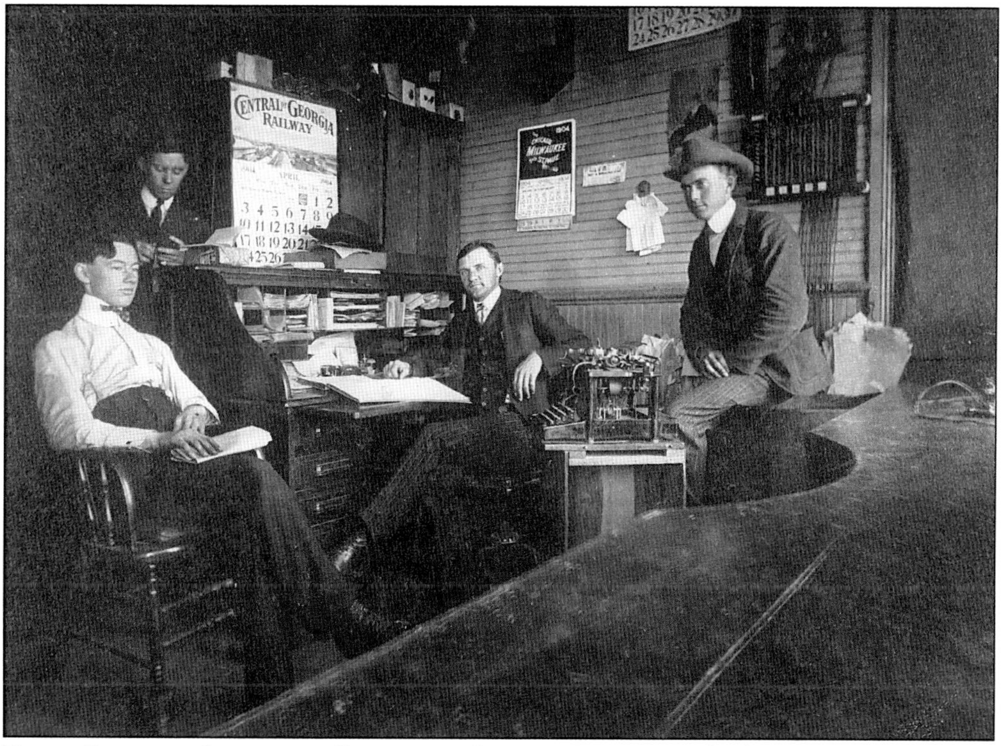

Frisco Railroad Station in Claremore, August 5, 1909. In the late 1860s, the railroads were granted land easements contingent upon a territorial form of government. The companies were tenacious in their efforts to obtain the land and thus were instrumental in the eventual opening of the land to white settlers. (Courtesy of Will Rogers Memorial.)

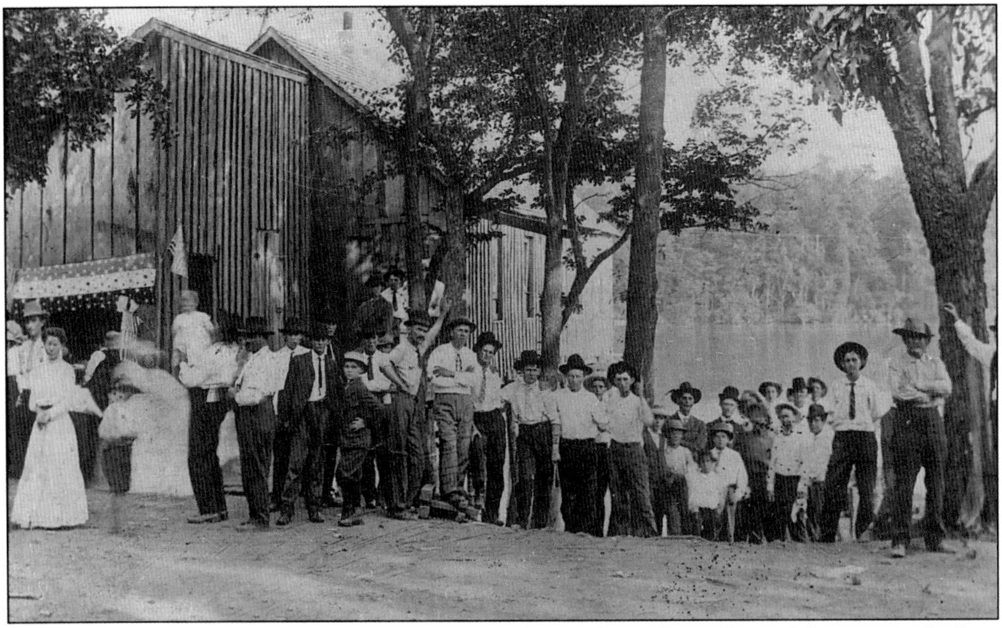

Verdigris Community Picnic, c. 1908. Yet another Independence Day celebration took place at Big Lake near the Verdigris community. The state of Oklahoma was not yet one year old, and patriotism was running high. It was a time to celebrate the booming growth in the Nation. (Courtesy of Rogers State College.)

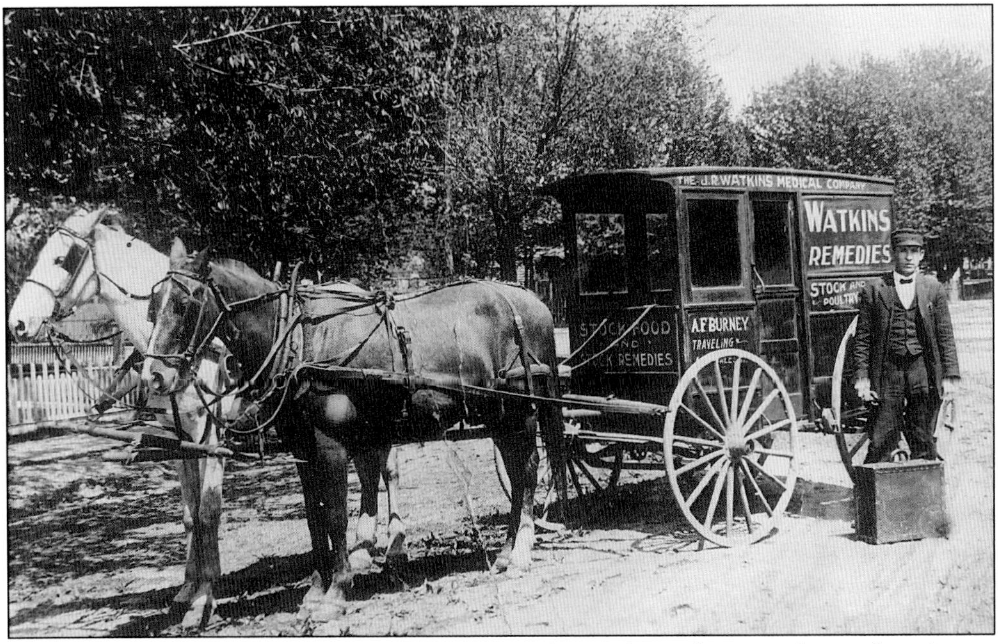

A. Frank Burney's Medical Wagon, c. 1912. A traveling salesman of animal medicines and feed, A. Frank Burney stands beside a wagon of the J.R. Watkins Medical Company. His horses await, with blinders on, beside a lovely example of a white picket fence. This picture was taken in late April, a most beautiful time of year in the Cherokee Nation. (Courtesy of Rogers State College.)

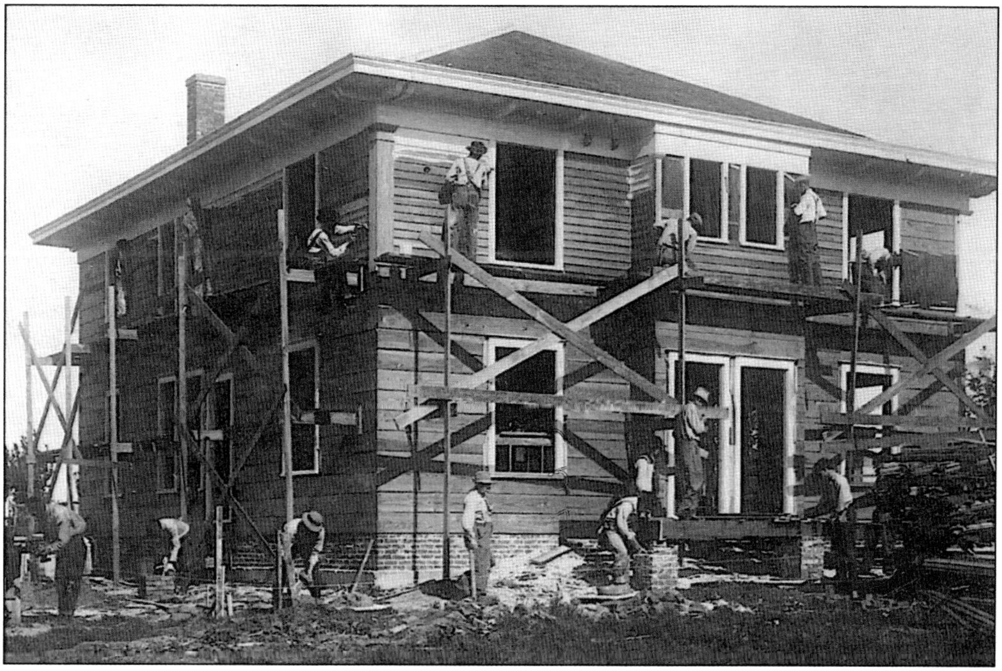

BUILDERS AT WORK IN THE CHEROKEE NATION, EARLY 1900S. A work crew of at least 14 finish out a two-story frame structure that is seated on a brick and concrete foundation. Outer siding is being added from the top down, as the upper portions receive a coat of white paint. This is thought to be a new dormitory at the Sequoyah High School near Tahlequah. (Courtesy of Cherokee National Archives.)

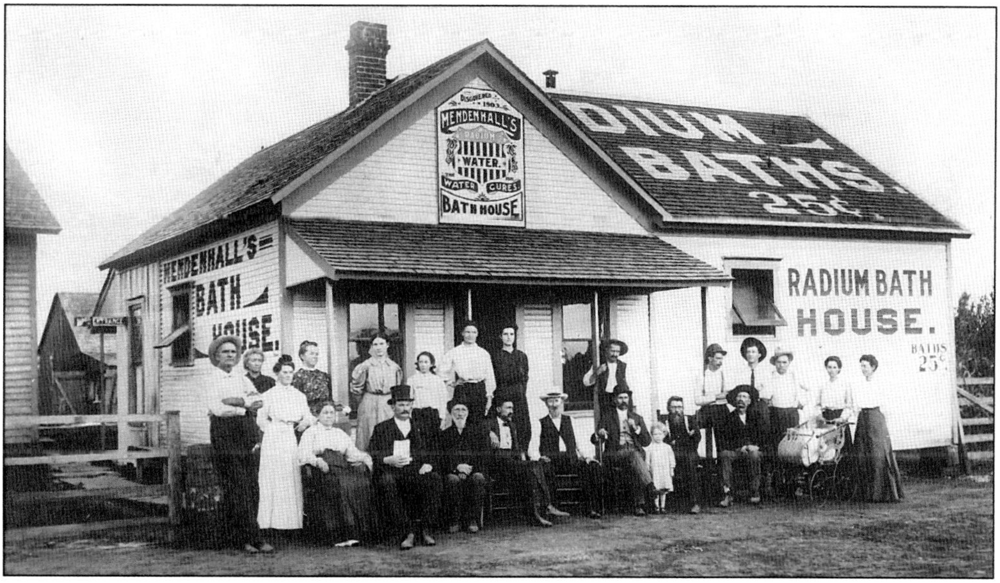

MENDENHALL'S BATH HOUSE, C. 1905. When mineral-rich radium wells were discovered in the Cooweescoowee district, entrepreneurs like the Mendenhalls set out to capitalize on nature's wealth. The building would be positioned over the water source and would contain interior structures to retain water. The radium bath was promised to cure all manner of illnesses at the cost of 25¢. (Courtesy of Rogers State College.)

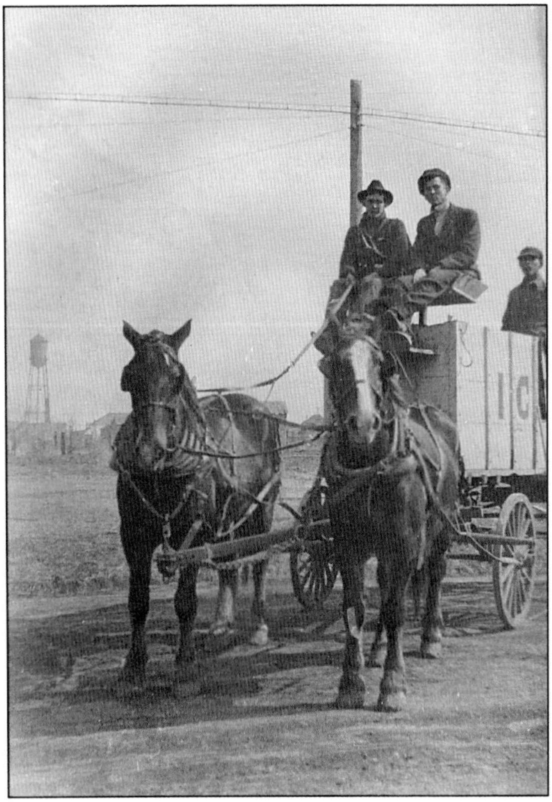

LIGHTNER'S ICE WAGON, C. 1914. Employee Harvey C. Helm (left) drives Lightner's ice wagon, a wooden vehicle designed to keep ice cold as blocks were delivered to waiting customers. In the far distance stands the community water tower. (Courtesy of Rogers State College.)

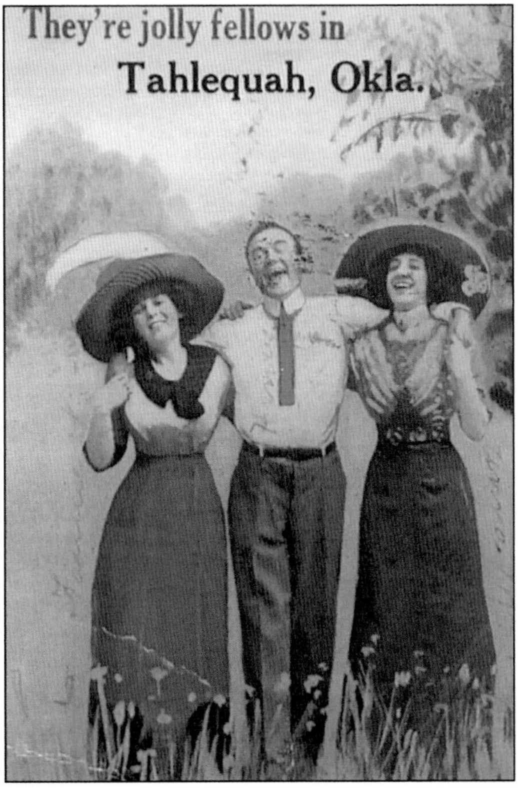

TAHLEQUAH POSTCARD, C. 1914. The message on this postcard from early statehood days bespeaks the spirit and community pride of Tahlequah's citizenry. The beauty of the area, with its sparkling water and lush hillsides, has attracted tourists for decades. (Courtesy of Cherokee Studies Institute.)

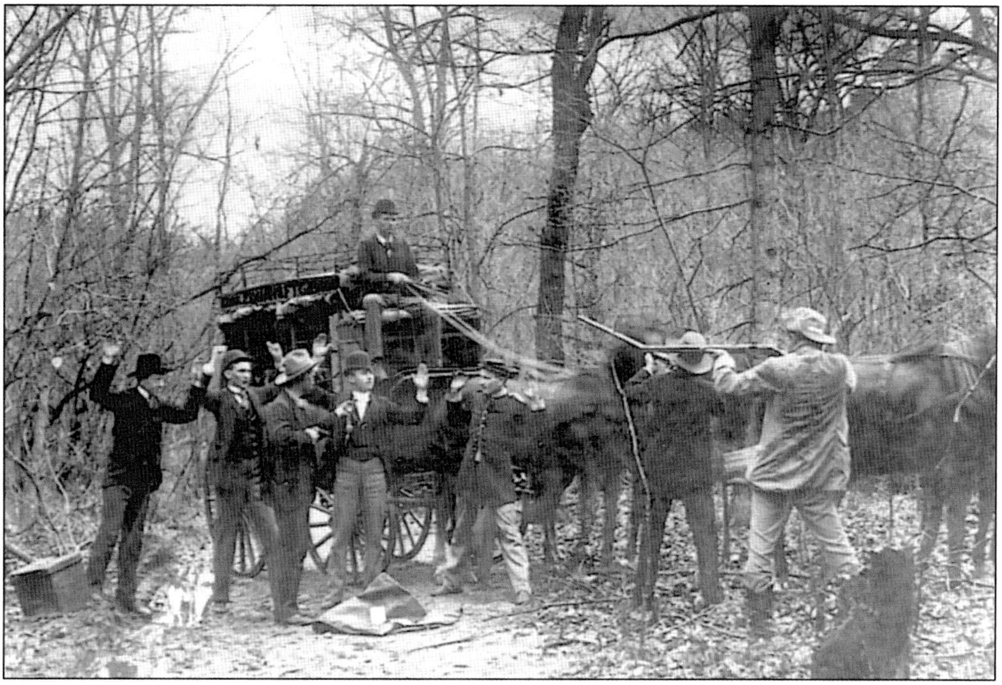

A Staged Holdup of a Stage, early 1900s. A bandit relieves a wealthy traveler of his watch and chain. Perhaps this photograph was taken to illustrate a story about the real outlaws who had frequented the area. Frank and Jesse James, the Dalton brothers, Belle Starr, and numerous other outlaws would retreat to the safety of Indian Territory to hide out and plan their raids. (Courtesy of Cherokee Studies Institute.)

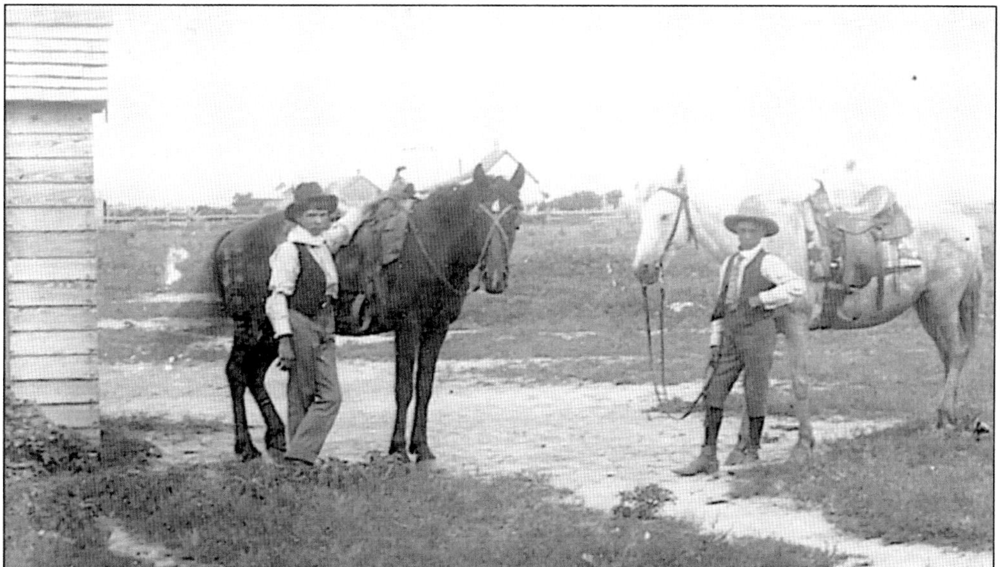

Two Friends with Horses, Late 1800s. The horse has been with the Cherokees for many decades and is described in accounts of Cherokees going well back in American history. Horses took precedence over all other stock animals when it came to value. (Courtesy of Cherokee National Archives.)

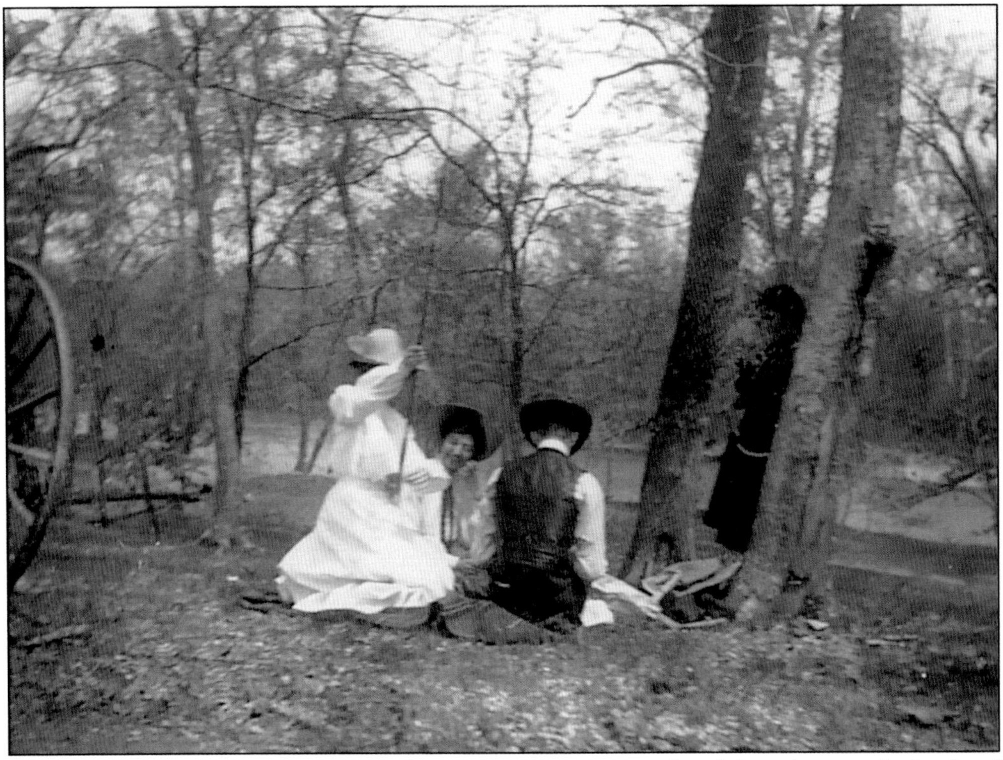

RELAXING ON THE ILLINOIS, C. 1906. A young woman prepares her fishing line on the banks of the peaceful Illinois River near Tahlequah. Some of the native game fish found there include sun perch, black perch, yellow perch, white crappie, black crappie, large mouth and small mouth bass, and several varieties of catfish. (Courtesy of Cherokee National Archives.)

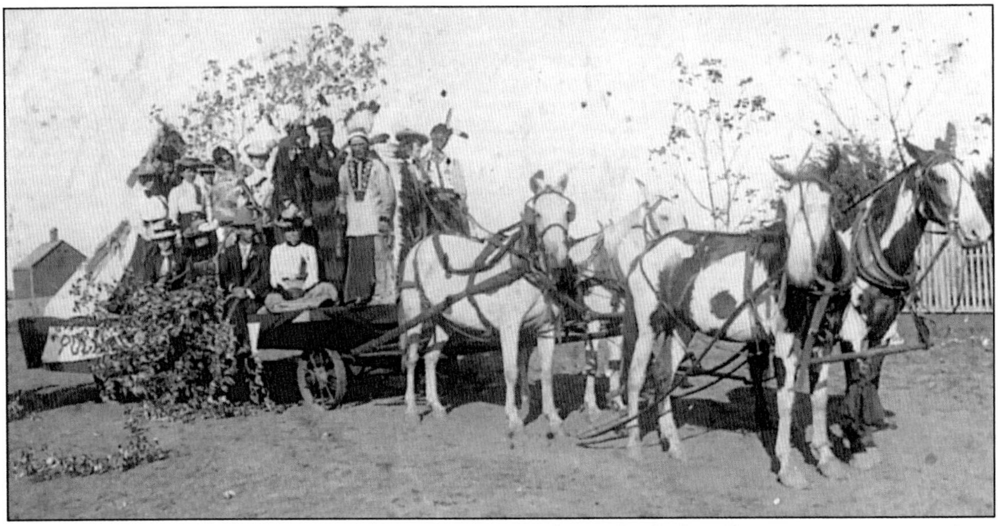

POCAHONTAS CLUB FLOAT, C. 1901. Atop a wagon drawn by Indian Paint ponies are members of the Indian Women's Pocahontas Club of Claremore, a group formed by Cherokee women in the Cooweescoowee district in 1899. Cherokee women throughout history have been a powerful force within the tribe, serving as both warriors and leaders. (Courtesy of Will Rogers Memorial.)

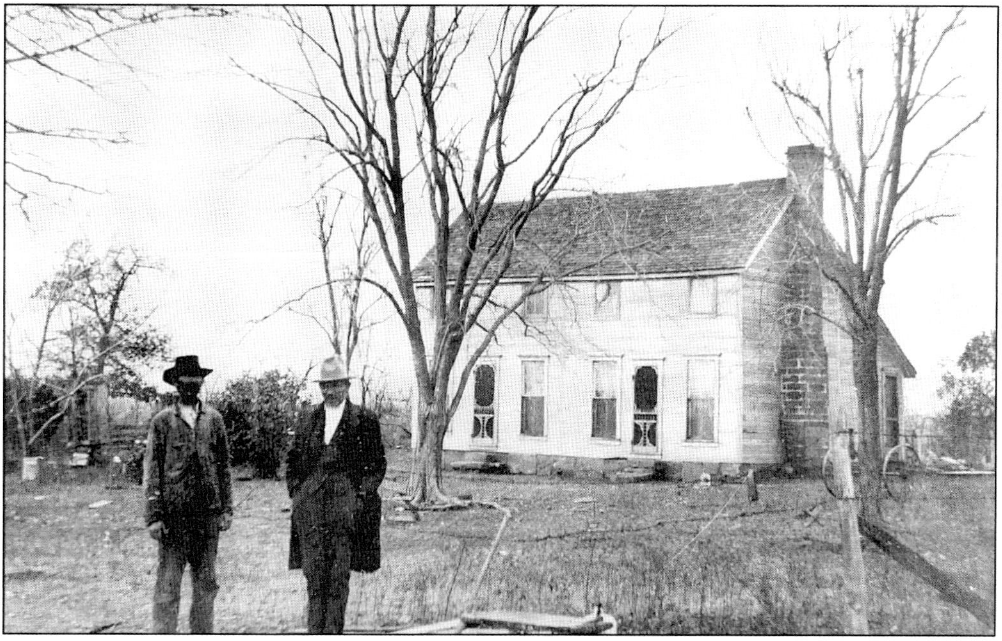

ED BEAN HOME, C. 1913. Ed Bean (left) and Napoleon Johnson stand outside Ed's house on Thanksgiving Day. This photograph captures the winter landscape in eastern Oklahoma. The house, with its native stone fireplace, sits on cleared land that was once deciduous forest. The distant trees with leaves are not evergreens, but oaks. The oaks retain their brown leaves most of the winter. (Courtesy of Rogers State College.)

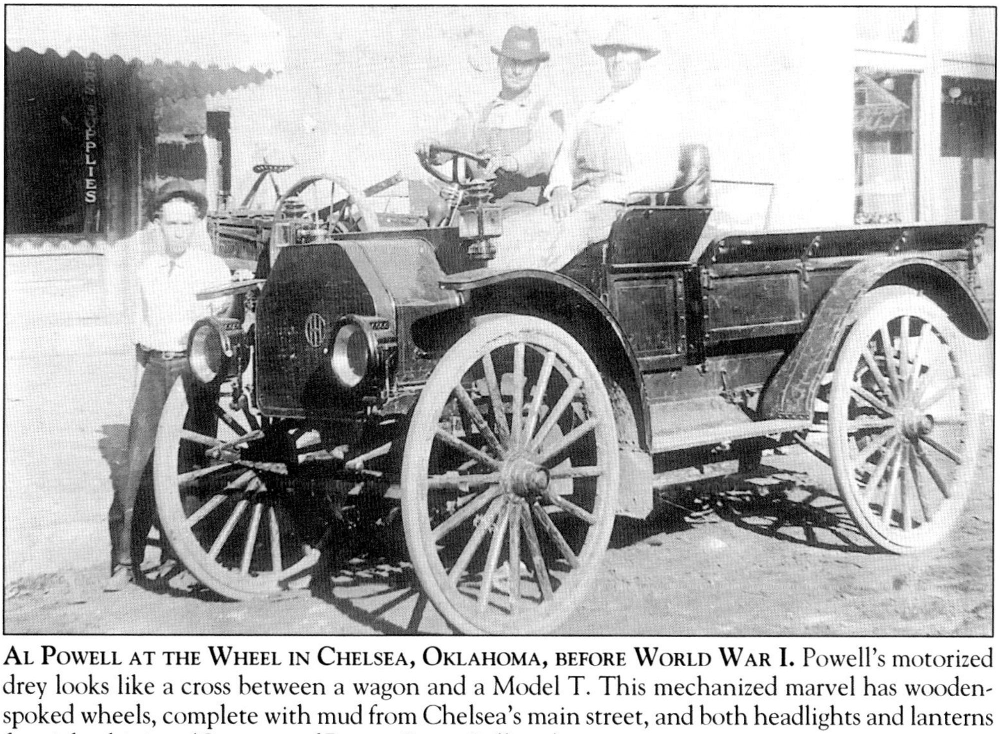

AL POWELL AT THE WHEEL IN CHELSEA, OKLAHOMA, BEFORE WORLD WAR I. Powell's motorized drey looks like a cross between a wagon and a Model T. This mechanized marvel has wooden-spoked wheels, complete with mud from Chelsea's main street, and both headlights and lanterns for night driving. (Courtesy of Rogers State College.)

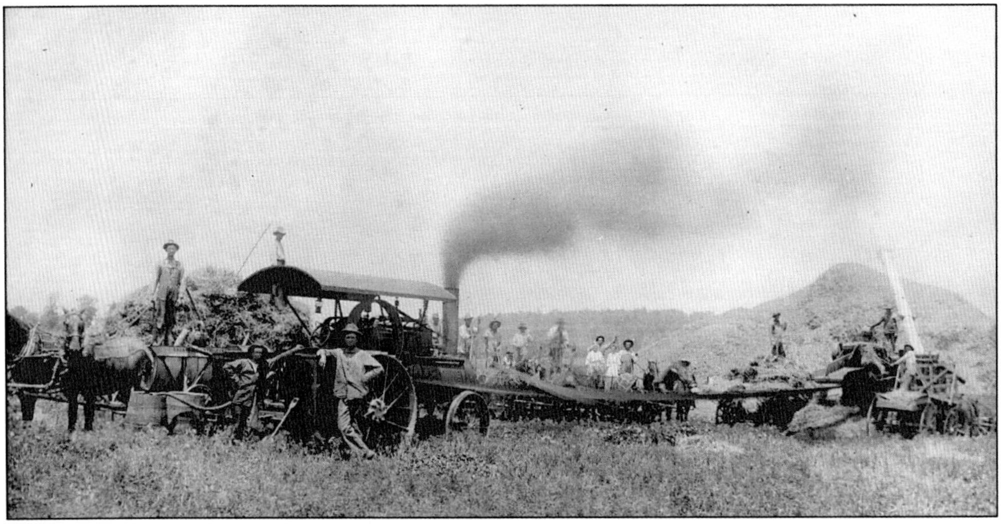

EARLY TEENS THRESHING MACHINE. Belching steam and creating mountains of straw, machines such as this were a boon to early farmers. The invention revolutionized wheat farming and provided jobs for citizens. Still the farmer had to deal with weather and the chance of too little, or too much, rainfall. (Courtesy of Rogers State College.)

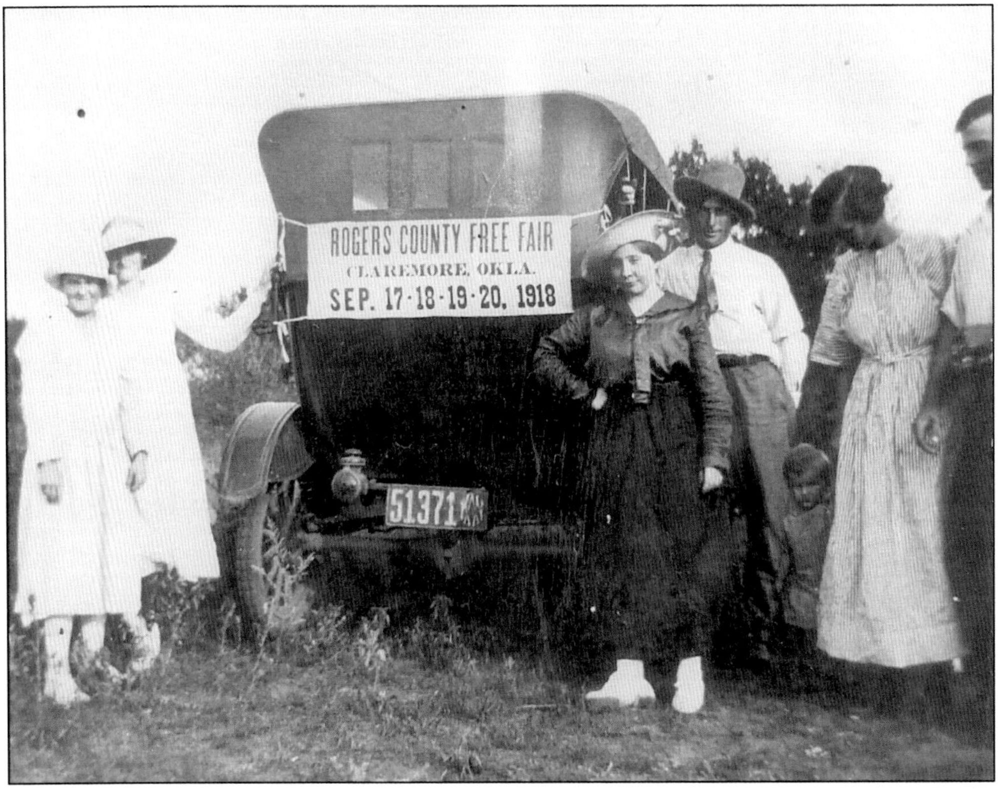

COUNTY FAIR VISITORS, C. 1918. Standing to the right of their car are Hattie, Denver, Lila, and Fred Moree. A tiny Moree looks out from behind Lila's skirt. Perhaps they are headed for the Rogers County Fair or want to attract more people there. The county fair remains a rich tradition in eastern Oklahoma. (Courtesy of Rogers State College.)

OIL RIG, C. 1913. This steam-powered contraption is in the process of creating the wealth for which parts of Oklahoma are known. Contractor Jim Cross is drilling near Catale, Oklahoma. From left to right are Jim Cross, Eve McKinnis, Hazin Preston, Jode Willbanks, and Bill Cross. (Courtesy of Rogers State College.)

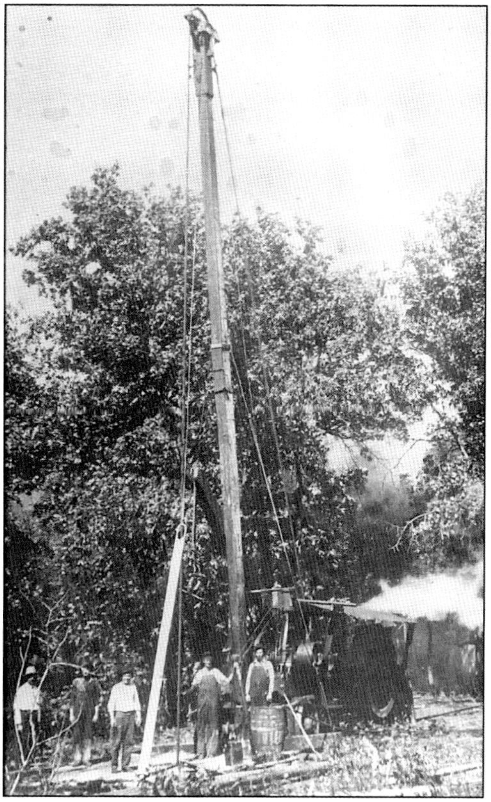

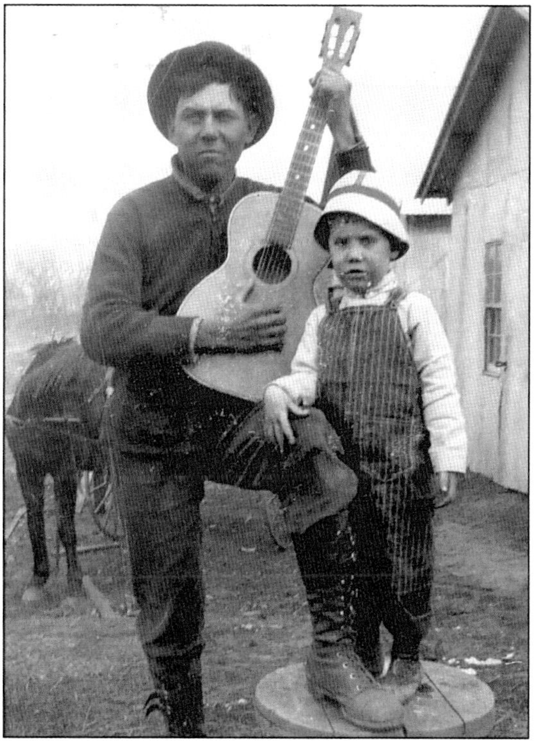

AN OOLOGAH MUSICIAN, C. 1914. Henry Lee Canada poses with his son Ray Elmo Canada outside their home in Oologah. According to family members, Henry was acquainted with Will Rogers, having been raised in and around the same area. (Courtesy of Duane Canada.)

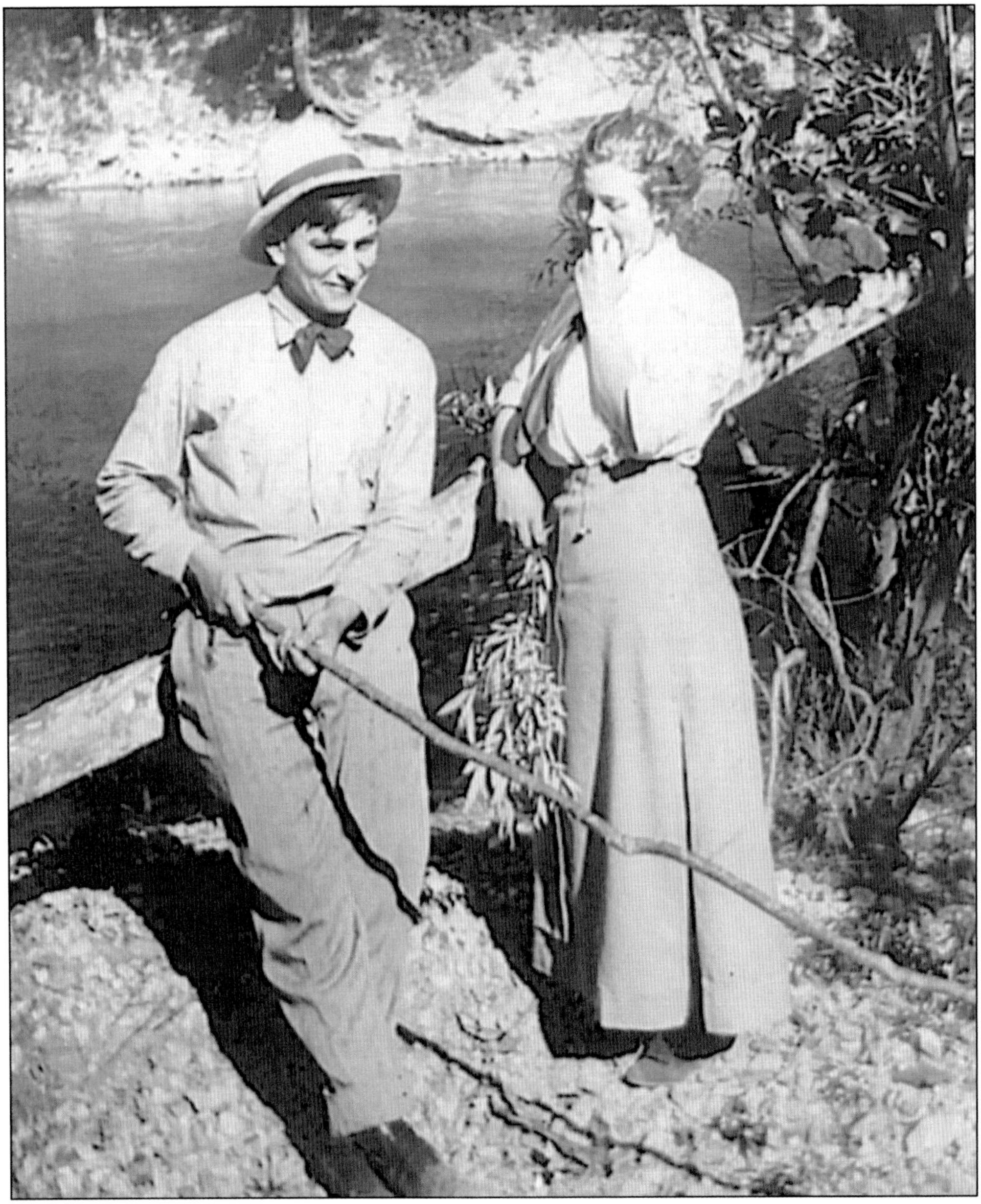

Oklahoma's Beautiful Illinois River, c. 1920. Robert Lee Sanders and a friend enjoy a sunny day on the Illinois River near Tahlequah. The Illinois begins in the Ozarks near Siloam Springs, Arkansas, and flows southwest through the Cherokee Nation and into the Arkansas River. On September 6, 1839, the Cherokee Council met at the Illinois River campgrounds. There they agreed to designate Tahlequah the capital of the Nation. As they had in their eastern homeland, Cherokees had a preference for valley lands. They settled near the rivers and creeks of Indian Territory. In the 1890s, Tahlequah had a city water hauler who took barrels of water from the Illinois to sell to residents. The barrels sold for 10¢ each. Residents from nearby cities and towns built summer homes on the river. In the early 1900s, a residential group organized Sequoyah Inn, a membership outing club where the wealthy went to relax. (Courtesy of Sally Sanders Finch.)

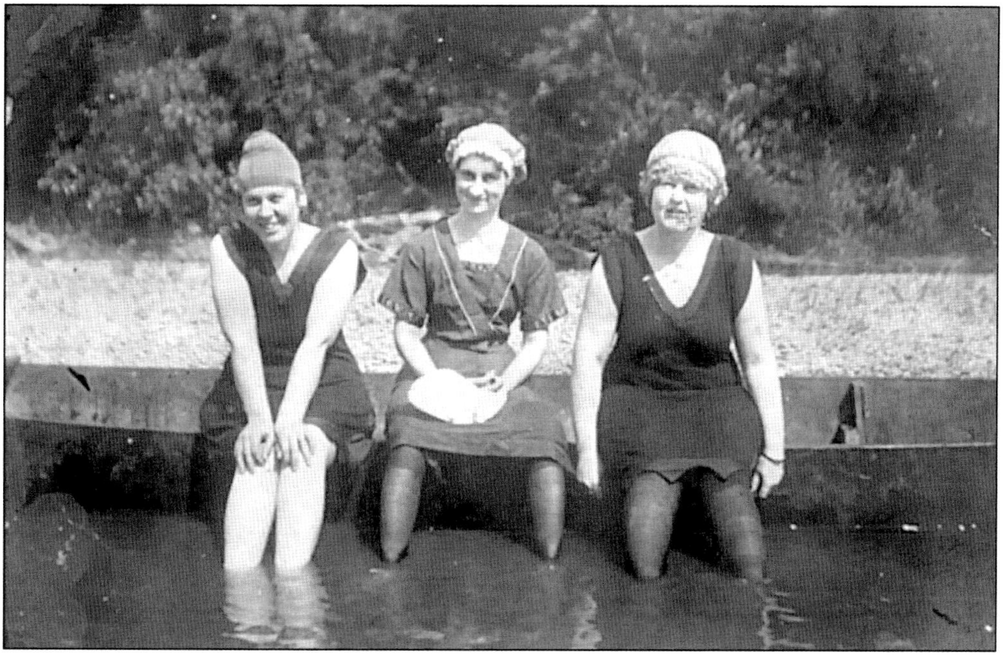

Bathers on the River, c. 1925. Friends Sally, Sadie, and Jane perch on the edge of their flat-bottom boat. Each is wearing proper bathing attire, complete with cap. The light area behind them is a gravel bar, a common sight along the Illinois River, Baron Fork Creek, and Spring Creek. (Courtesy of Cherokee National Archives.)

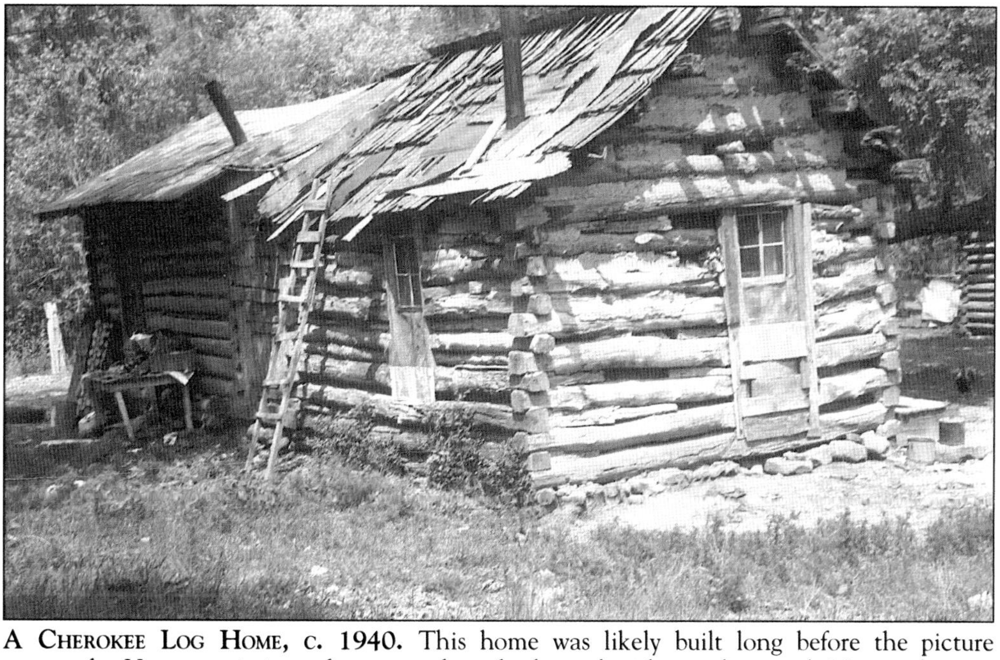

A Cherokee Log Home, c. 1940. This home was likely built long before the picture was made. However, it is modern enough to be heated with wood or coal. Notice the two stove pipes rising above the roof. The house would contain materials from the land, such as hand-cut logs and rock. Even the ladder appears to be homemade. (Courtesy of Cherokee National Archives.)

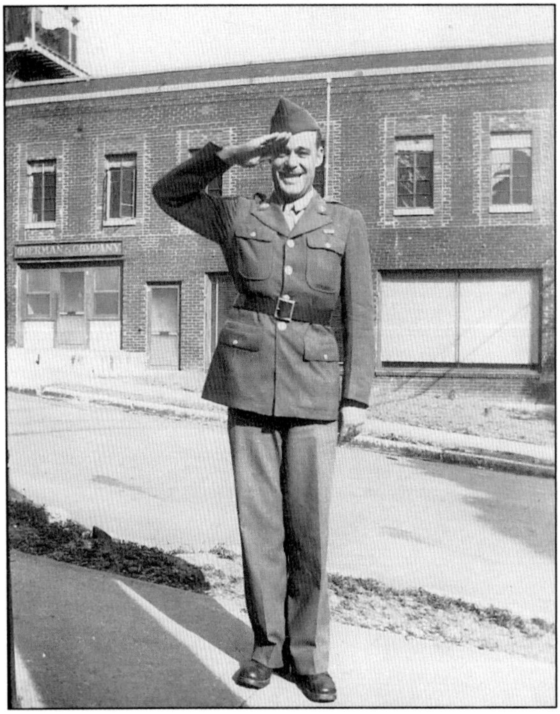

Judd Dickenson, c. 1940. Cale Gideon "Judd" Dickenson salutes the camera. Judd was a popular figure in Cherokee County, having been raised on the south side of Tahlequah. Thought a daredevil, he would streak through the streets on his motorcycle, often with passengers hanging on the back. (Courtesy of Ralph and Loretta Dunham.)

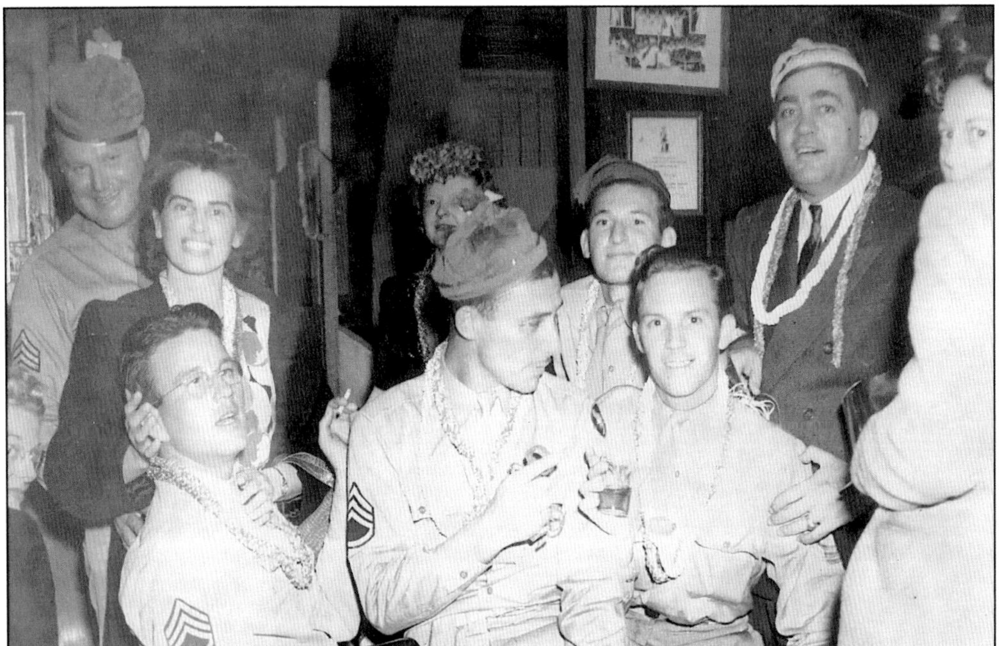

A Weekend in Miami, World War II. Sitting center front, with the hat and cold beer, is Cherokee Hank Baker. After retirement, Hank lived in Texas but traveled every summer to the Cherokee capital. There he volunteered his summer months at the Cherokee Heritage Center, overseeing the grounds crew and making repairs to the facilities. He continued this volunteer work well past the age of 80. (Courtesy of Hank Baker.)

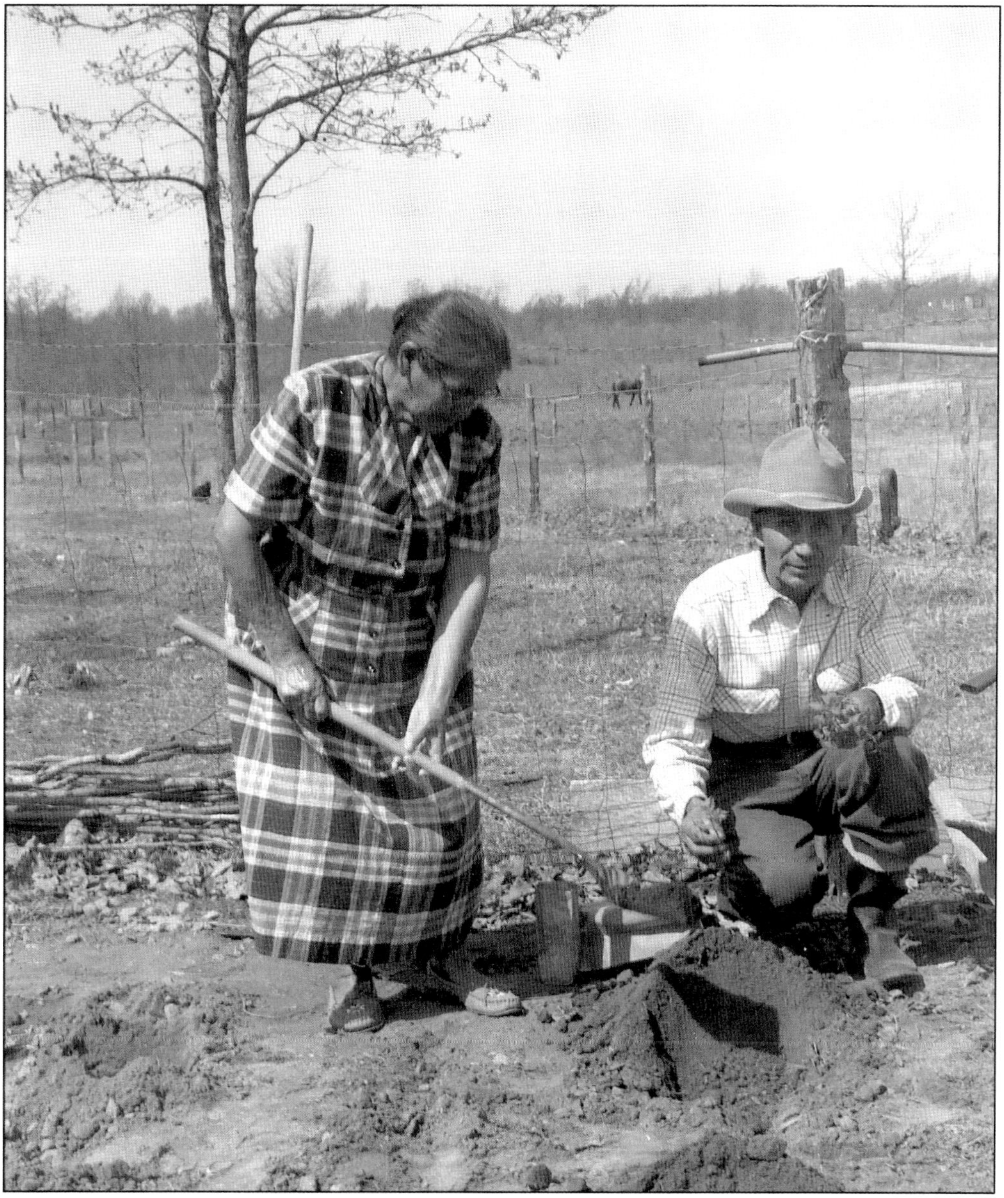

PLANTING TOMATOES, C. 1950. Cherokee County residents Mr. and Mrs. Charlie Smith are preparing their garden for tomato plants. Before the agricultural depression of 1919, cotton was the major crop in the county. Within ten years the price of cotton fell to less than 5¢ per pound. Conditions for farmers continued to worsen when the county was stricken by drought in the early 1930s. The county population dwindled and mortgage foreclosures increased on family farms. The ground in eastern Oklahoma is so rocky one would think it impossible to grow crops. But the soil is fertile and perfect for growing particular crops, such as strawberries. No strawberries compare to those grown in Adair County. Its county seat, Stilwell, is known as the "Strawberry Capital of the World." In Sequoyah County, Sallisaw is the "Black Diamond Watermelon Capital." The hot, dry days of late July and August intensify the sweetness of these big, luscious melons. But perhaps tastiest of all are the homegrown tomatoes of summer, a staple on the Cherokee table. (Courtesy of Cherokee National Archives.)

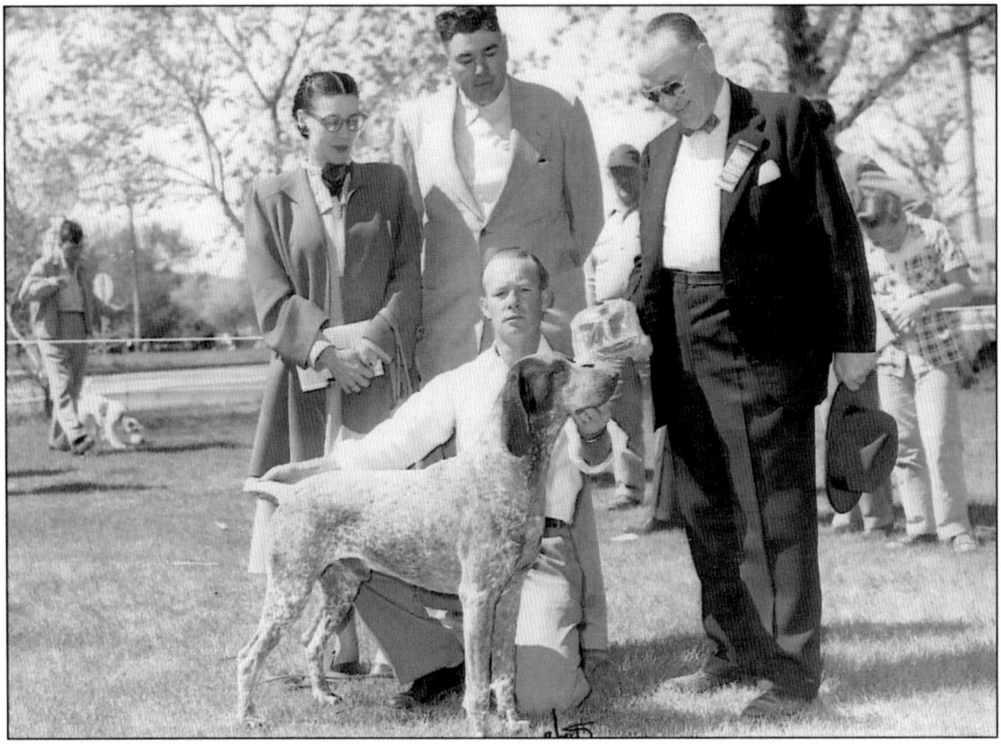

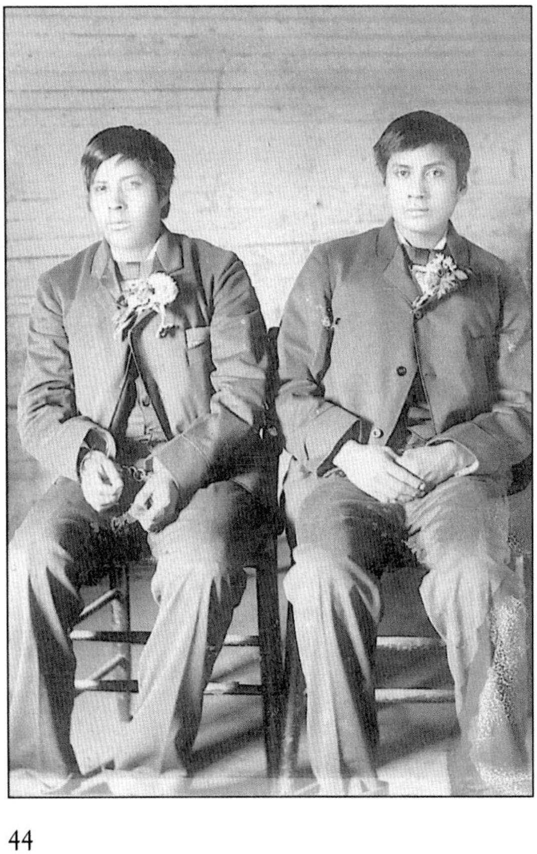

DOGBREEDER SARAH MAYES MCGILBREY, c. 1940. Original enrollee Sarah McGilbrey looks on as an official judges the merits of her dog. Standing beside her is her husband, a professional wrestler of Creek heritage. (Courtesy of Sally Sanders Finch.)

TWIN CHEROKEE TEENAGERS, EARLY 1900s. This pair looks almost identical, even down to the necktie and boutonniere. One could wonder if they are going to a church service, a funeral, or a wedding. On closer inspection, however, it seems more likely they are going to court. Look between the wrists of the young man on the left. The chain linking handcuffs is clearly visible. (Courtesy of Cherokee National Archives.)

Three

EDUCATION

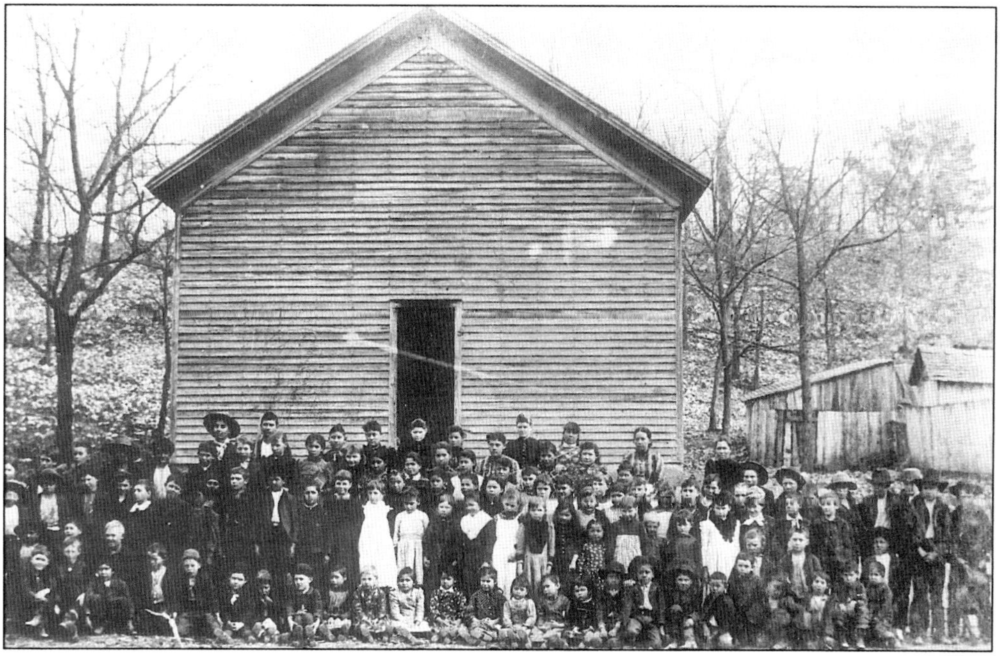

FIRST SCHOOL IN TAHLEQUAH, c. 1874. Practically the first order of business in the reunited Cherokee Nation was a plan for educating children. By 1841, the National Council voted in a public school system controlled by a board of education. In 1845, James M. Payne became superintendent of schools. In 1846, Caleb Covel was appointed the first teacher of the first public school in the city of Tahlequah. The school was built on the east bank of the town branch, in what is now the city park, not far from the Capitol Square. There elementary-aged children were taught reading, writing, and mathematics. However, graduation from the school did not prepare a student to enter the fine colleges back east. The council appropriated funds to construct two seminaries, one for boys and one for girls, which were secondary schools like the high schools of today. The seminaries were built a mile apart at Park Hill. Made of local brick and stone, the sides measured 185 feet by 109 feet. Parts of the buildings were three stories high. Both opened in May 1851. (Courtesy of Cherokee Studies Institute.)

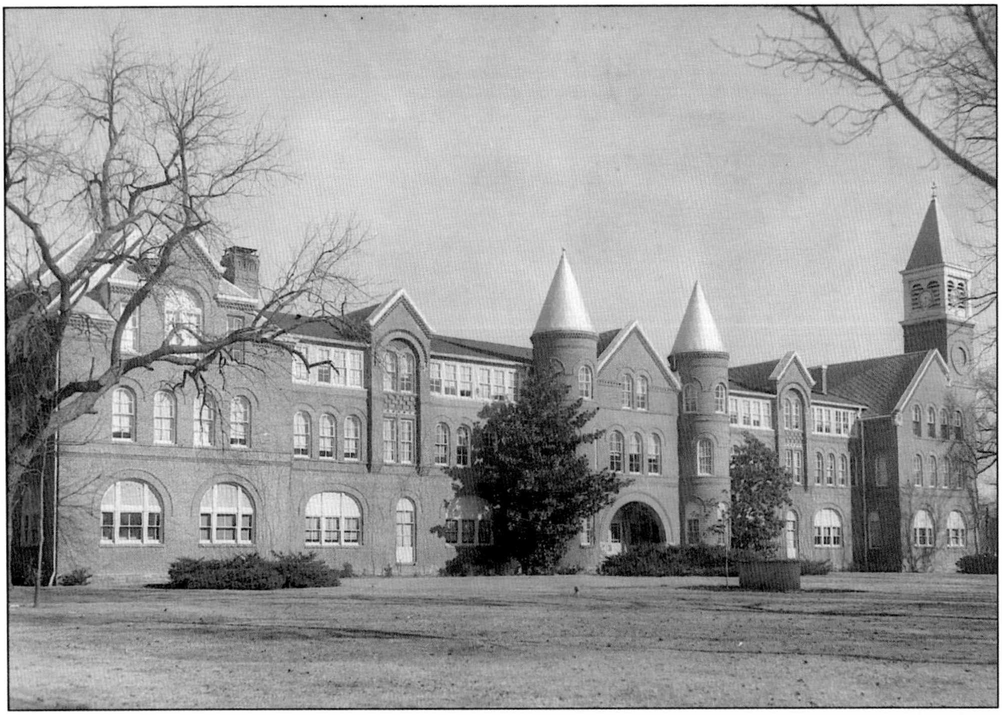

Old Cherokee Female Seminary, c. 1945. This magnificent structure was completed in Tahlequah on April 18, 1889, after the seminary at Park Hill burned in 1887. Tahlequah citizens wanted the seminary built there. With their donations, 40 acres on the north side of town were purchased to accommodate the school. The school had steam heat, hot and cold running water, and could accommodate 250 students. (Courtesy of Cherokee National Archives.)

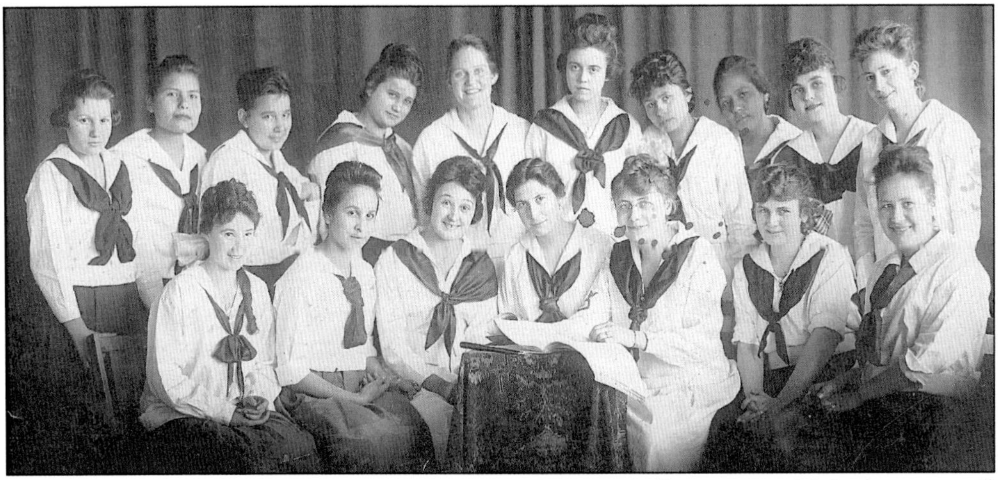

Girls Glee Club at Bacone College, c. 1918. Bacone College was established to serve all the Five Civilized Tribes. Pictured, from left to right, are (seated) Wynifred Cornatzer, Helen Tiger, Martha Harris, pianist Miss Wallace, director Miss Olson, Johnnie Mae Duncan, and Edna Hakeah; (standing) Neva Winton, Margaret Chewie, Minnie Walker, Mattie Henderson, Elizabeth Harris, Irene Lovette, Lizzie Lovette, Minnie Tiger, Winnie Harris, and Bessie Daniel. (Courtesy of Cherokee National Archives.)

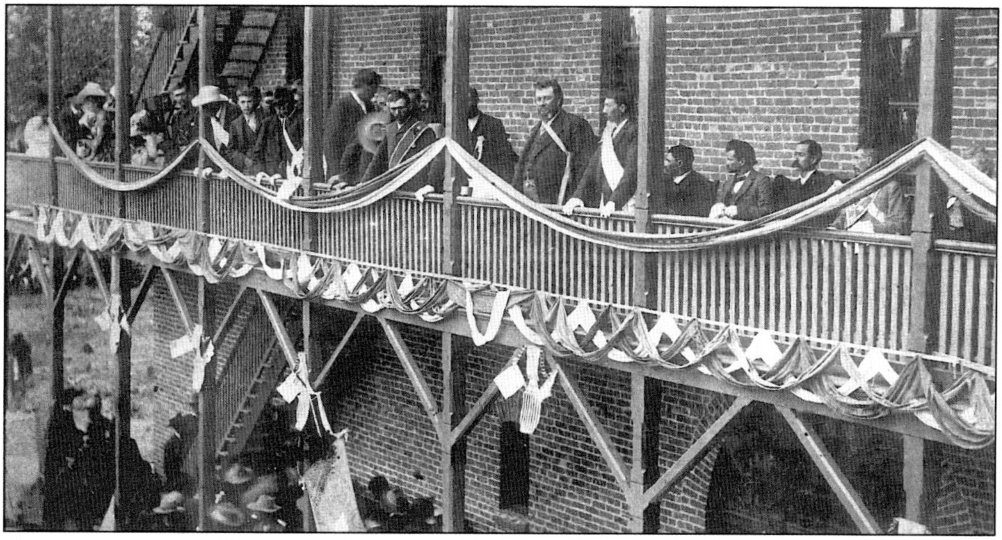

DEDICATION OF THE SEMINARY, MAY 7, 1889. The gala opening of the new Cherokee Female Seminary drew the largest crowd ever assembled in Tahlequah. The visitors enjoyed speeches by Chief Joel B. Mayes and other prominent citizens. The Tahlequah Cornet Band led a procession that included the Masons, Odd Fellows, Sunday school classes, Cherokee Male Seminary students, and many more. (Courtesy of Cherokee Studies Institute.)

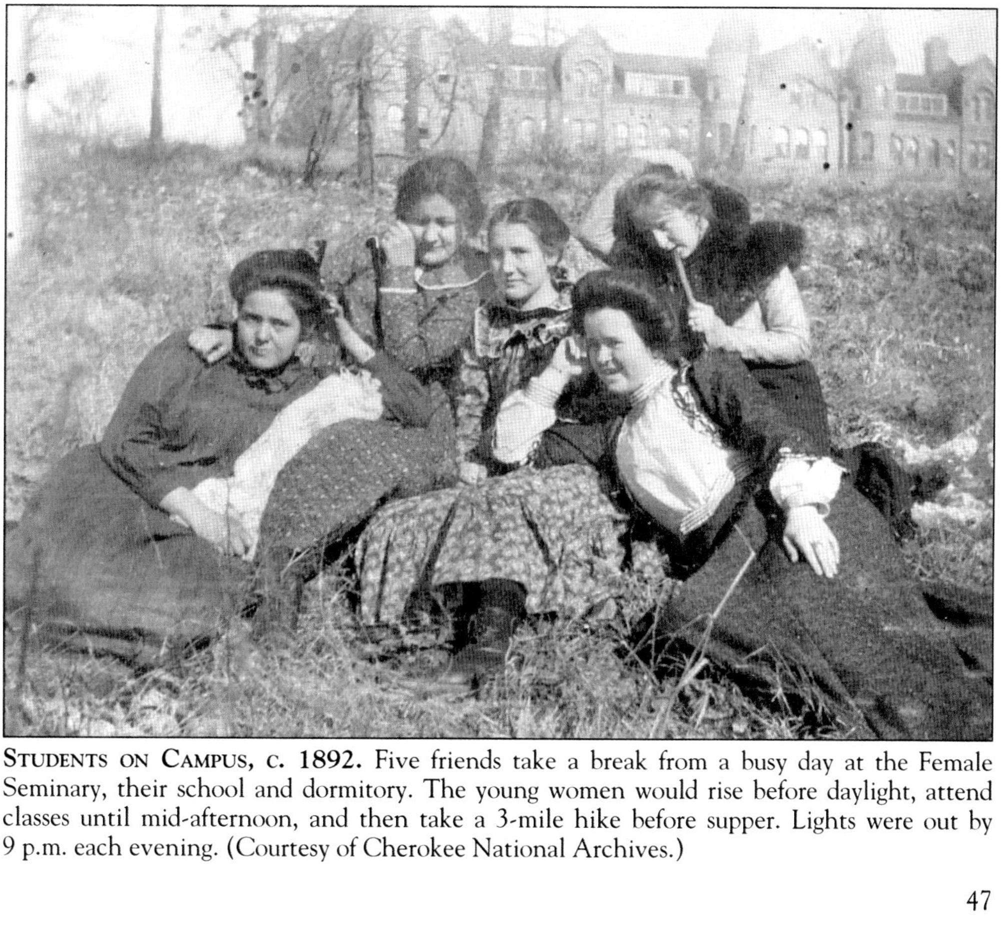

STUDENTS ON CAMPUS, C. 1892. Five friends take a break from a busy day at the Female Seminary, their school and dormitory. The young women would rise before daylight, attend classes until mid-afternoon, and then take a 3-mile hike before supper. Lights were out by 9 p.m. each evening. (Courtesy of Cherokee National Archives.)

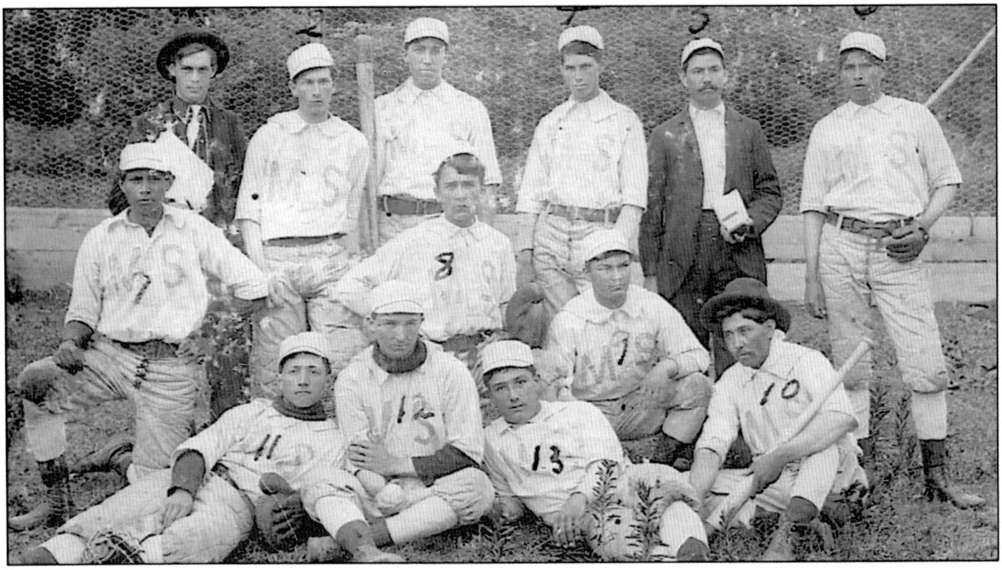

Cherokee Male Seminary Baseball Team, c. 1897. Number six is Big Bush Groves, and number seven is his twin brother Little Bush. It is said that Big Bush once threw nine strikes in a row, putting out three batters in a game against Muskogee's Kendall College. Cherokees have a natural knack for this game, and it is an integral part of community life. (Courtesy of Cherokee National Archives.)

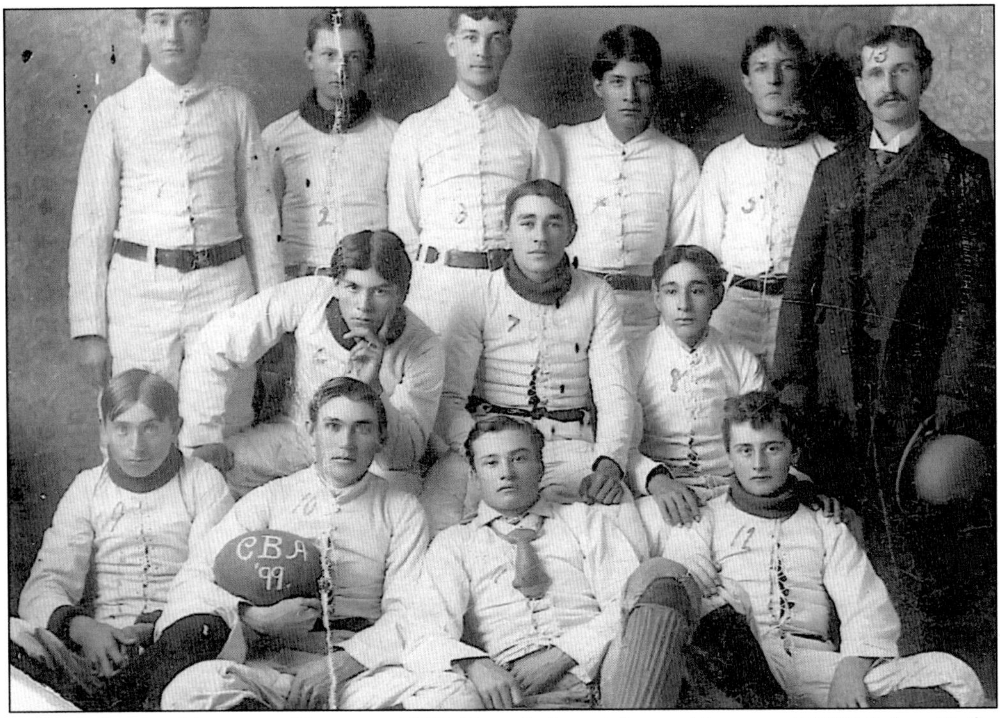

Male Seminary Football Team, c. 1899. From left to right are (front row) Will Baker, Rufus Johnes, Rufus Goodwin, and New Mayes; (second row) Johnson Cunningham, Dennis McNair, Sam Lacy, and Professor Parks; (back row) Roby Wilkenson, Louie Branch, Hiram Thompson, Charles Pritchett, and Alton Brimes. (Courtesy of Cherokee National Archives.)

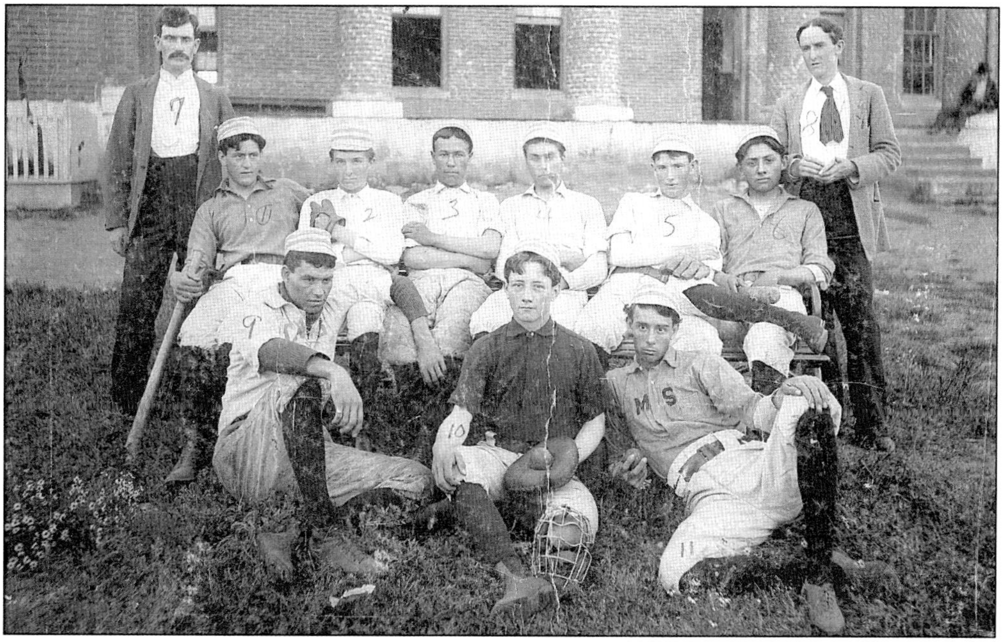

BALL TEAM AT THE MALE SEMINARY, C. 1900. The Cherokee Male Seminary was constructed of bricks made at a kiln in the Cherokee Nation and with local stone. The construction cost $60,000. The seminary opened in May 1851. Only Cherokees were admitted. The classes were rigorous and included Latin, geometry, rhetoric, astronomy, chemistry, and religion. (Courtesy of Cherokee National Archives.)

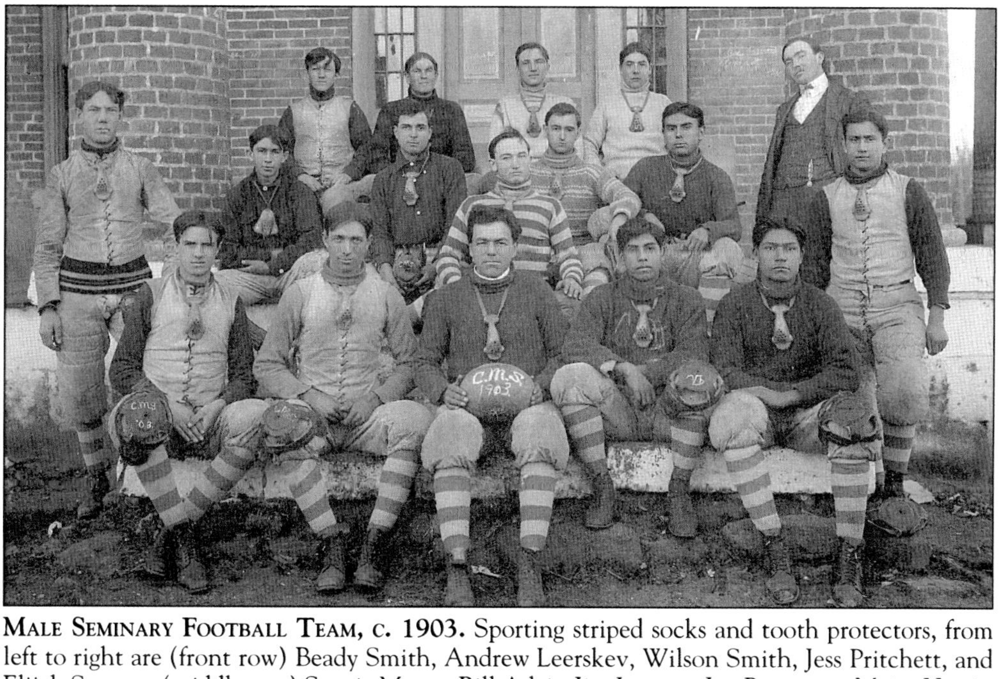

MALE SEMINARY FOOTBALL TEAM, C. 1903. Sporting striped socks and tooth protectors, from left to right are (front row) Beady Smith, Andrew Leerskev, Wilson Smith, Jess Pritchett, and Elijah Scraper; (middle row) Soggie Mayes, Bill Adair, Jim Lowery, Joe Patterson, Major Harris, Houston Ballard, and Bob Fields; (back row) Frank Martin, Jesse James, Fuller Alexander, Paddy Mayes, and W.T. Scott. (Courtesy of Cherokee National Archives.)

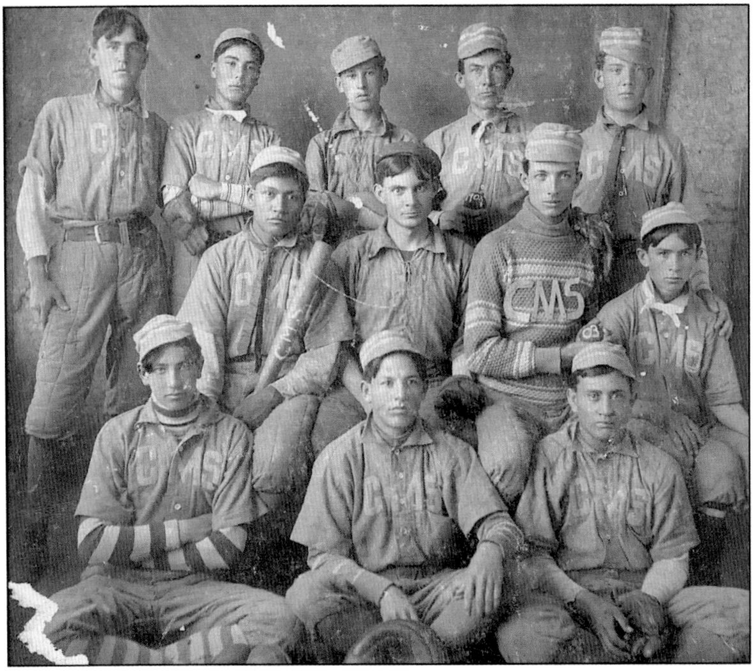

Male Seminary Baseball Team, c. 1903. Pictured, from left to right are (front row) Bob Ironside, Clarence Markham, and Bob Fields; (second row) Elijah Scraper, Claud Duncan, Andrew Lesgrove (holding '03 ball), and Bill Adair; (back row) Joe Adair, Adair Mayes, Bruce Ross, Jim Sanders, and Soggy Mayes. (Courtesy of Cherokee National Archives.)

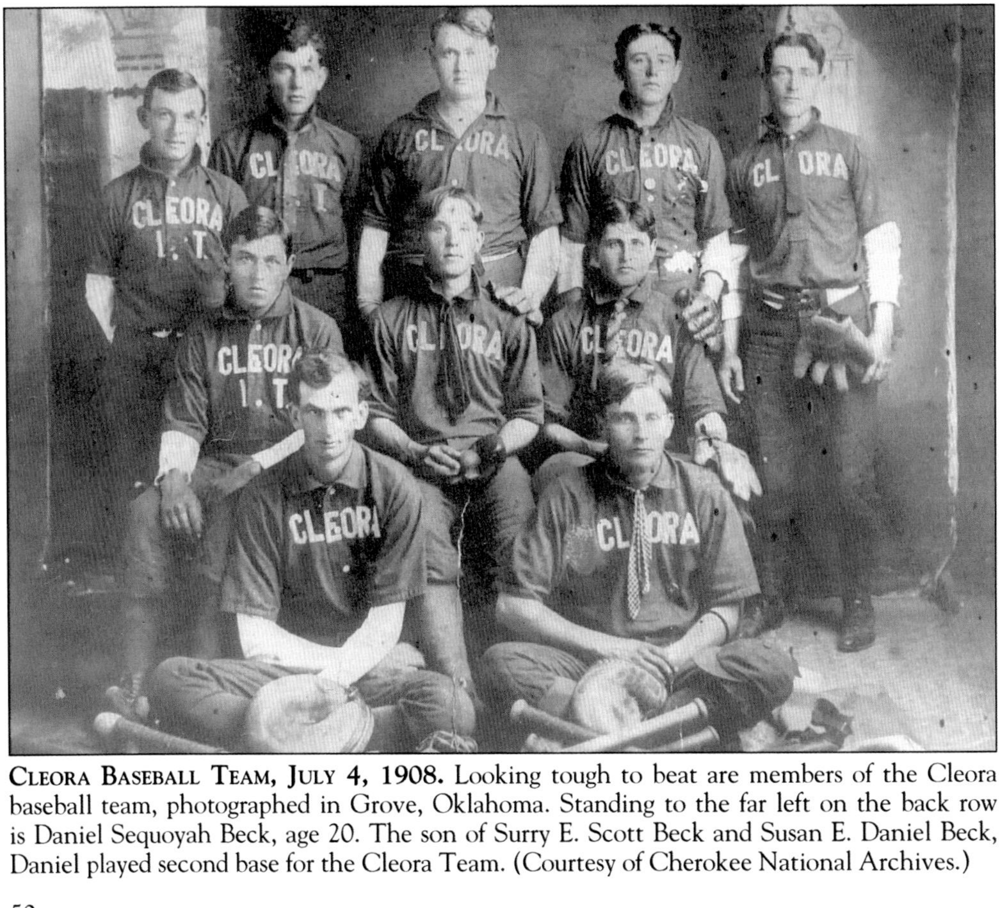

Cleora Baseball Team, July 4, 1908. Looking tough to beat are members of the Cleora baseball team, photographed in Grove, Oklahoma. Standing to the far left on the back row is Daniel Sequoyah Beck, age 20. The son of Surry E. Scott Beck and Susan E. Daniel Beck, Daniel played second base for the Cleora Team. (Courtesy of Cherokee National Archives.)

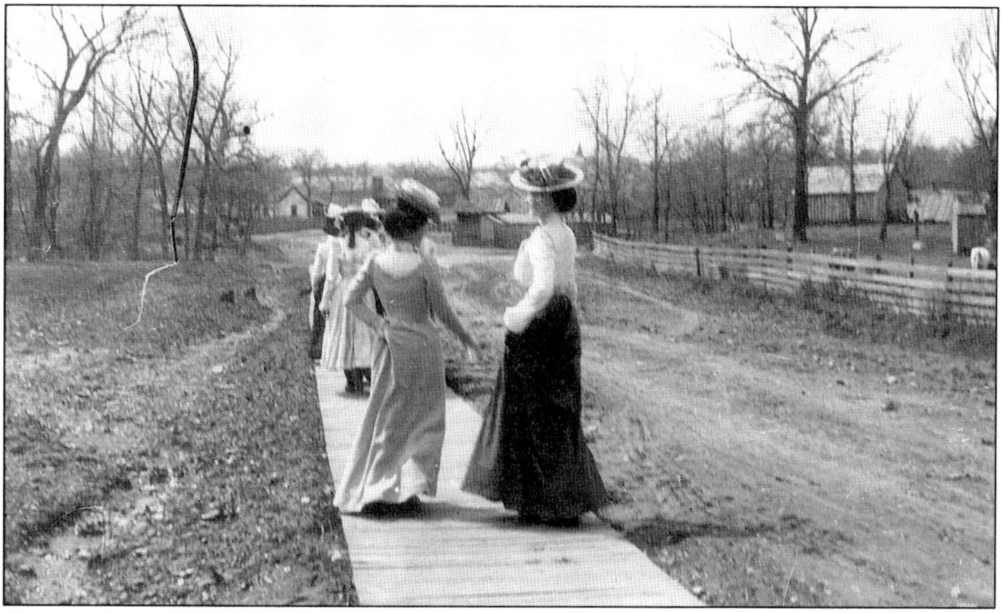

ON THE BOARDWALK IN TAHLEQUAH, C. 1902. Students and teachers at the south end of town walk along the boardwalk toward the Female Seminary. The distant clock tower of the building can be seen just above the woman's hat to the right. This picture, taken by Jennie Ross, gives an excellent view of the outskirts of the city. (Courtesy of Cherokee National Archives.)

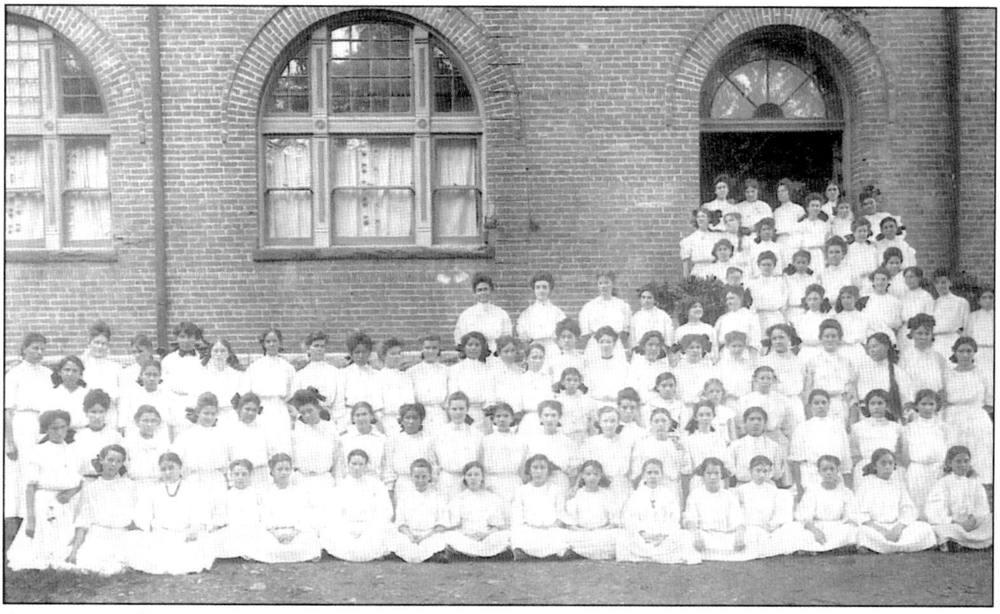

ARITHMETIC PUPILS, FEMALE SEMINARY, C. 1908. Miss Beulah Edmondson was the teacher, and she was assisted by Janana Ballard. Little did they know that a year later the State of Oklahoma would be operating their school. The state purchased the Female Seminary and the land and opened Northeastern Normal School on September 14, 1909. In 1919, the school was upgraded to Northeastern State Teachers College and offered its first bachelors degrees. (Courtesy of Cherokee National Archives.)

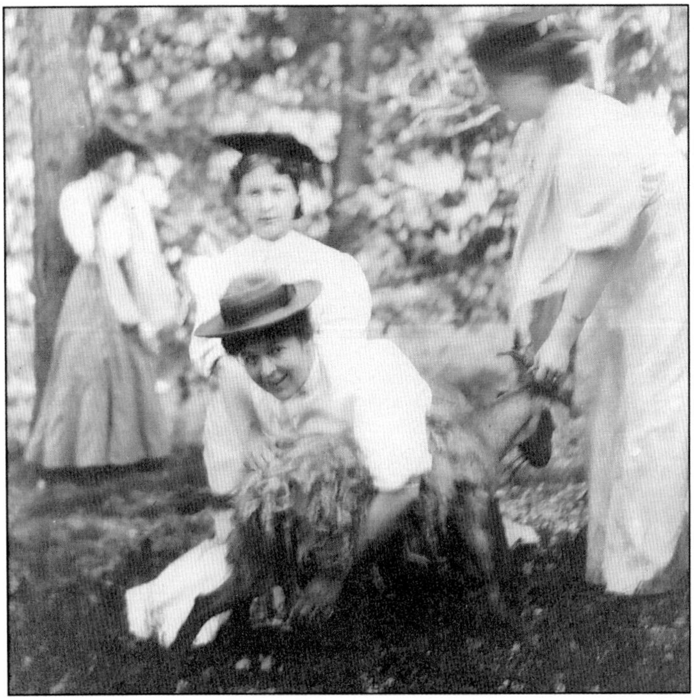

A SEMINARY TEACHER HAD MANY JOBS, C. 1899. Cherokee Female Seminary instructor Miss Mosser displays her goat-milking skills as a student named Vera holds the goat by the horns. Chores such as this were simple facts of life at the turn of the century. (Courtesy of Cherokee National Archives.)

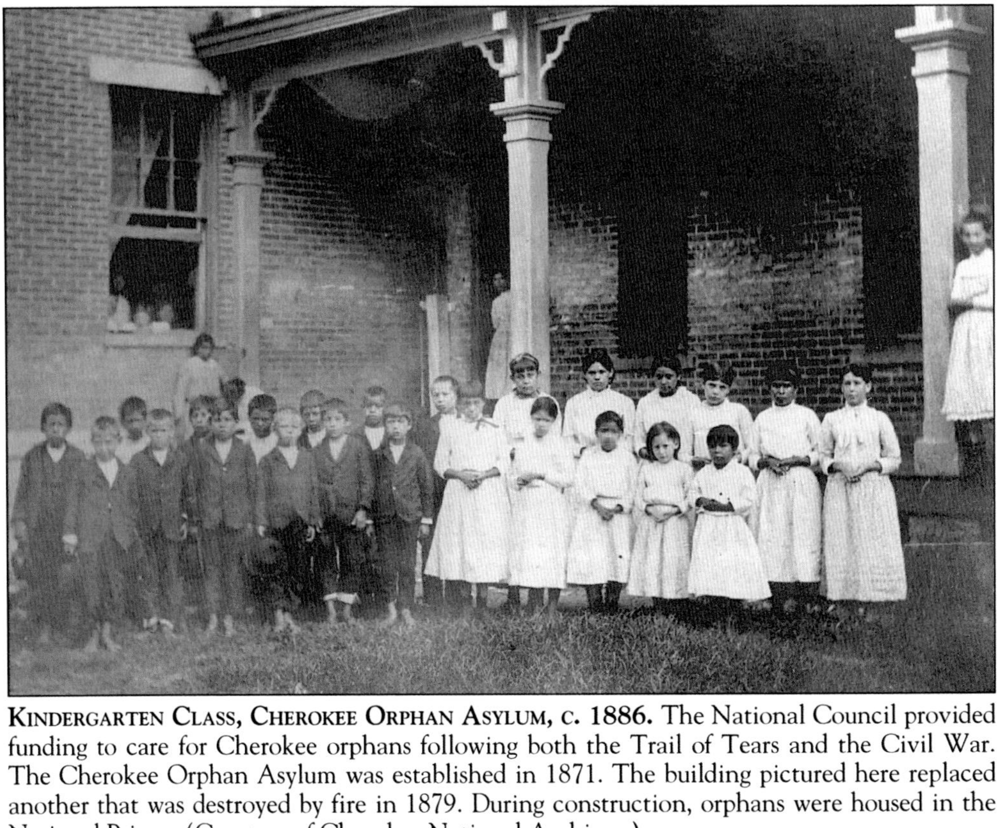

KINDERGARTEN CLASS, CHEROKEE ORPHAN ASYLUM, C. 1886. The National Council provided funding to care for Cherokee orphans following both the Trail of Tears and the Civil War. The Cherokee Orphan Asylum was established in 1871. The building pictured here replaced another that was destroyed by fire in 1879. During construction, orphans were housed in the National Prison. (Courtesy of Cherokee National Archives.)

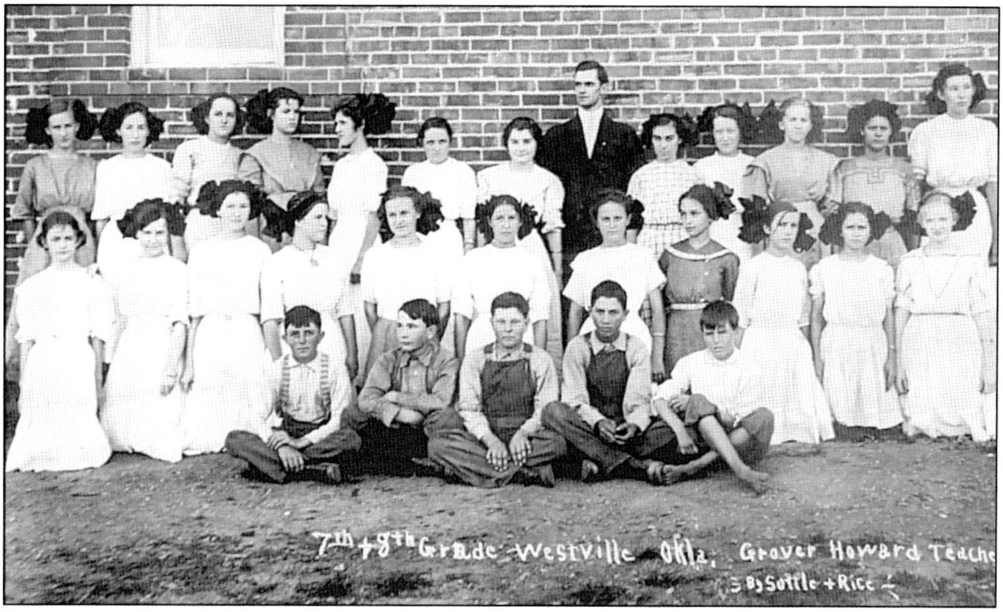

WESTVILLE, OKLAHOMA STUDENTS, EARLY 1900S. Standing outside their school are the seventh and eighth grade students of Westville, Oklahoma. A small Adair County community, Westville had an economy that centered around the lumber industry and fruit production. In 1920, over 150 train car loads of apples were shipped from Westville, and in 1951, there were over 500 acres of grape vineyards and berry patches. (Courtesy of Cherokee National Archives.)

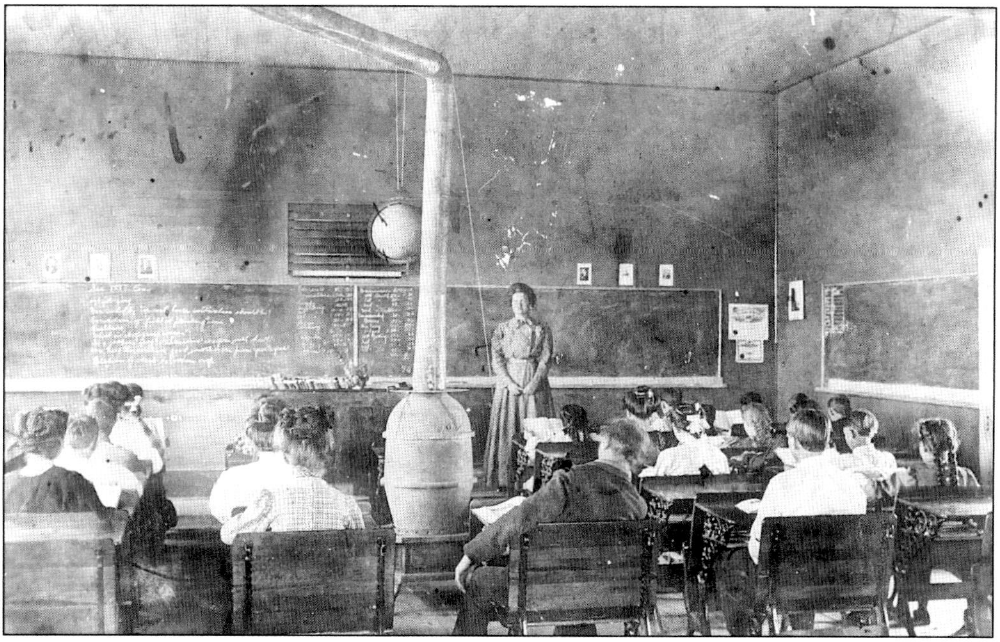

VERDIGRIS SCHOOL ROOM, C. 1908. This elementary school room looks much like the classrooms of today. However, there could be up to eight grades represented by these students. The older children sit near the back of the room. Notice the long stove pipe, suspended globe, and the handiwork of the wooden and iron desks. (Courtesy of Rogers State College.)

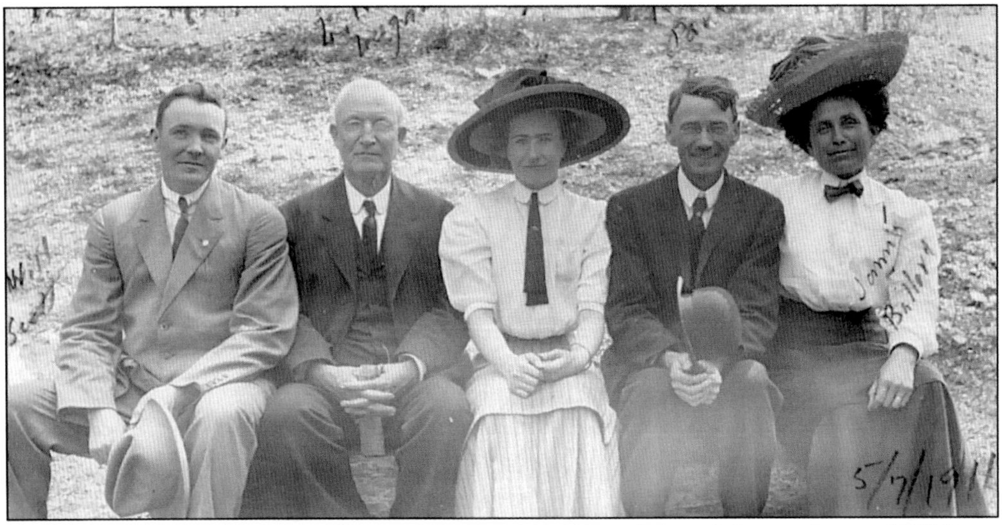

TEACHERS AND PREACHERS IN TAHLEQUAH, C. 1903. Seated, from left to right, are Will Scott and L.M. Logan, teachers at the Cherokee Male Seminary; Will's sister Susie Scott; Methodist minister James Parks; and Janana Ballard, teacher at the Cherokee Female Seminary. (Courtesy of Cherokee National Archives.)

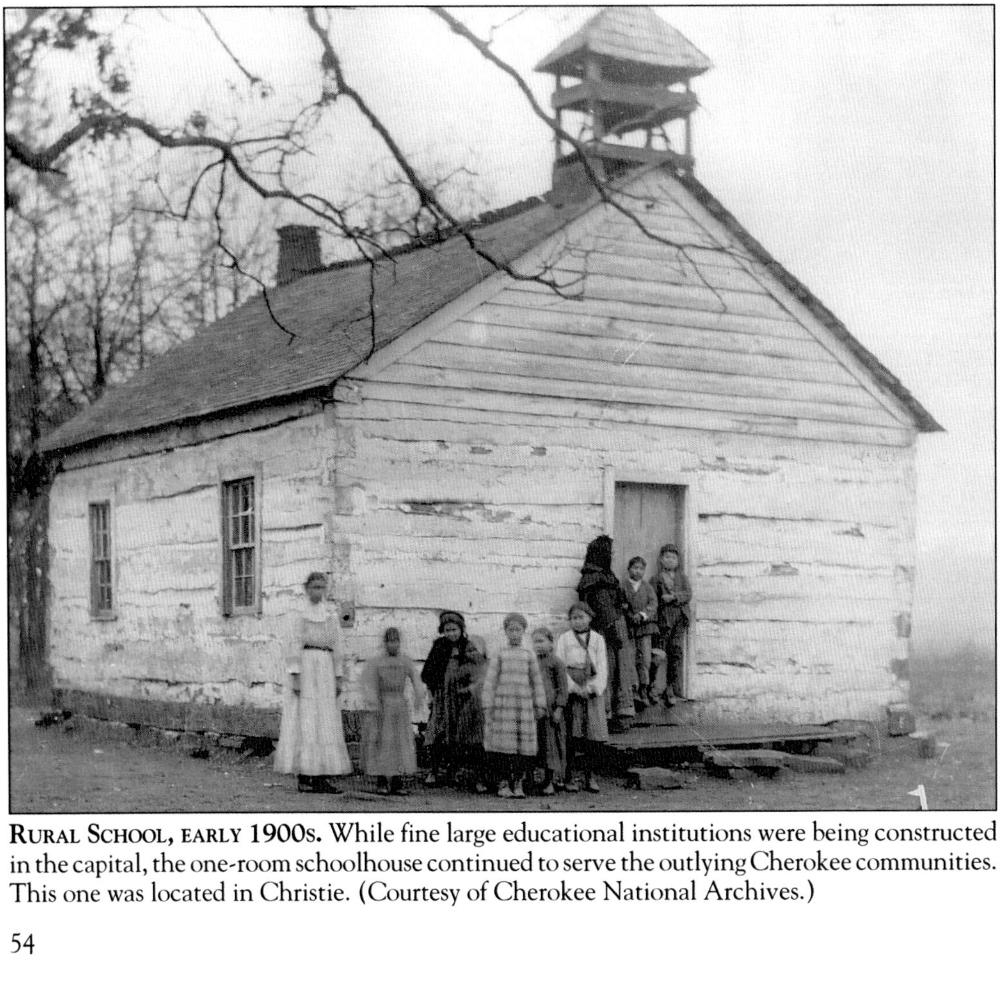

RURAL SCHOOL, EARLY 1900S. While fine large educational institutions were being constructed in the capital, the one-room schoolhouse continued to serve the outlying Cherokee communities. This one was located in Christie. (Courtesy of Cherokee National Archives.)

ROUNDBALL PLAYERS, c. 1914. These Tahlequah Central High School basketball players look feminine in their uniforms, but they were formidable opponents on the court. Pictured are Myrtle Leitch, guard, and center Maud Cooper, holding the ball. (Courtesy of Cherokee National Archives.)

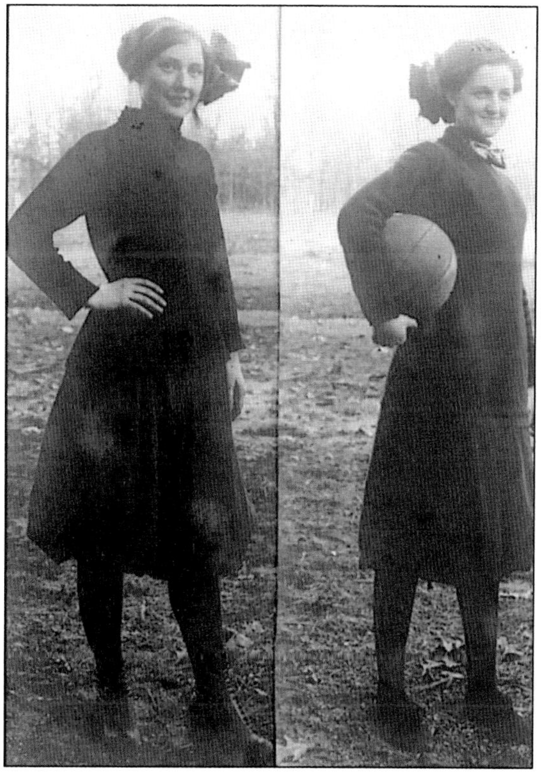

SCHOOL OFFICIALS IN ROGERS COUNTY, c. 1925. This office in the old Rogers County Courthouse was home to School Superintendent F.E. Lamons and Deputy Miss Nannie Lipe. Notice the old electric fan and light fixture. (Courtesy of Rogers State College.)

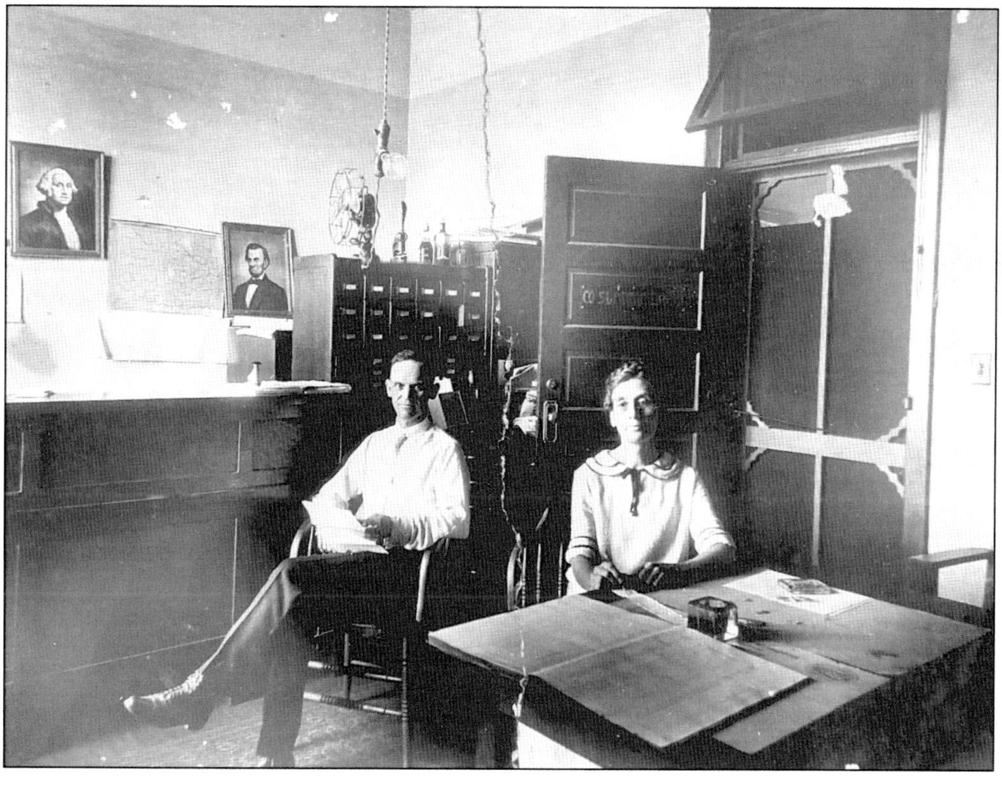

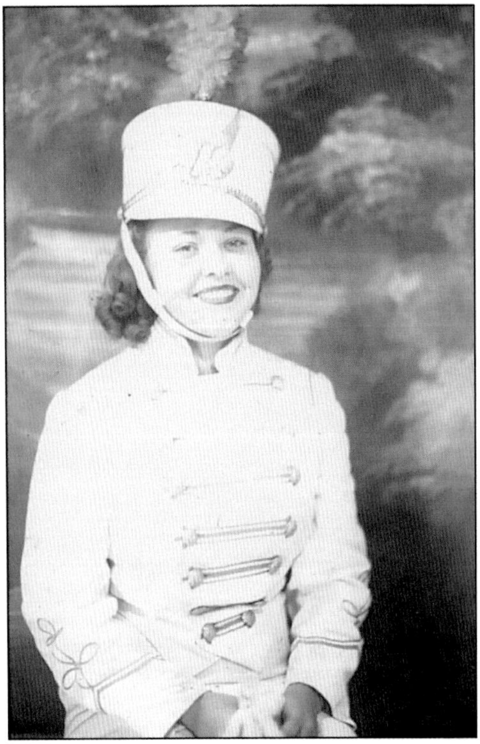

DRUM MAJOR JEWEL CRABTREE, C. 1935. Those who remember her say that Jewel Crabtree was a feisty, friendly, and popular student at the high school in Tahlequah. She is shown here in her drum major uniform. (Courtesy of Ralph and Loretta Dunham.)

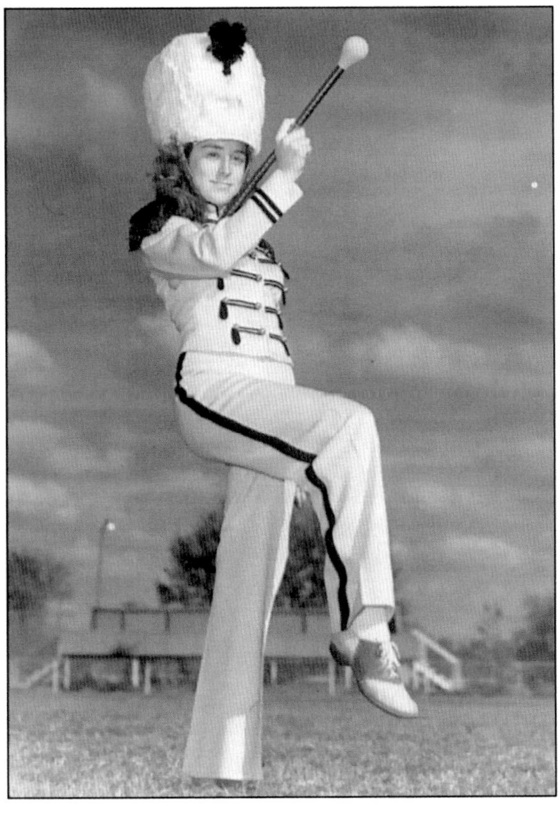

SALLY SANDERS FINCH, C. 1947. Before she became a Finch, Sally Sanders was a highly skilled drum major for her high school band. Her uniform was just as elaborate as the ones seen today. Sally is a direct descendant of Principal Chief Joel B. Mayes. (Courtesy of Sally Sanders Finch.)

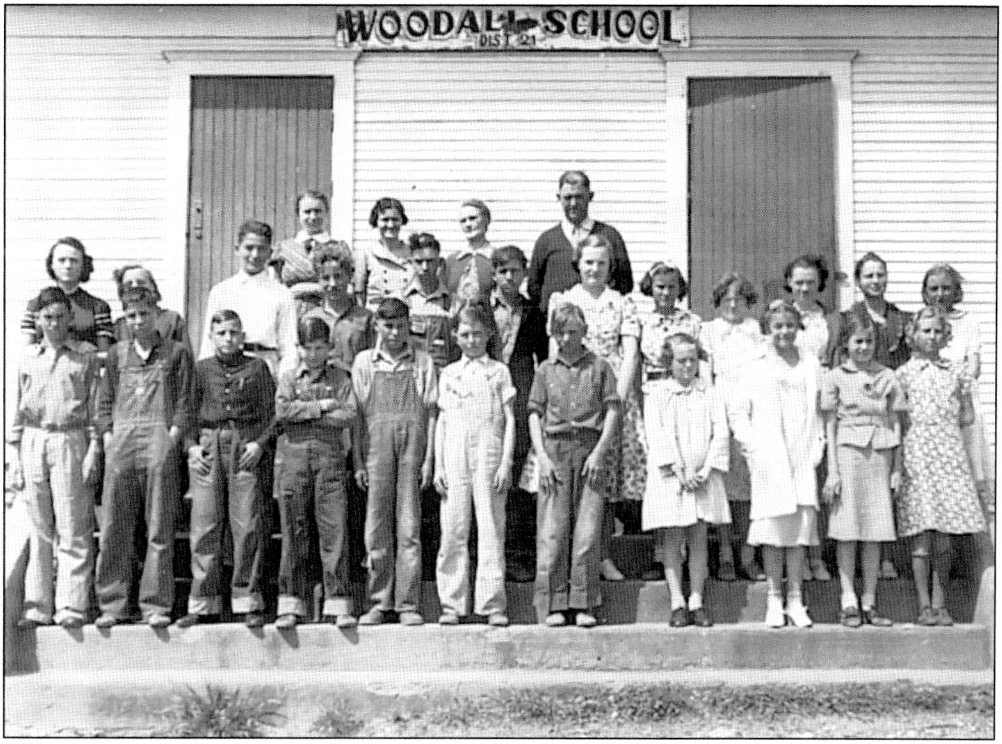

Woodall School, c. 1948. Students from the Woodall community gather on the front steps of the Woodall School. Woodall is a pleasant area a few miles southwest of Tahlequah. As in numerous rural schools in the area, students will attend through the eighth grade and then transfer to the Tahlequah school system. (Courtesy of Cherokee National Archives.)

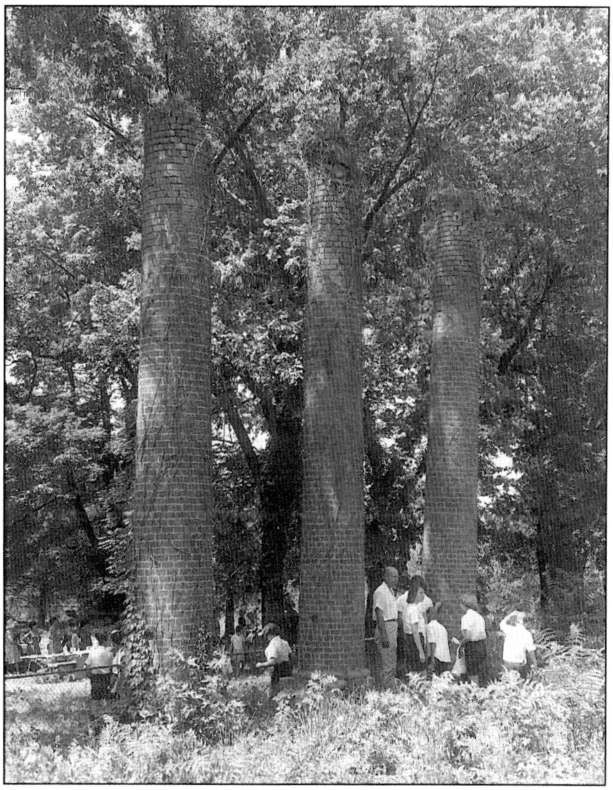

Female Seminary Ruins at Park Hill. On Easter Sunday, April 10, 1887, the original Cherokee Female Seminary at Park Hill caught fire and was totally destroyed. It is said that even the school bell was consumed by the heat. The three columns shown here are all that remain. This wooded area will become the park-like grounds of the Cherokee Heritage Center. (Courtesy of Cherokee National Archives.)

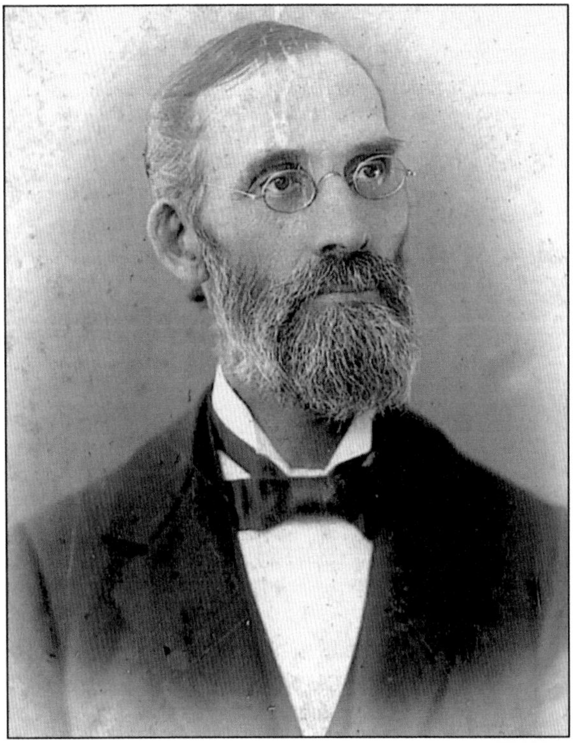

BAPTIST MISSIONARY EVAN JONES, c. 1860. Reverends Jesse Bushyhead and Lewis Downing were students of Evan Jones at Valley Town, North Carolina, in the 1820s. Jones journeyed with the Cherokees across the Trail of Tears and reestablished the Baptist Mission Church in Indian Territory. There Jones worked as an activist abolitionist before and during the Civil War. (Courtesy of Cherokee National Archives.)

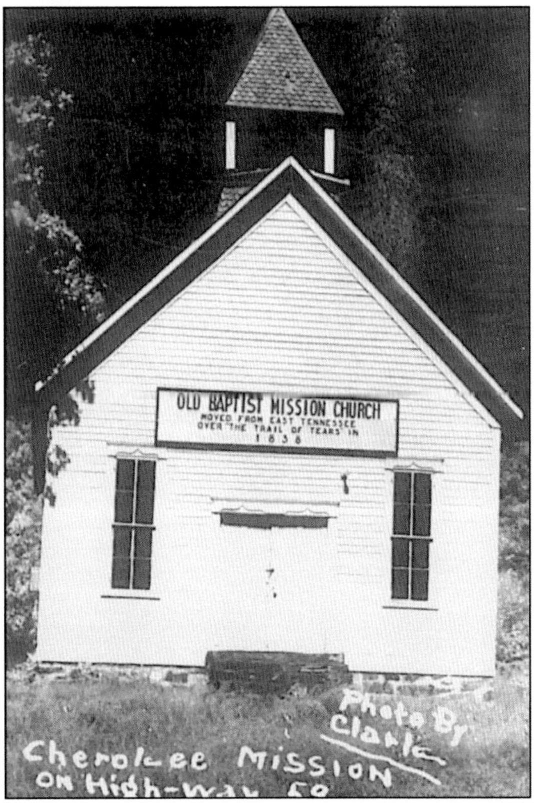

CHEROKEE MISSION, c. 1910. The sign reads, "Old Baptist Mission Church, moved from East Tennessee over the Trail of Tears in 1838." From this building, Evan Jones issued the *Cherokee Messenger*, a magazine printed in both Cherokee and English. Here he helped to organize "The Pins," a group of Cherokees opposed to slavery who had frequent skirmishes with Southern sympathizers. (Courtesy of Cherokee Studies Institute.)

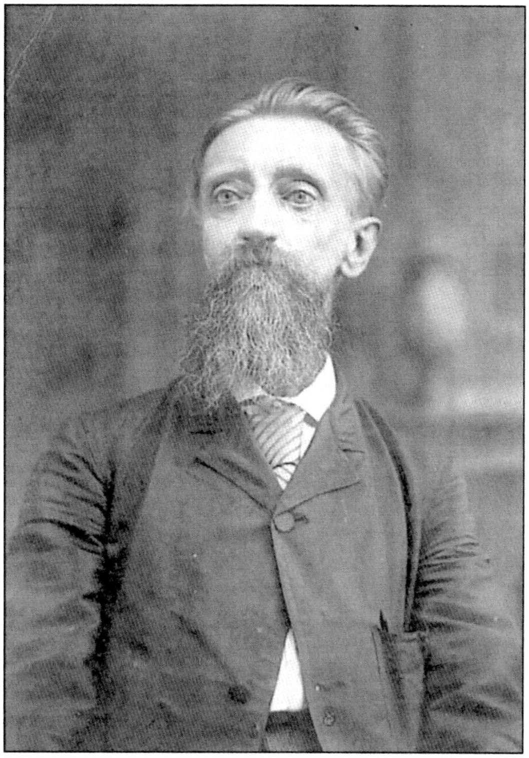

MORAVIAN, MR. WRIGHTS, c. 1875. Moravian missionaries enthusiastically helped deliver Sequoyah's syllabary to the Cherokees in the 1820s. They traveled with the tribe to Indian Territory during the removal. There they built New Springplace near the present-day Oaks community. The mission was burned during the Civil War. Until it could be rebuilt, classes were held in Park Hill's Female Seminary dining hall. (Courtesy of Cherokee National Archives.)

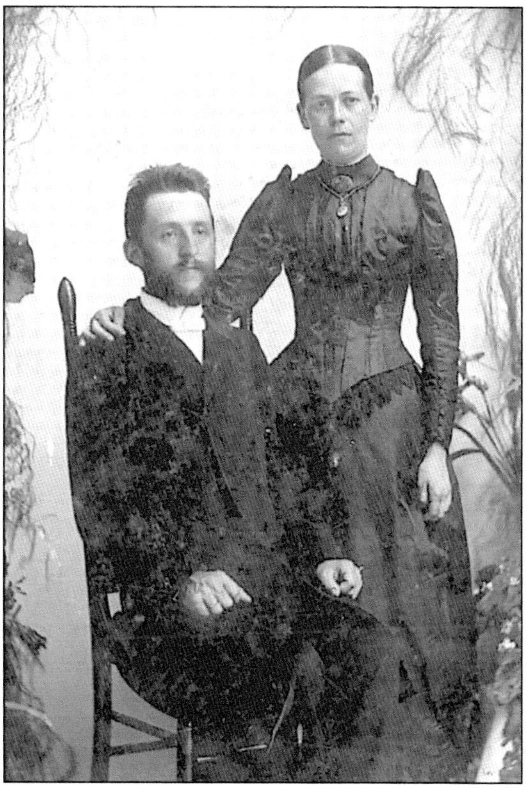

MORAVIANS, MR. AND MRS. BECK, c. 1880. Around 1800, radical changes of philosophy took place in the eastern Cherokee Nation. Until then, Cherokees had resisted both white education and the Christian religion. But a new desire for knowledge led to the first mission school, operated by the Moravian missionaries. Religious studies were allowed only if they remained secondary to mathematics, reading, and writing. (Courtesy of Cherokee National Archives.)

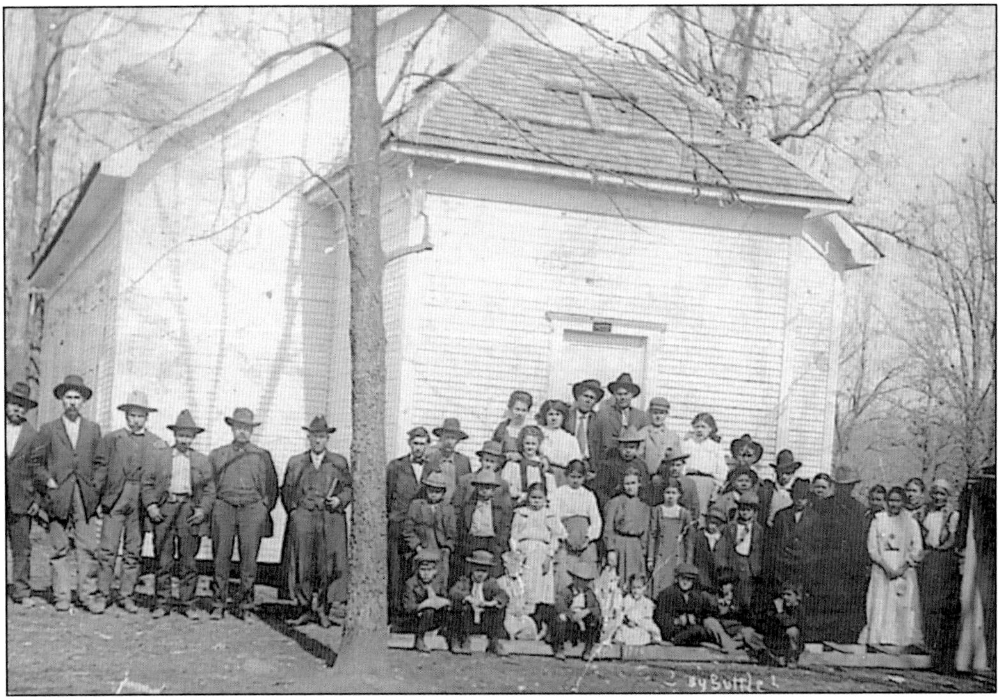

Rural Cherokee Church, c. 1900. Original Cherokee settlements were usually situated near fresh streams of water. As more families gathered, rural communities were formed and given names. Some might be fortunate enough to have a store, but practically all had a church such as the one shown here. Today, services in the Cherokee language are enjoyed in several community churches. (Courtesy of Lena Fourkiller.)

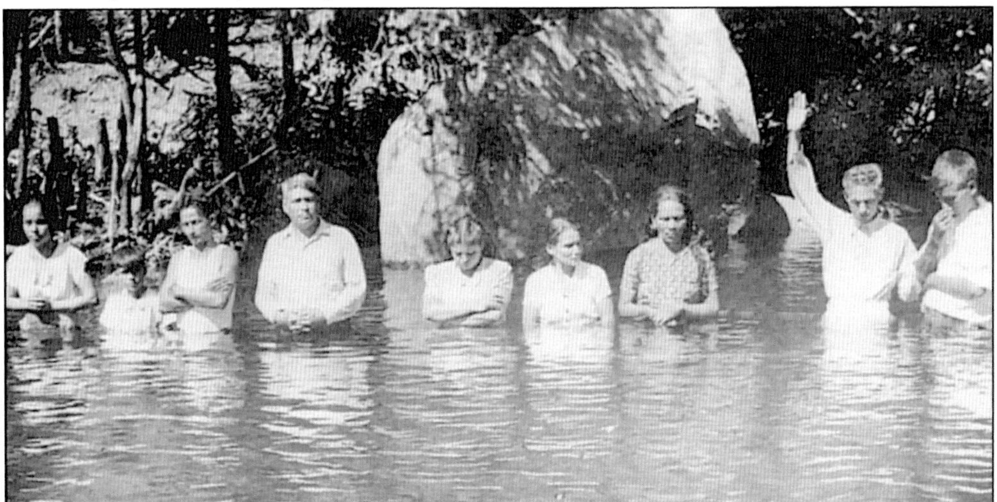

Cold Water Baptism in Welling, Oklahoma. Even on the hottest day in August, Baron Fork Creek runs crisp and cold thanks to the abundance of springs that feed its waters. These believers are being baptized the old-fashioned way, by being totally immersed in the cold water. It is still common to happen upon a baptism service on creeks and rivers in the Cherokee Nation. (Courtesy of Cherokee Studies Institute.)

Four

Community

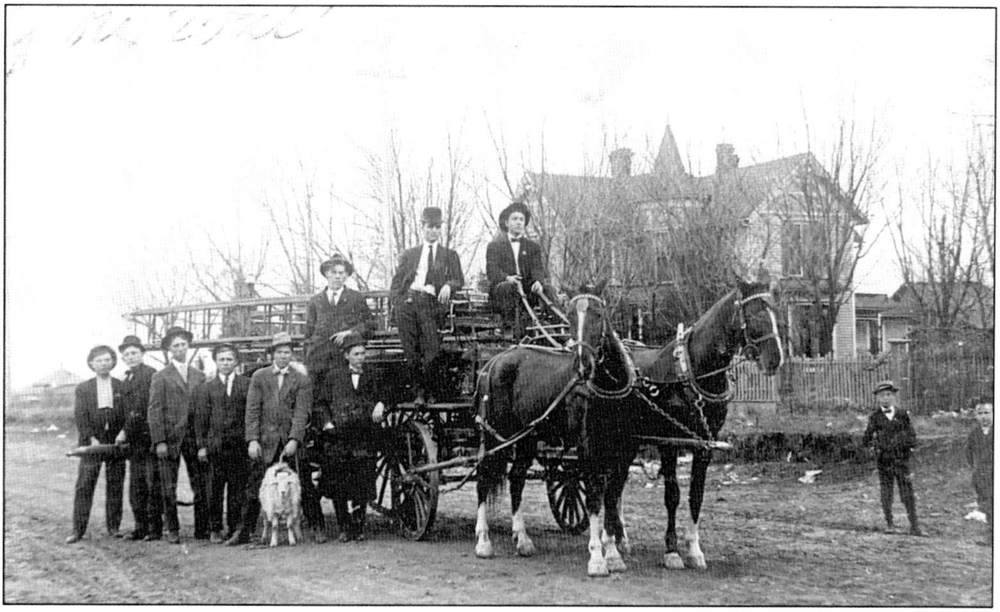

Claremore Fire Wagon, c. 1908. A horse-drawn fire wagon pauses before a fine home in Claremore. The gentleman second from left holds the heavy nozzle that directs the water. Perhaps the goat is a mascot for the firefighters. The wagon and team of horses would have cost up to $1,700 or $1,800, an essential investment for the growing city. The city of Claremore got its name from the chief of a band of Osage living near the Verdigris River. He was called "Clah-Mo," or Clermont in English. Old Settler Cherokees who raised cattle in the vicinity did not get on well with the Osage. Soon, missing cattle were traced to the Osage camp. Cherokee Chief Spring Frog led Cherokees armed with rifles against Osages with arrows. The match was no contest. Clermont became a Cherokee settlement. The families gradually moved eastward to be nearer the Frisco railroad in the 1870s. A spelling error recorded the name of the post office as Claremore, and the name has remained with the city ever since. (Courtesy of Rogers State College.)

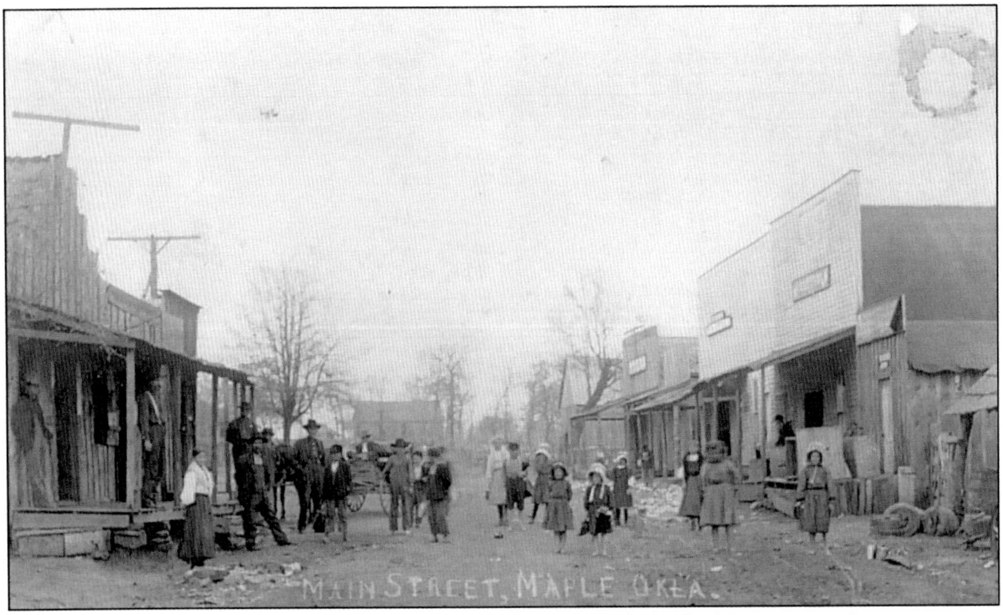

MAIN STREET OF MAPLE, c. 1909. The small town of Maple looks like a scene from a western movie. One of the buildings once served as the first courthouse for the Sequoyah district of the Cherokee Nation. From there it was moved to Sallisaw, the present county seat. (Courtesy of Sequoyah County Historical Society.)

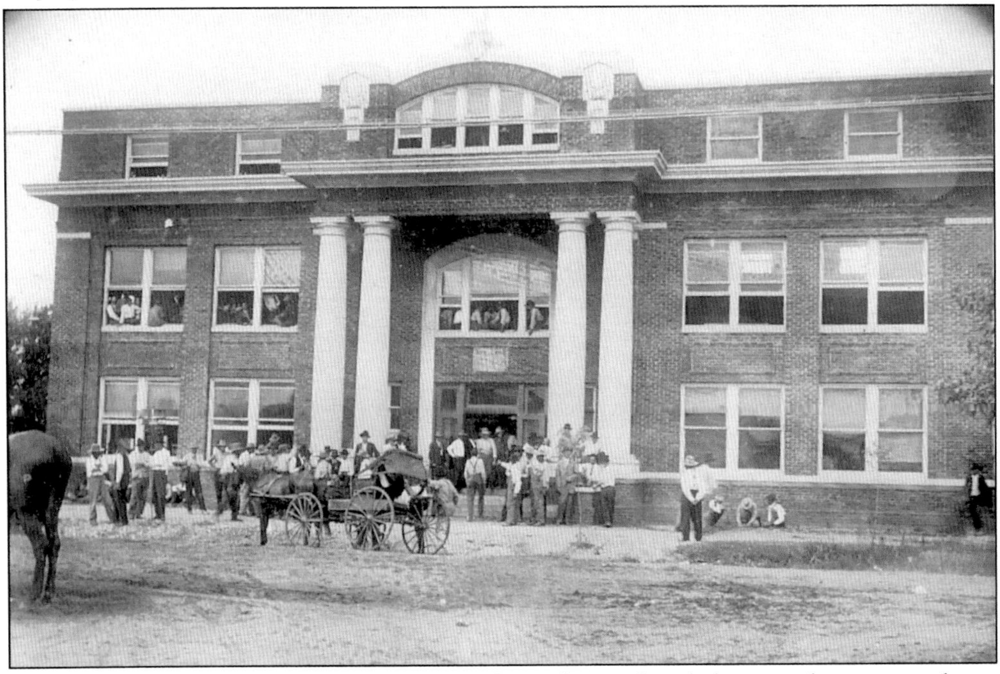

SEQUOYAH COUNTY COURTHOUSE, c. 1914. In early statehood this courthouse was always bustling with activity. Citizens are even seated in the window sills, looking out over the town. Sallisaw, Oklahoma, acquired this fine building in 1914. In later years the beautiful white columns were encased in bricks, perhaps to attain a more modern look. (Courtesy of Sequoyah County Historical Society.)

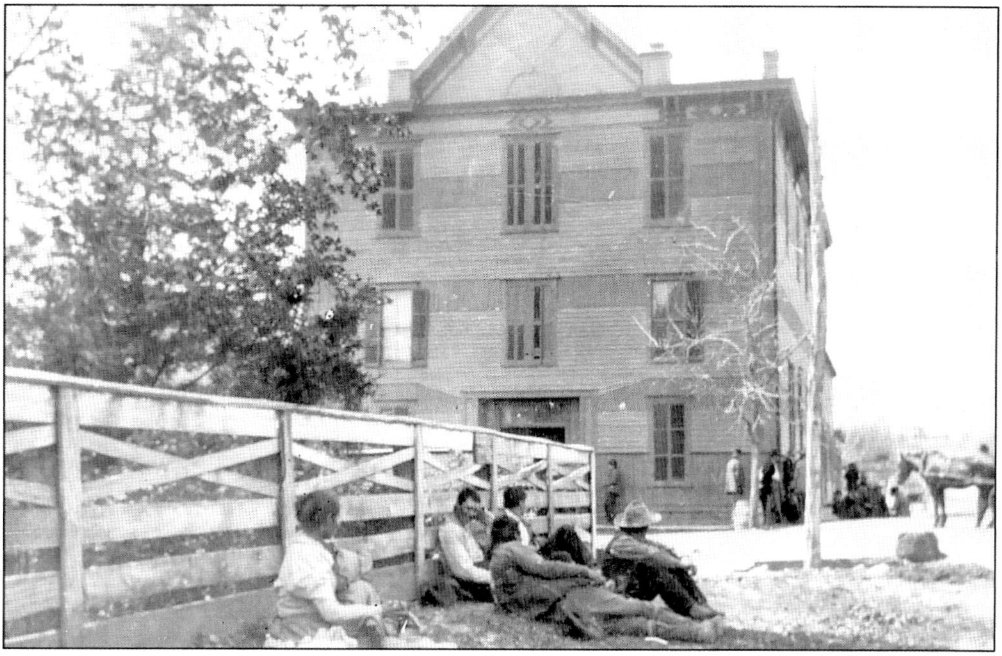

UNITED STATES COURTHOUSE, C. 1901. This imposing frame structure served as a federal courthouse in Indian Territory. Notice the people relaxing against the board fence. Perhaps they await an appointment inside. Within a few years and with the coming of land allotment, the courthouse will become a busy place indeed. (Courtesy of Cherokee National Archives.)

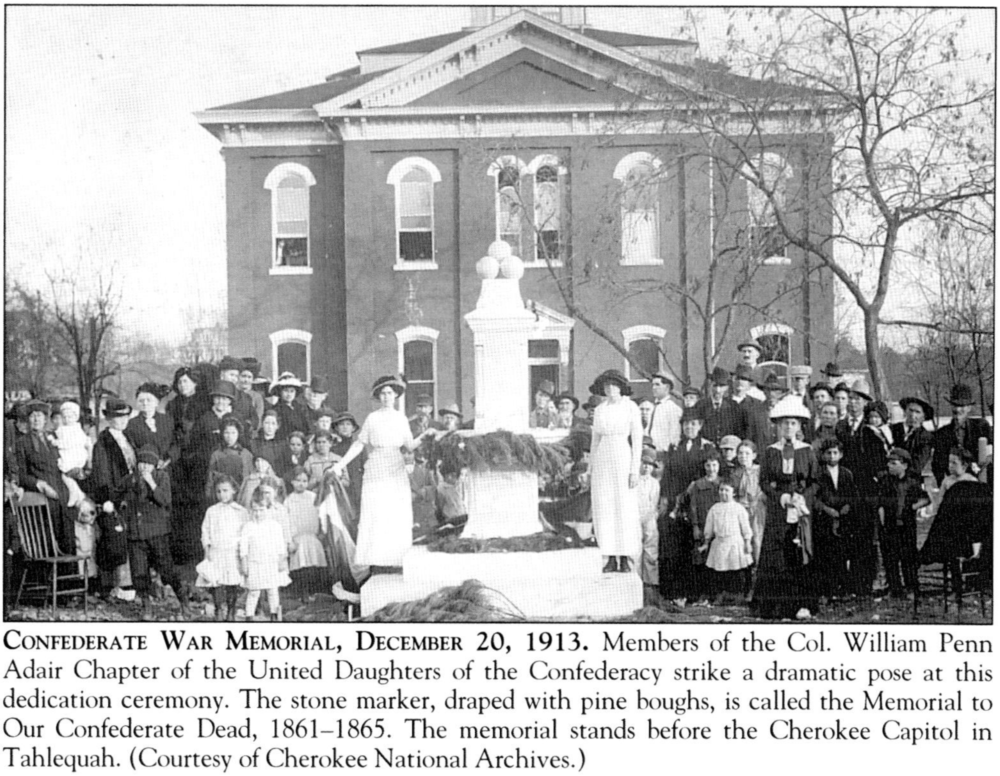

CONFEDERATE WAR MEMORIAL, DECEMBER 20, 1913. Members of the Col. William Penn Adair Chapter of the United Daughters of the Confederacy strike a dramatic pose at this dedication ceremony. The stone marker, draped with pine boughs, is called the Memorial to Our Confederate Dead, 1861–1865. The memorial stands before the Cherokee Capitol in Tahlequah. (Courtesy of Cherokee National Archives.)

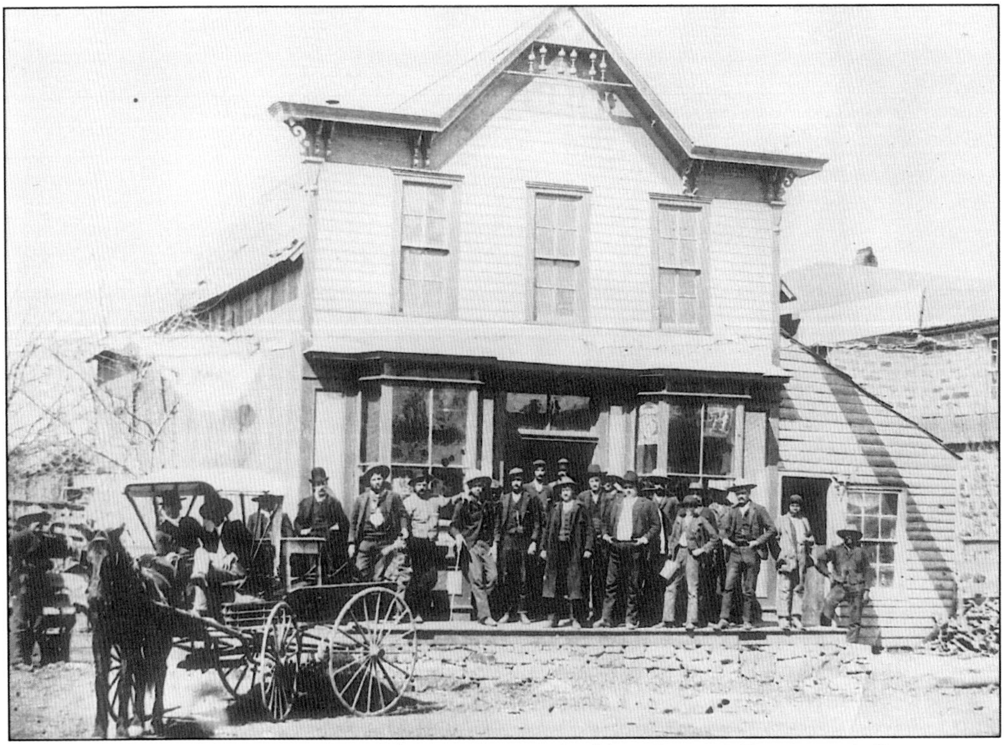

Brown's Drug Store, c. 1892. This impressive building housed Brown and Company, a drug store opened in Tahlequah in 1889. The venture was a partnership between M.R. Brown and Dr. Joe M. Thompson. Later the store would add a $600 soda fountain. On through the 1960s, the major drug stores in town featured full service soda fountains. (Courtesy of Cherokee Studies Institute.)

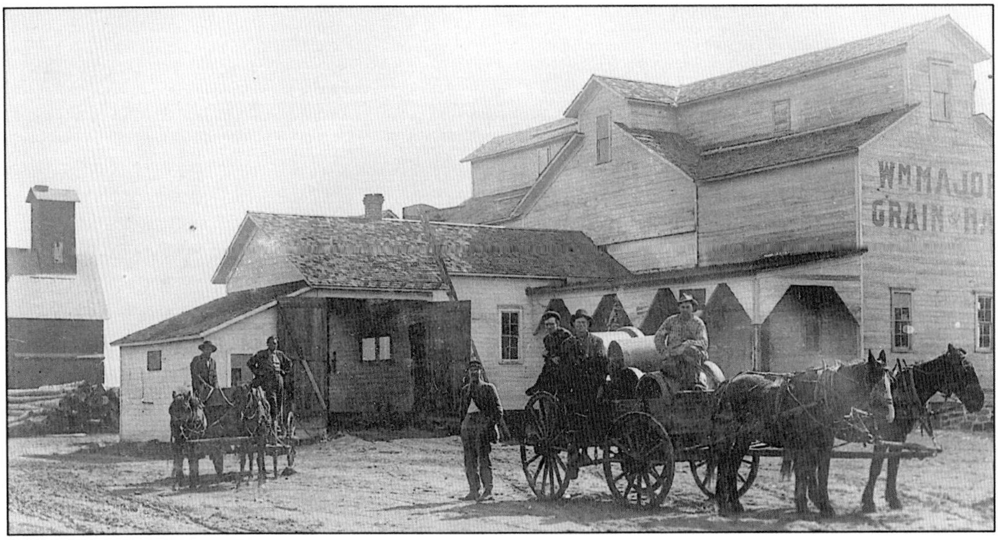

Bushyhead Grain Elevator, c. 1907. The grain and feed establishment was, and still is, an essential part of commerce in rural farming communities. The town of Bushyhead was founded in 1898 and named for Dennis W. Bushyhead, principal chief of the Cherokee Nation. (Courtesy of Rogers State College.)

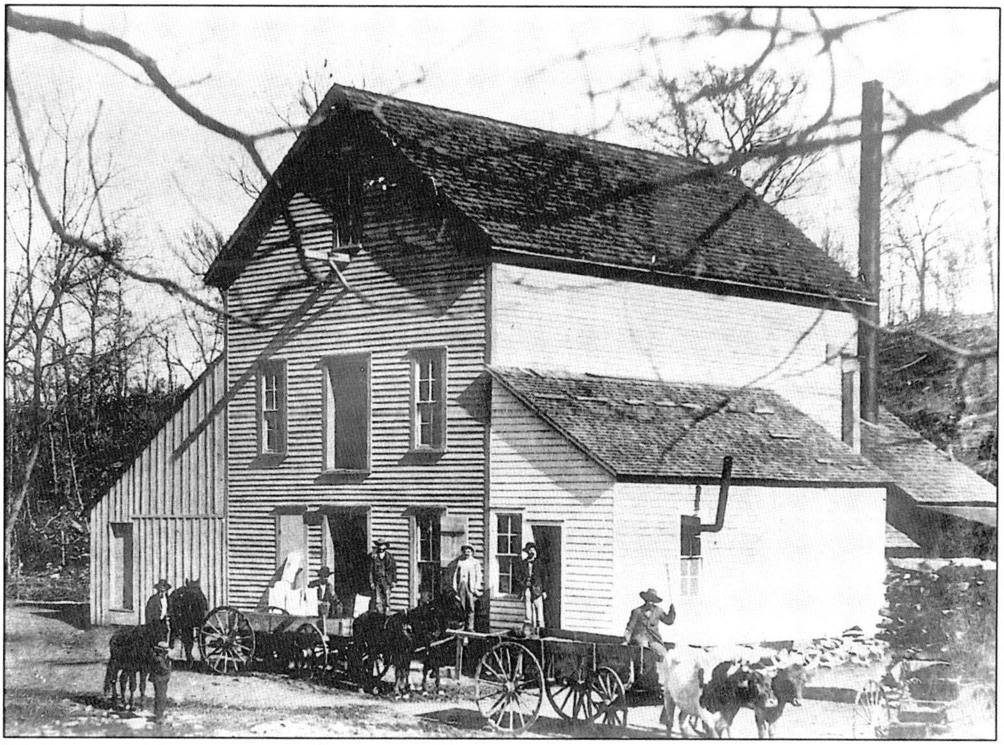

McSpadden Mill, c. 1890. The McSpadden Grist and Flour Mill was located on the southeast side of Tahlequah, along Bear Creek (commonly called the town branch). Notice that the wagon in front is being pulled by a team of oxen. (Courtesy of Cherokee Studies Institute.)

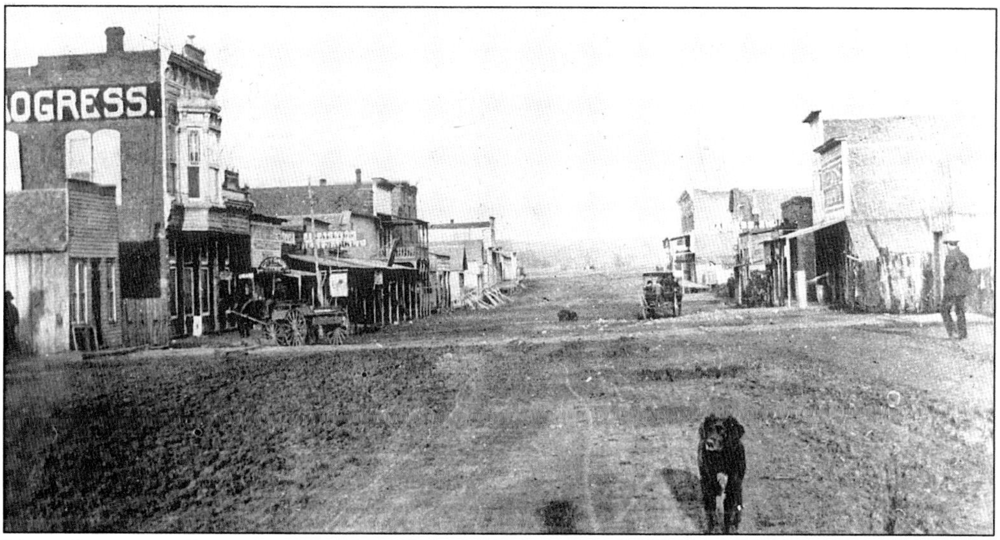

Main Street in Claremore, Indian Territory, c. 1895. From humble beginnings grow great cities. In 1890, the town of Claremore, formerly Clermont, had only 200 residents. Claremore's claims to fame are America's favorite son Will Rogers and Lynn Riggs, author of *Green Grow the Lilacs*. The play inspired the hit musical *Oklahoma!* by Rodgers and Hammerstein. (Courtesy of Will Rogers Memorial.)

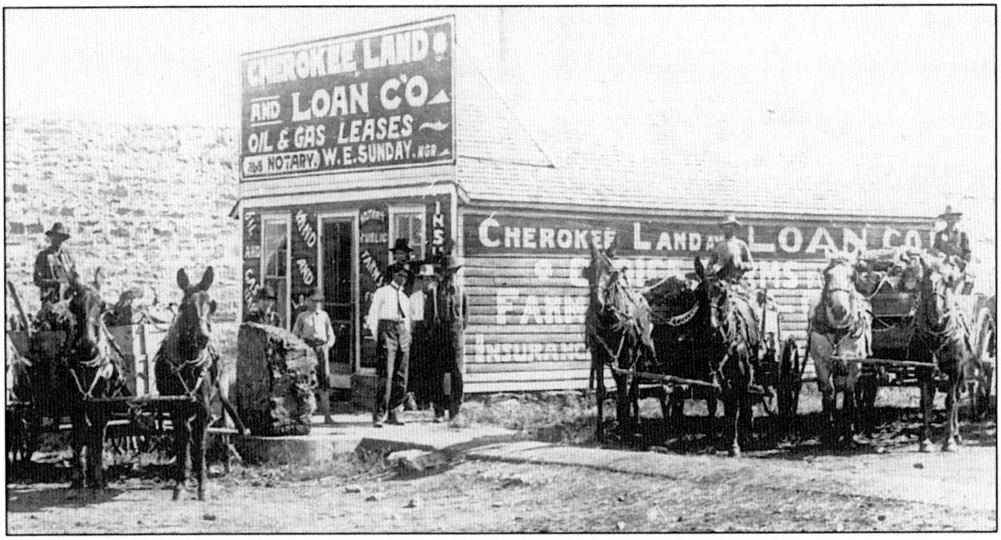

OOLOGAH'S CHEROKEE LAND AND LOAN COMPANY, C. 1900. Uncle Ed Sunday, the first mayor of Oologah, operated a coal mine outside the town. The horses and wagons pictured here have been conscripted to haul the coal to the railroad. The Cherokee Land and Loan Company was owned by W.E. Sunday, shown on the porch in his white shirt. (Courtesy of Will Rogers Memorial.)

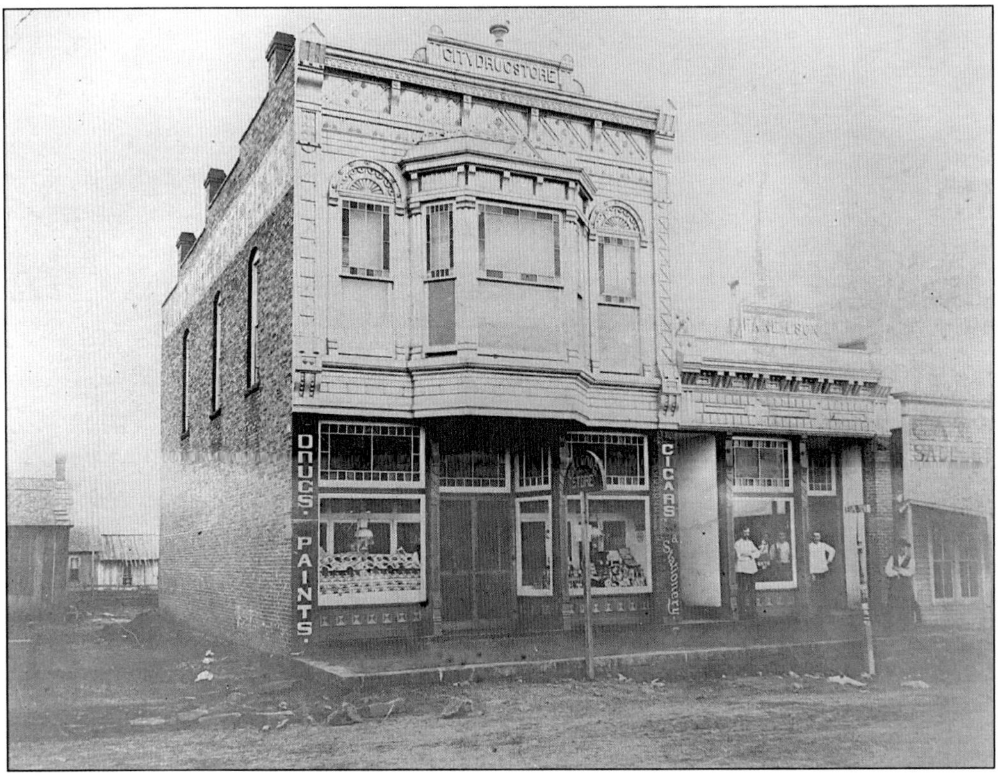

EARLY ARCHITECTURE, C. 1912. Claremore's City Drugstore boasts its inventory of drugs, paints, stationery, and cigars. The building's upper facade is a beautiful example of the ornate decor of the period. (Courtesy of Rogers State College.)

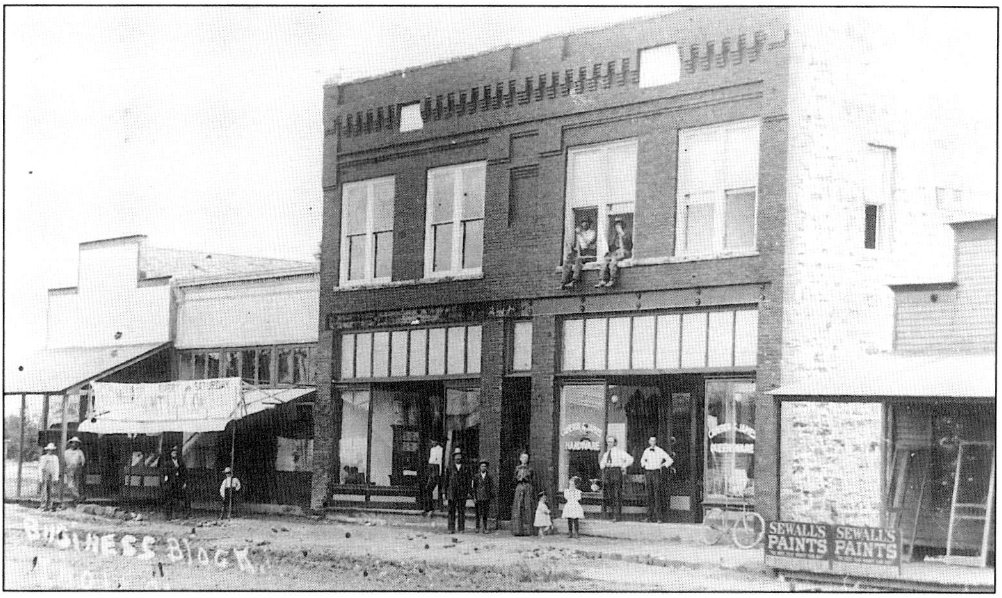

BUSINESS BLOCK OF INOLA, C. 1910. One large brick-and-stone building is flanked by simple western storefronts in the farming community of Inola. The town was founded in 1890. Its name is taken from the Cherokee word meaning "black fox." A number of Mennonite farmers settled on the land surrounding Inola. (Courtesy of Rogers State College.)

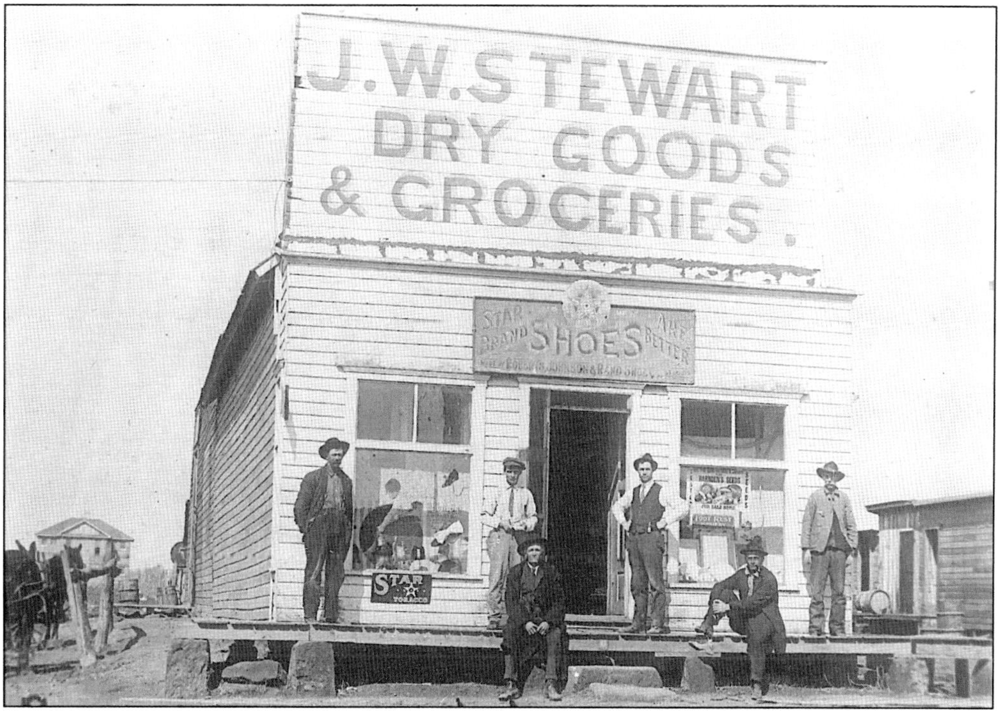

CLOTHING AND GROCERY STORE, C. 1911. Bushyhead residents could enjoy one-stop shopping at the J.W. Stewart Dry Goods and Grocery Store. From left to right are (seated) Coony Whitman and Witt Robertson; (standing) P.E. Cantrell, Dalton Stewart, owner J.W. Stewart, and Boma Fox. (Courtesy of Rogers State College.)

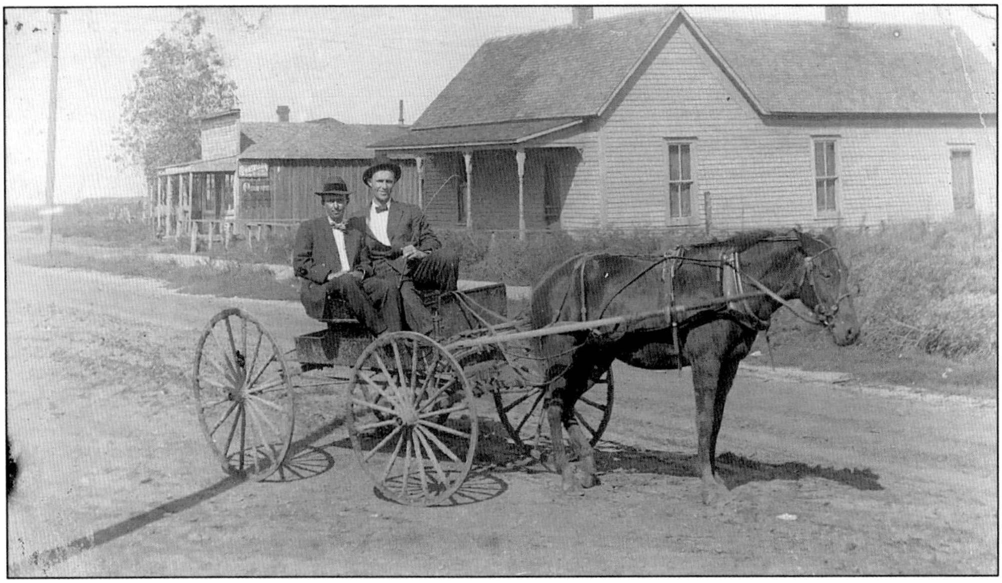

Postal Workers, c. 1915. Residents of rural communities received their mail from carriers driving wagons like the one shown here. This mode of transportation was used as late as the 1920s. Notice the telephone pole in the upper left. (Courtesy of Ralph and Loretta Dunham.)

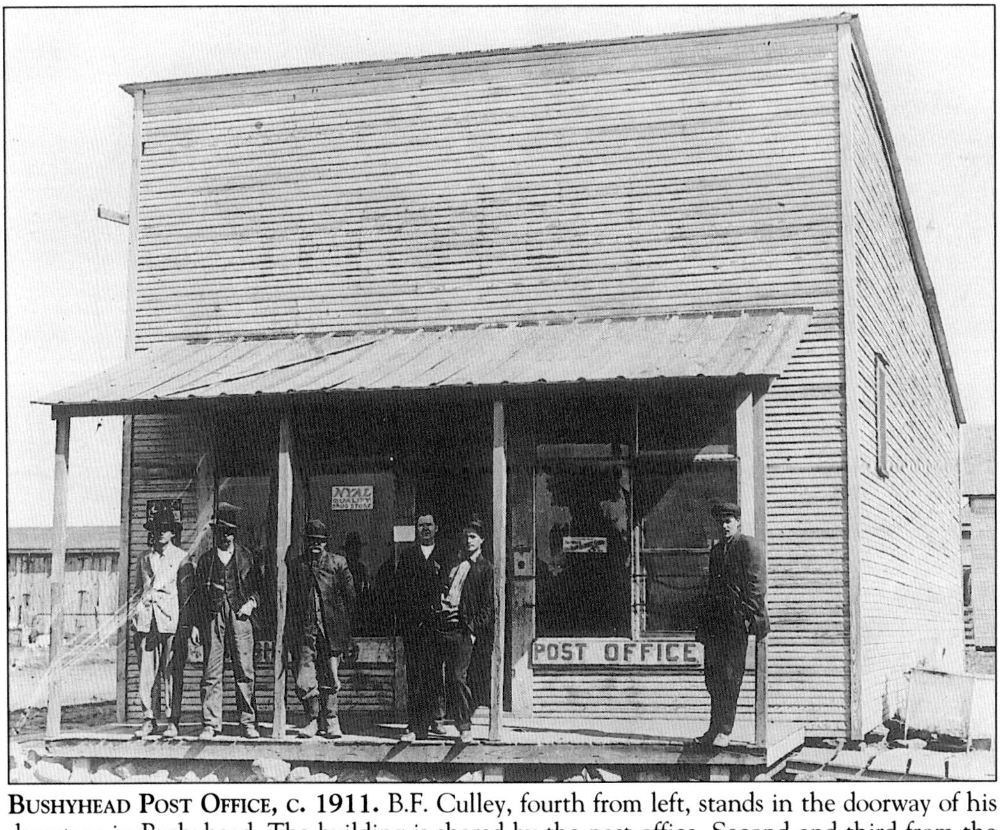

Bushyhead Post Office, c. 1911. B.F. Culley, fourth from left, stands in the doorway of his drugstore in Bushyhead. The building is shared by the post office. Second and third from the left are P.E. Cantrell and Charley Robison. (Courtesy of Rogers State College.)

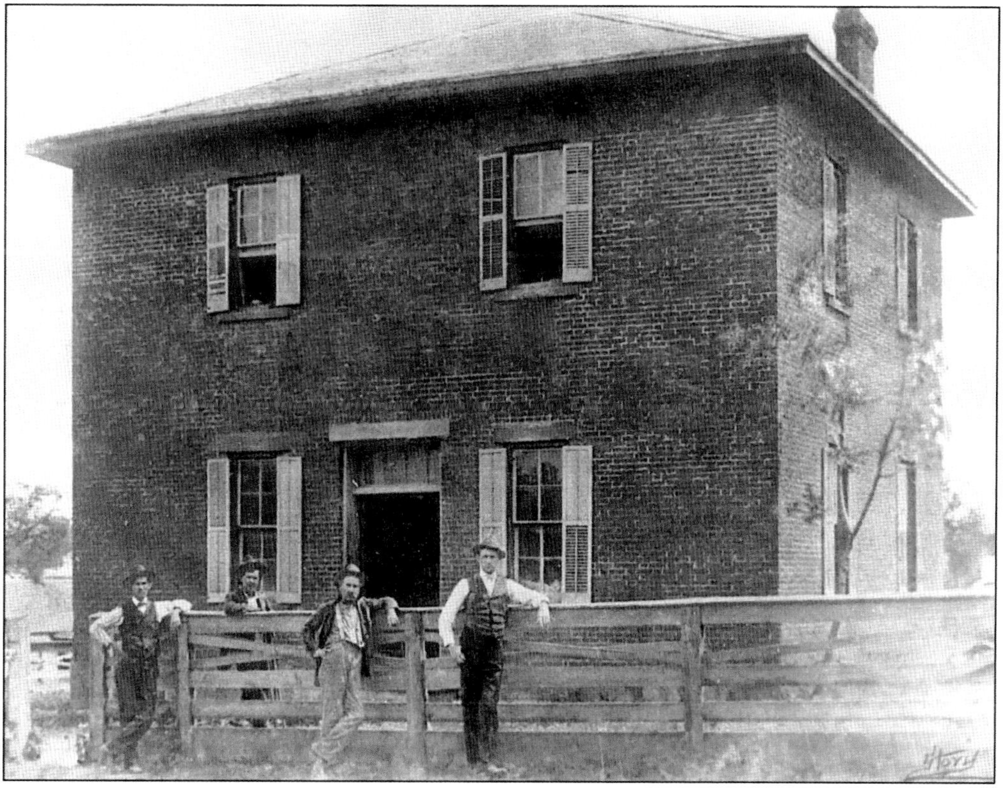

CHEROKEE SUPREME COURT BUILDING, LATE 1800s. The Cherokee Supreme Court building, built in the 1840s and still standing in the capital city of Tahlequah, is the oldest public building in Oklahoma. The bricks were fired in a kiln erected for the Cherokees by members of the Mormon church. (Courtesy of Cherokee National Archives.)

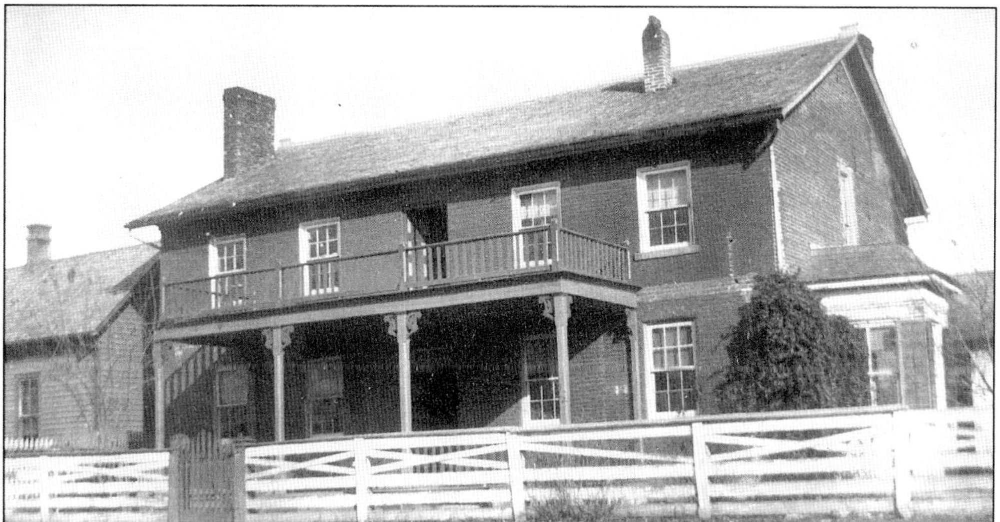

THE NATIONAL HOTEL, LATE 1800s. Another of Tahlequah's brick structures from the 1840s, the National Hotel was first operated by Mrs. Richard Taylor. A rival hotel in town, the Wolfe, was built of logs and run by Jesse Wolfe. (Courtesy of Cherokee National Archives.)

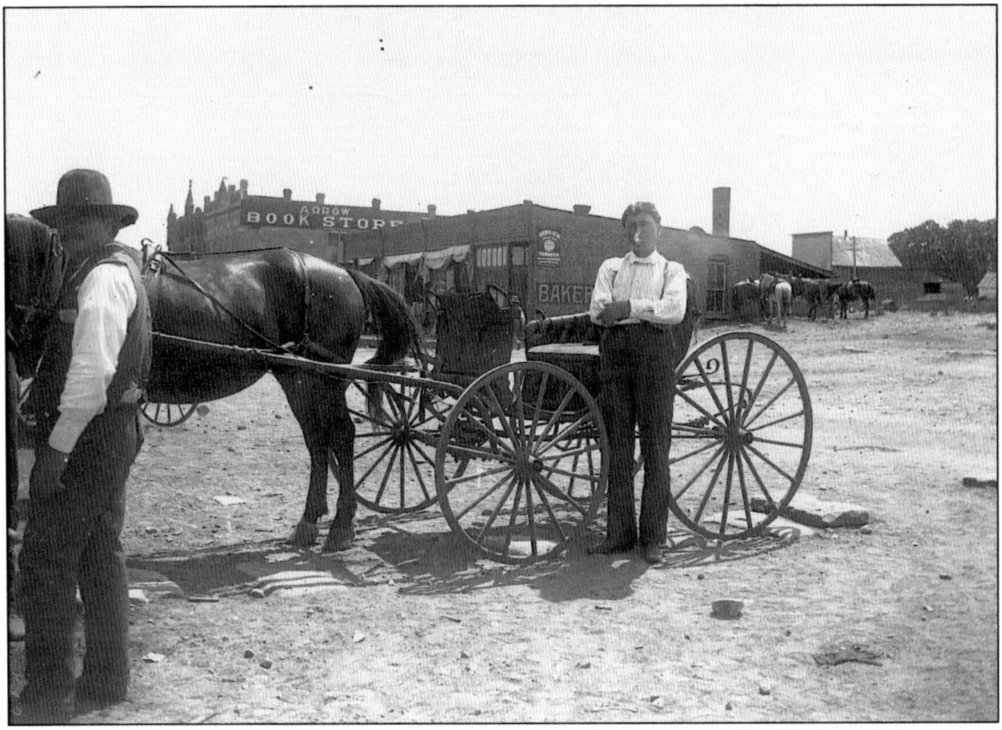

City Street Scene, c. 1900. For years the horse and buggy served well the inhabitants of Indian Territory. This one looks lightweight and built for speed. Notice the businesses across the road, the Arrow Bookstore and a bakery. (Courtesy of Cherokee National Archives.)

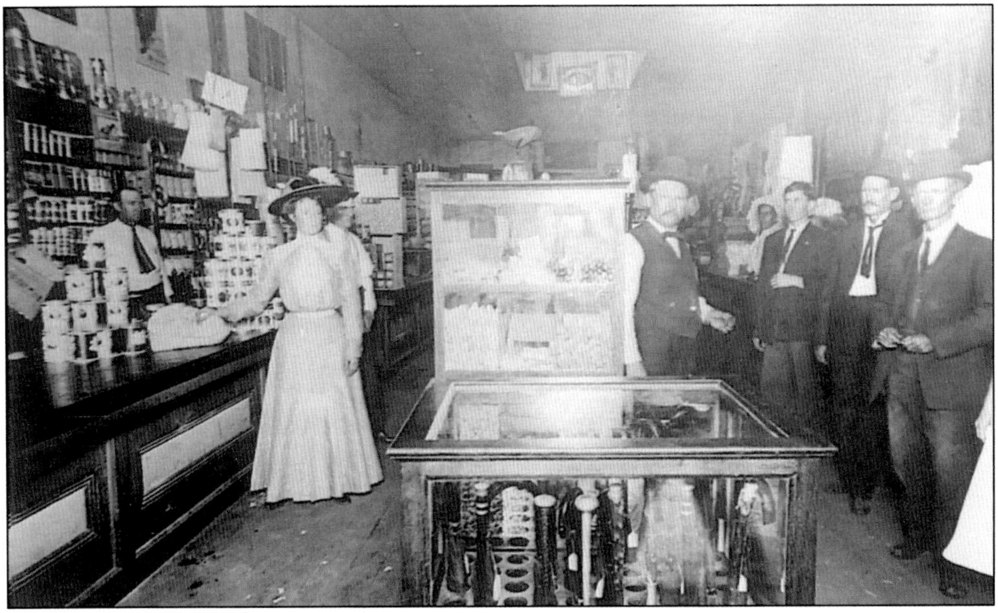

Inside the Stapler Store, c. 1880. One of the prominent markets in early Tahlequah was the J.W. Stapler and Son store. At the end of the Civil War, John Stapler returned from the safety of the East with a stock of goods, opening the business in 1865. (Courtesy of Cherokee Studies Institute.)

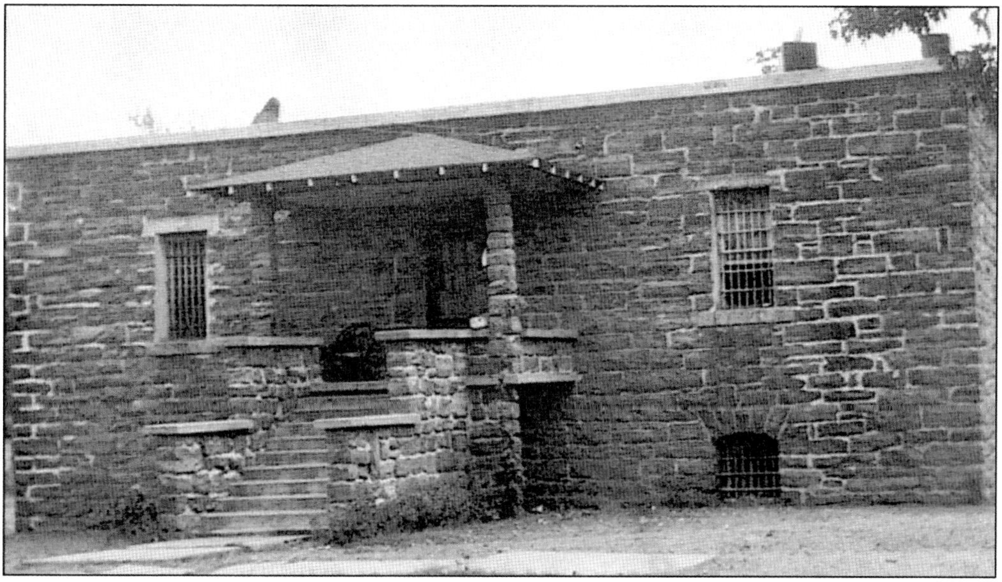

The Old Cherokee National Prison. This stone penitentiary, completed in 1874, held the Nation's hardened and dangerous prisoners. Those condemned to death faced the gallows on the back side of the building. The prisoners were overseen by the Cherokee high sheriff. But the sheriff had no authority over white criminals who roamed freely through Indian Territory. (Courtesy of Cherokee Studies Institute.)

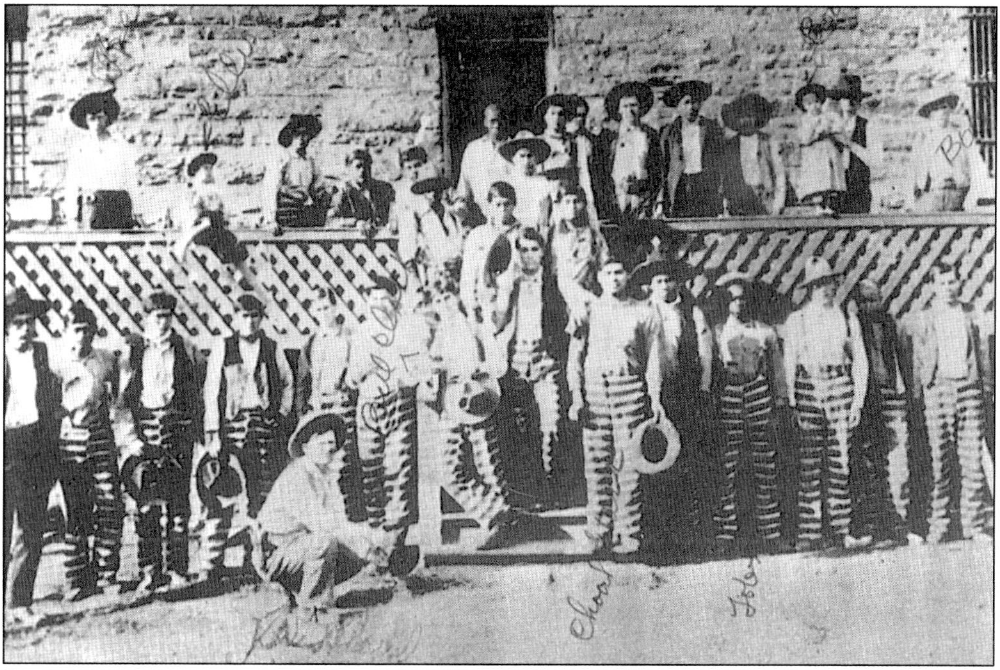

Prisoners in the Yard, c. 1896. Before the prison facility was in place, criminals were punished by public whipping, flogging, and sometimes hanging. These prisoners are being taught working skills, such as shoemaking, blacksmithing, and wagon making. They are in good health and well fed. However, a few will be sentenced to die for capital offenses. (Courtesy of Cherokee Studies Institute.)

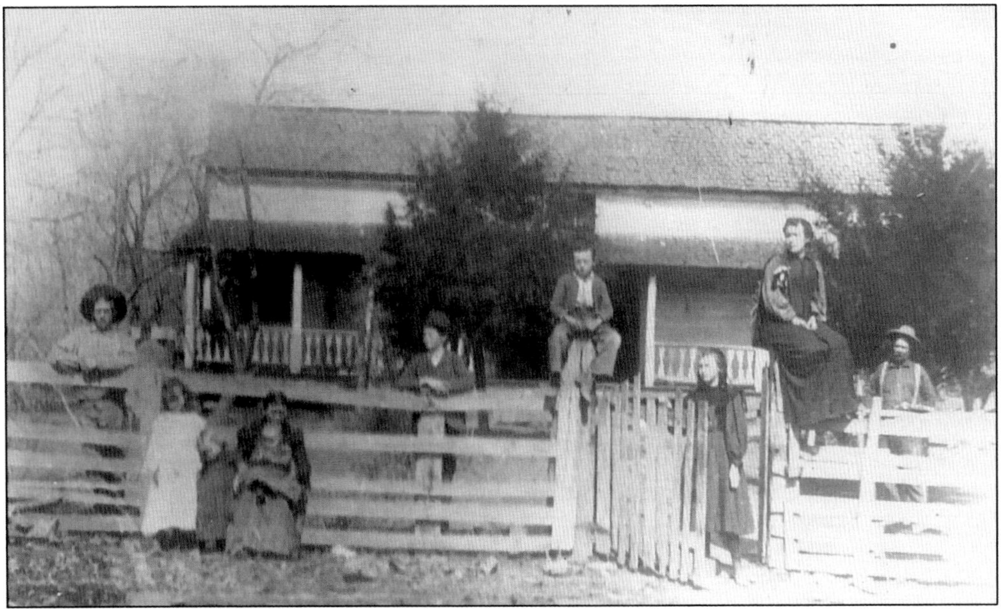

STAGECOACH STOP, C. 1889. Located near Vian, this building is the oldest standing stagecoach stop in Oklahoma. Built by Jack "Squam" Miller, who crossed the Trail of Tears, the home became known as the "88 Way Station." The property became the allotment land of Mary Miller Waters (holding baby). George Deerskin Waters, far right, served as a Cherokee senator and court interpreter. (Courtesy of Lisa LaRue Tennison.)

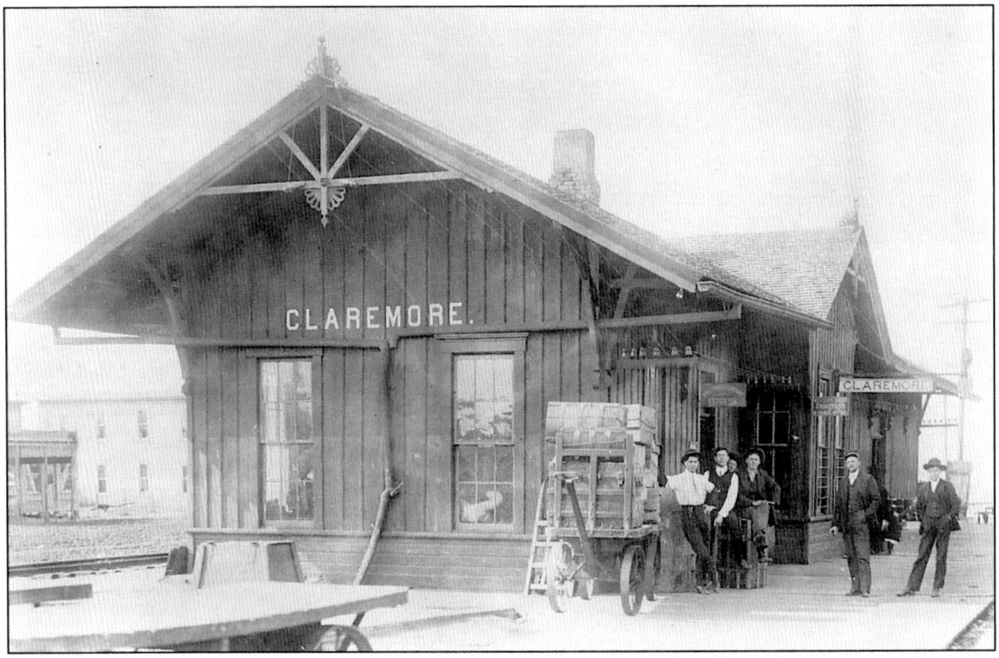

FRISCO DEPOT IN CLAREMORE, INDIAN TERRITORY, C. 1904. Railroad employees await the train at Claremore's Frisco Depot. Among those pictured are railroad agent F.G. Griswold, cashier J.K. Mettert, assistant Lon Burd, and messenger Howard Hale. Note the telegraph wires strung over the entryway. (Courtesy of Rogers State College.)

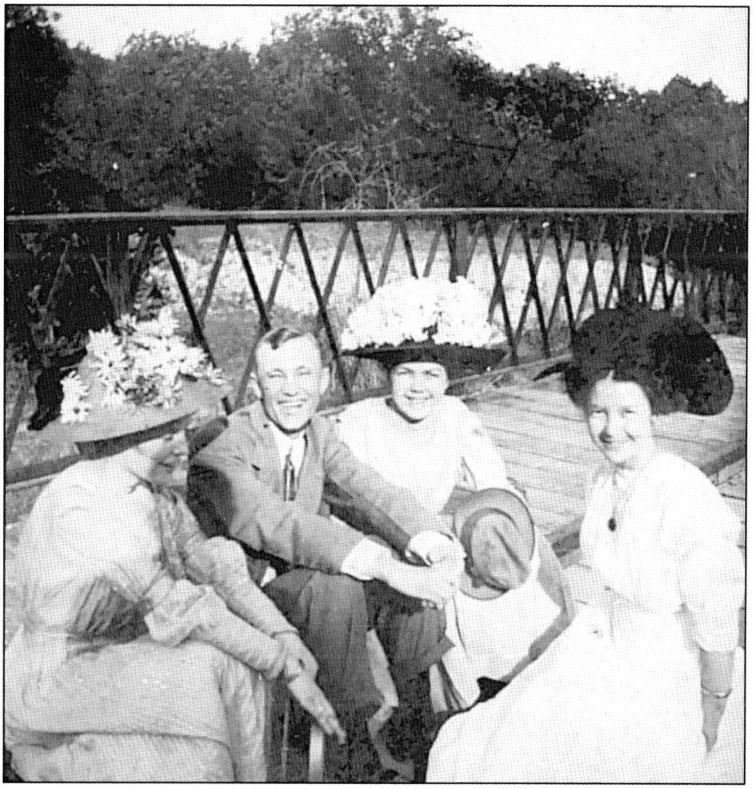

An Outing with Friends, early 1900s. Three fashionable young ladies surround their grinning gentleman escort on a lovely day in Indian Territory. Decked out in the latest hats and clothing, all appear to be enjoying the natural beauty of eastern Oklahoma. (Courtesy of Ralph and Loretta Dunham.)

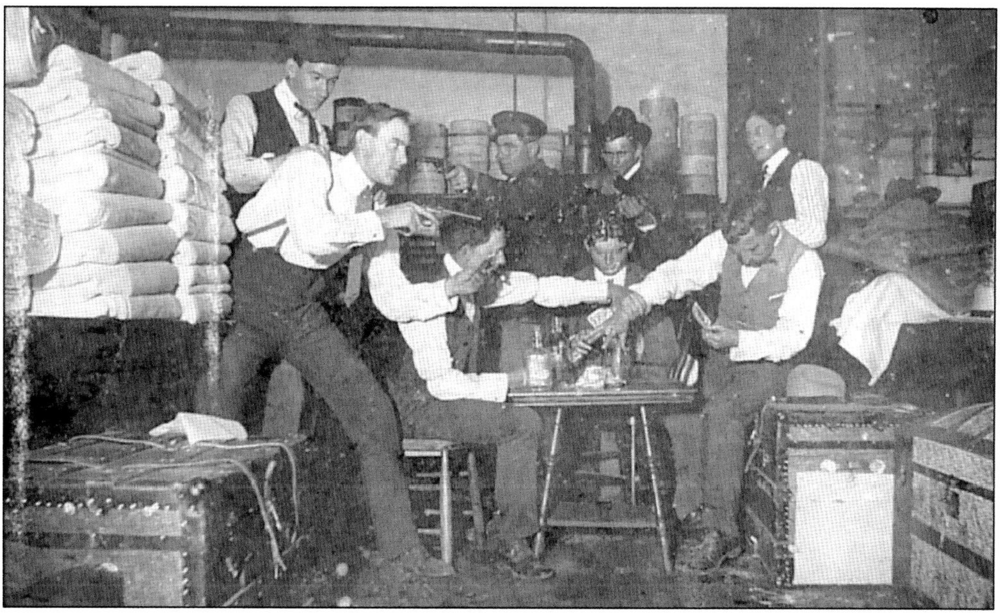

Back Room Intrigue, early 1900s. An illegal gambling and drinking operation appears to be underway here in some merchant's back room, purely in jest, of course. After the Civil War, bootlegging and whiskey running made up the majority of crimes committed in Indian Territory. Running illegal alcohol was a part-time job for some citizens on through the 1940s. (Courtesy of Ralph and Loretta Dunham.)

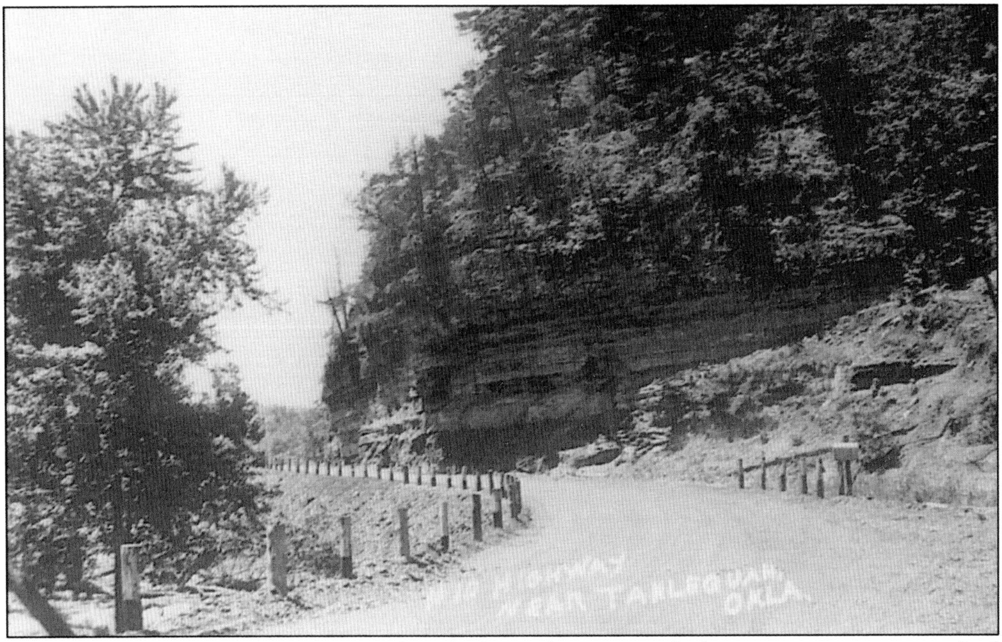

State Highway 10, c. 1930. Even though the surface is gravel, there is a protective guardrail along this curve on Oklahoma's Highway 10 near Tahlequah. The scenic road ran from Tahlequah along the river and north to Jay, the Delaware County seat. (Courtesy of Cherokee Studies Institute.)

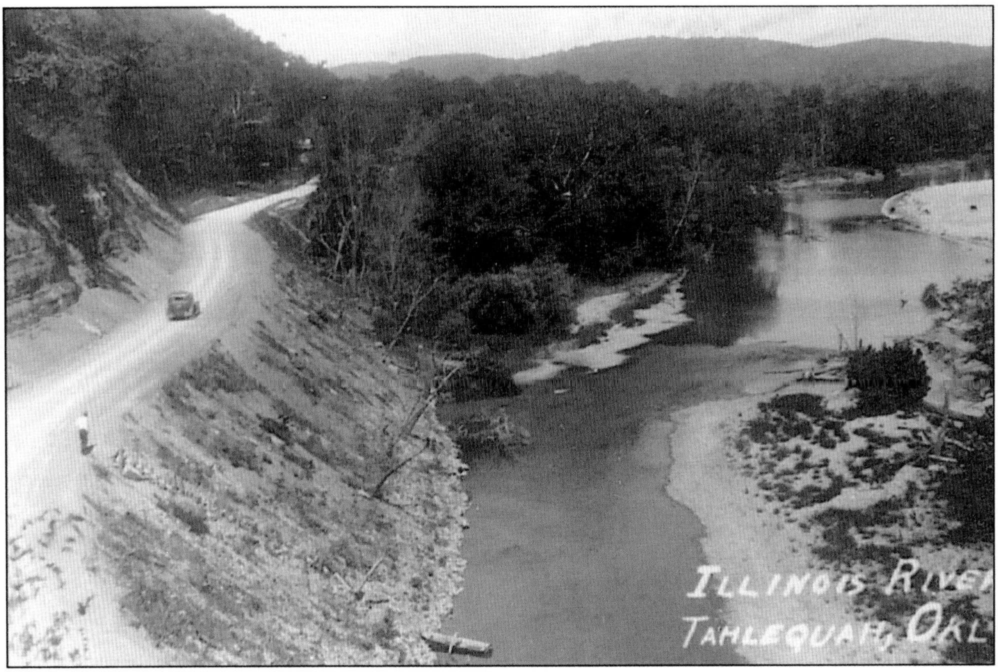

Scenic Illinois River, c. 1931. The pedestrian on the highway is heading for wooden steps down the steep bank of the Illinois River to his waiting boat. Since the 1840s, visitors have been drawn to the pristine waters of the Illinois. Each winter, bald eagles from the north migrate to the river for the good fishing it provides. (Courtesy of Cherokee Studies Institute.)

HUCKLEBERRY SHELL, C. 1953. Sequoyah County law officer Huckleberry Shell served as sheriff of Sequoyah County from 1953 to 1954. He served between the terms of E.W. Floyd (below). Huckleberry's hometown was Marble City, so named for the marble quarry that still operates there. (Courtesy of Sequoyah County Historical Society.)

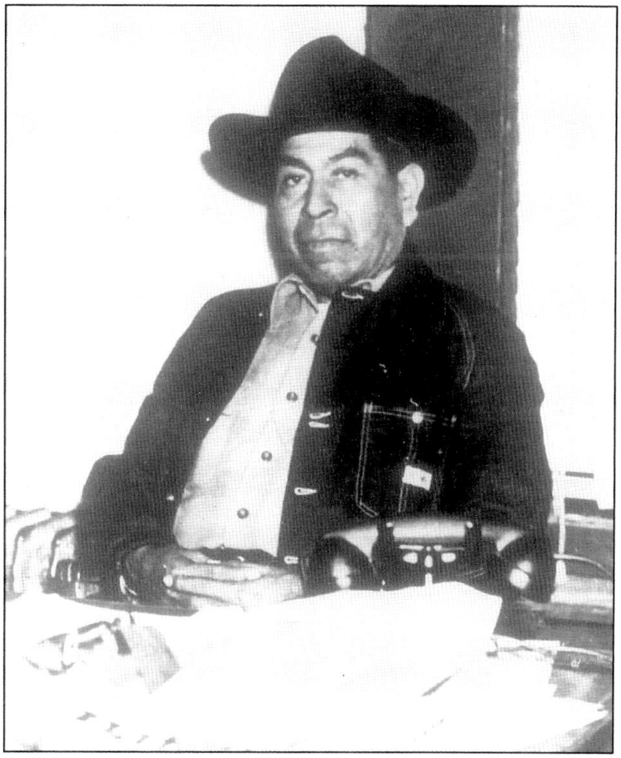

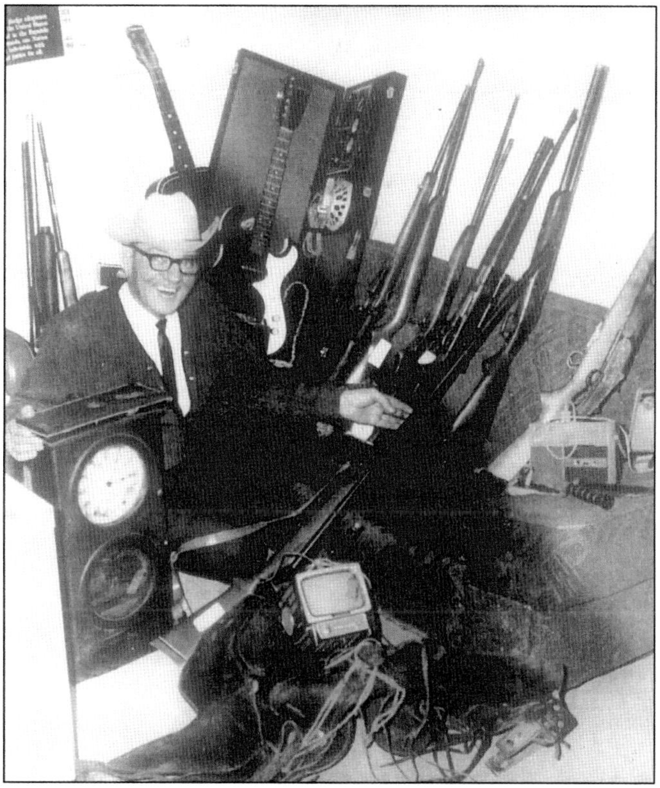

E.W. FLOYD, C. 1955. Sequoyah County sheriff E.W. Floyd displays a cache of confiscated goods. Floyd served as sheriff for 20 years. He finally retired in 1970. A Sallisaw, Oklahoma native, Floyd was the brother of famed outlaw Pretty Boy Floyd. (Courtesy of Sequoyah County Historical Society.)

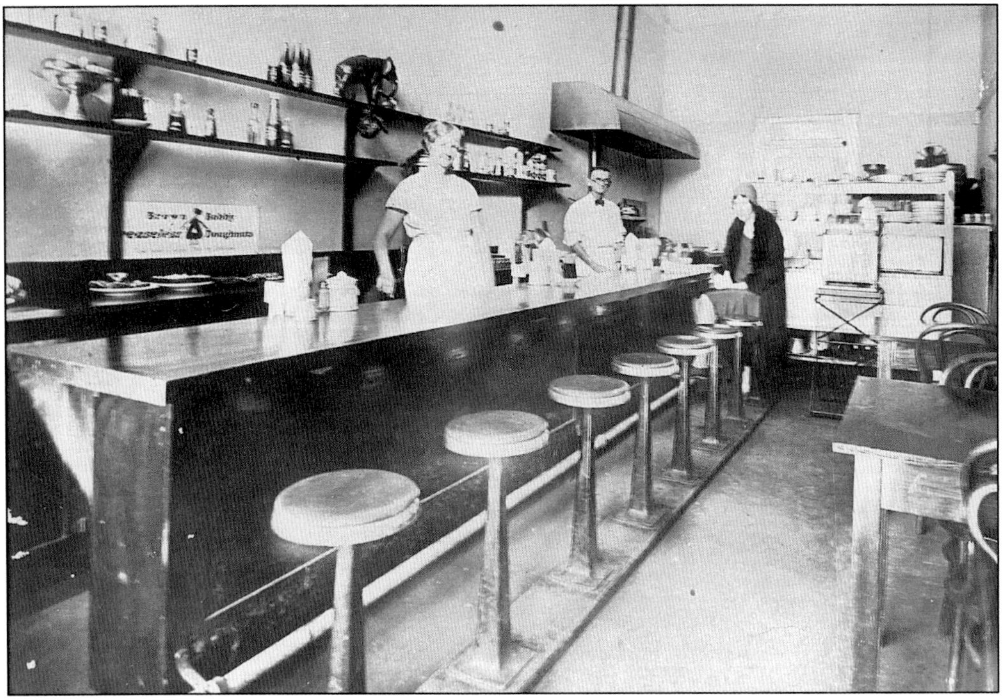

CLAREMORE'S LANDRUM CAFÉ, C. 1926. Situated in a long, narrow building, the Landrum Cafe offered eight barstools and two dining tables. Near the back is the well-equipped kitchen area. Behind the counter stands Harriet Almeda Landrum and her cook Floyd. Seated at the bar is Harriet's sister Sammie. (Courtesy of Rogers State College.)

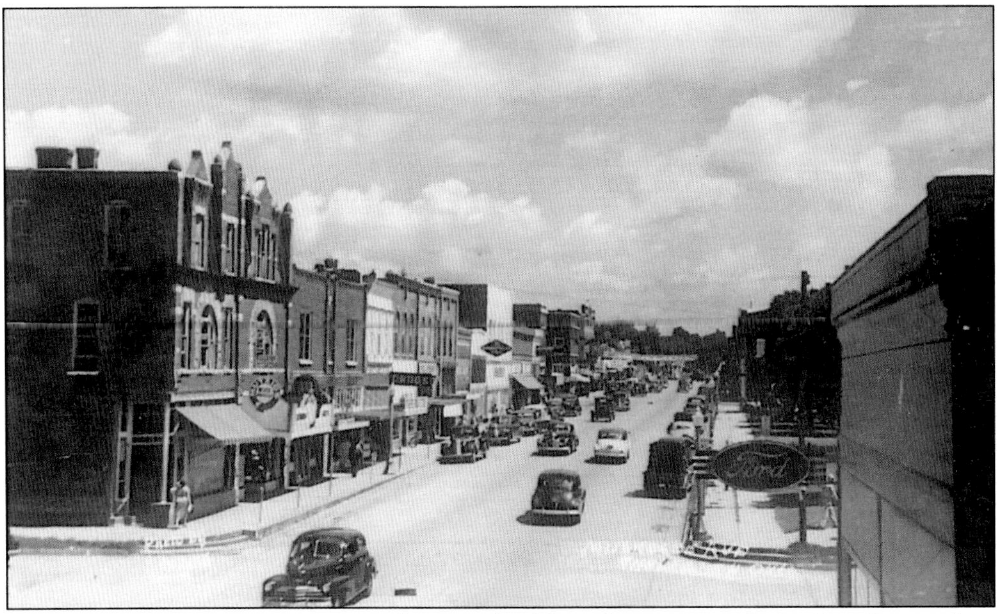

DOWNTOWN TAHLEQUAH, C. 1945. The city of Tahlequah experienced a building boom when World War II ended. This was due, in part, to veterans returning to attend Northeastern State College. From 1940 to 1950, the population grew from 3,027 to 4,750. (Courtesy of Cherokee Studies Institute.)

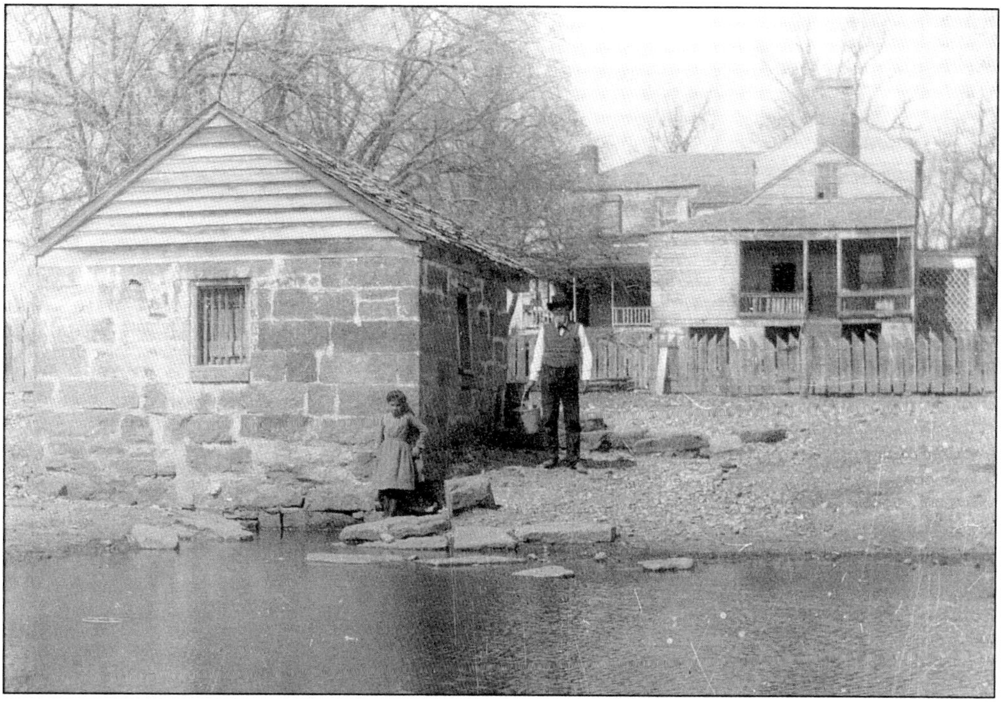

ROSS FAMILY MEMBERS AT THE MURRELL MANSION, LATE 1800S. Robert Bruce Ross collects a pail of water from the spring house at the Murrell home. The young lady is Annie Ross (Piburn). Robert Bruce Ross attended the Cherokee Male Seminary and served in the Union Army. He was later a sheriff, a senator, and a postmaster. (Courtesy of Cherokee National Archives.)

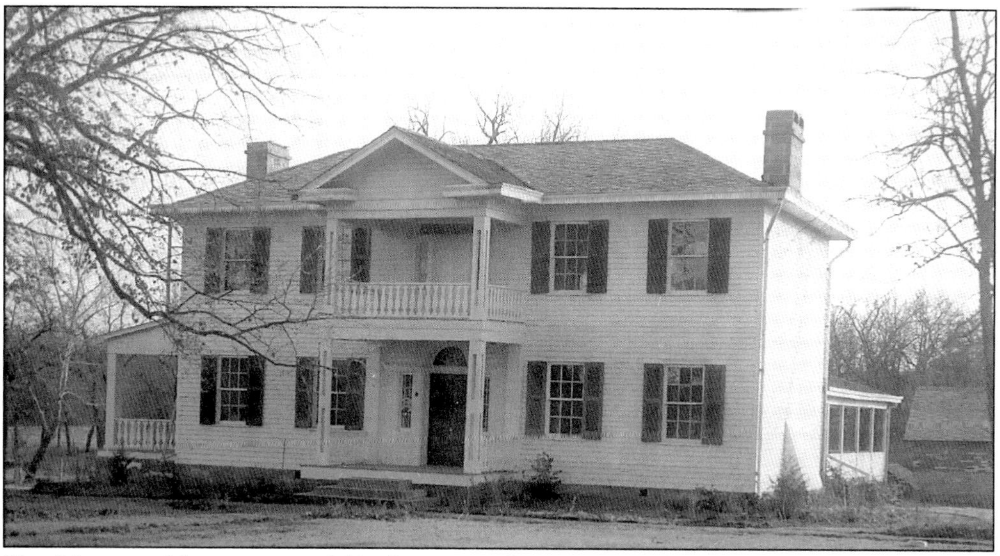

THE MURRELL MANSION, C. 1950. Constructed a century earlier, the mansion is a reminder of the antebellum lifestyle in pre-Civil War days. Virginia merchant George Murrell built the home for his Cherokee wife, Minerva Ross. He called the mansion "Hunter's Home." Some say the home survived the Civil War because George was a Mason admired by Stand Watie, enemy of the Ross family. (Courtesy of Cherokee National Archives.)

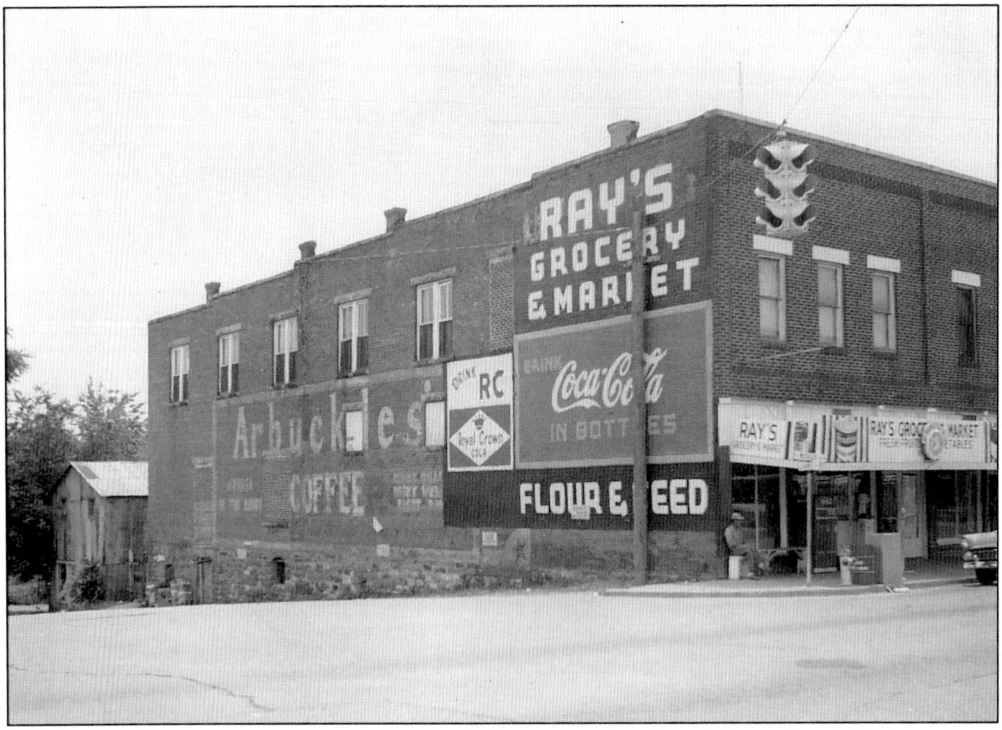

Ray's Grocery, Downtown Tahlequah. The ornate facades of the early 1900s have been replaced by simple, more modern brickwork. Ray's Grocery was one of the last of the downtown food stores. Soon the big chain stores, like Safeway and IGA, built away from the main street, providing easy access and parking. (Courtesy of Cherokee National Archives.)

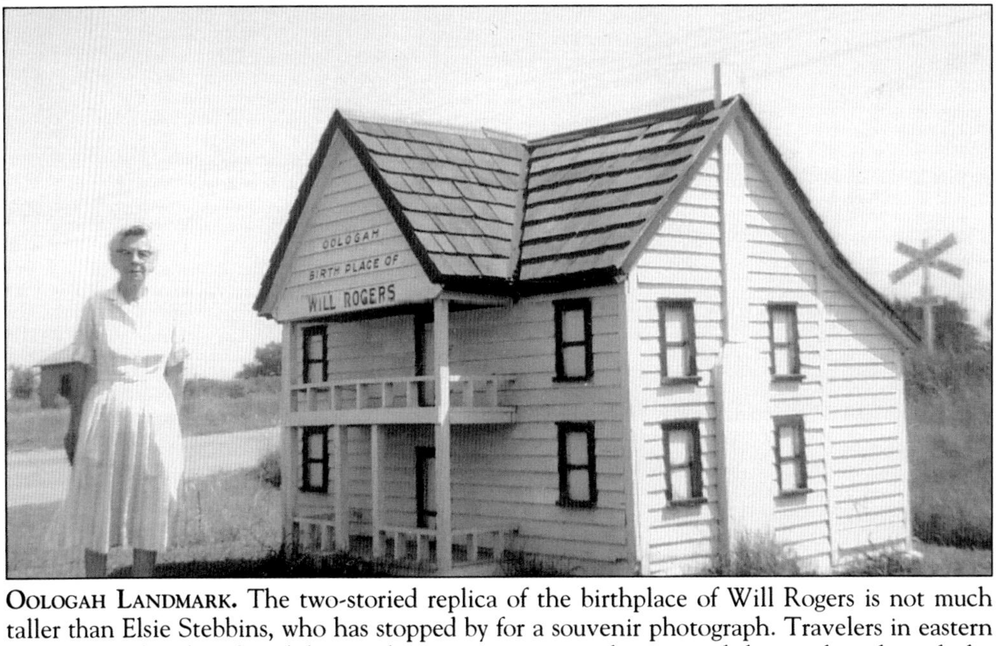

Oologah Landmark. The two-storied replica of the birthplace of Will Rogers is not much taller than Elsie Stebbins, who has stopped by for a souvenir photograph. Travelers in eastern Oklahoma, like Elsie, found the tiny home an interesting diversion while traveling through the Cherokee Nation. (Courtesy of Cherokee National Archives.)

Five

Government

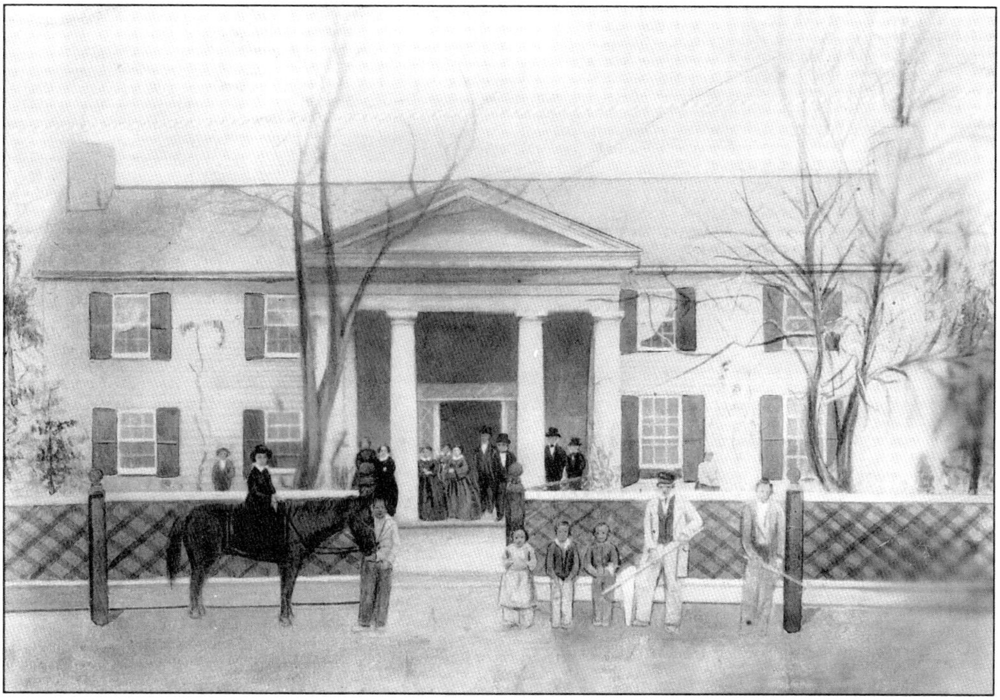

Rose Cottage, c. 1850. An artist has captured the grandeur of Rose Cottage, the residence of Principal Chief John Ross in Park Hill, Indian Territory. Ross built the mansion after his arrival there on the Trail of Tears. In addition to the home, Ross's property was equipped with stables, a laundry, a blacksmith, a dairy, and 1,000 apple trees. For 1 1/2 miles, the fences leading to the drive were planted in roses. Behind Ross's home lay the cottages for his slaves. Ross, and others like him, enjoyed the lifestyle of the Southern aristocracy before the days of the Civil War. Park Hill was a showplace, known as the "Athens" of Indian Territory. But war brought the community to its knees and it never did fully recover. The magnificent Rose Cottage was reduced to ashes. Ironically, it was not destroyed by Union forces, but by Confederate general Stand Watie, so great was his hatred for Ross. (Courtesy of Cherokee National Archives.)

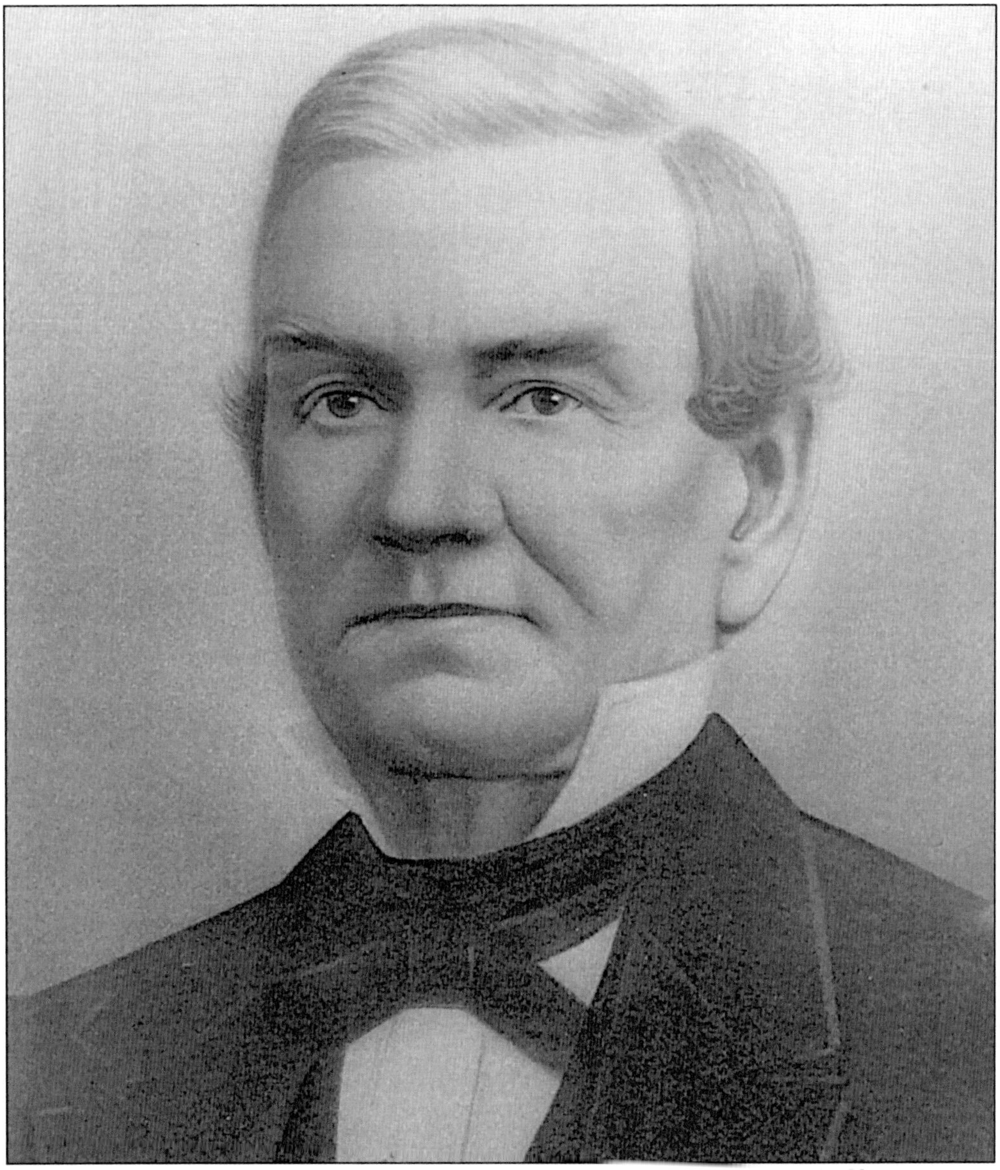

PRINCIPAL CHIEF JOHN ROSS, SERVED 1828 TO 1866. John Ross, one-eighth Cherokee, was born October 3, 1790, at Ross Landing (now Chattanooga), Tennessee. His great-grandmother was a full-blood of the Bird Clan who married a Scot named Shorey. Brought up with full-bloods who traded at his father's store, Ross identified with the Cherokee people. At adulthood, he was given the Cherokee name, Cooweescoowee. At 19, Ross began dealings with Cherokees who had gone west. He fought under Andrew Jackson at the Battle of Horseshoe Bend against the Creeks. Ross was a delegate to Washington to arrange the Treaty of 1816, which established the borders of the eastern Cherokee lands. As Congress pushed for removal west, Ross helped defeat their efforts. Ross was elected principal chief in 1828, a position he held his entire life. When removal was inevitable, Ross got permission for Cherokees to direct the travel. In the Civil War, he preached neutrality until Union troops pulled out of Indian Territory, then he reluctantly sided with the South. Ross passed away in Washington, D.C., on August 1, 1866. (Courtesy of Cherokee National Archives.)

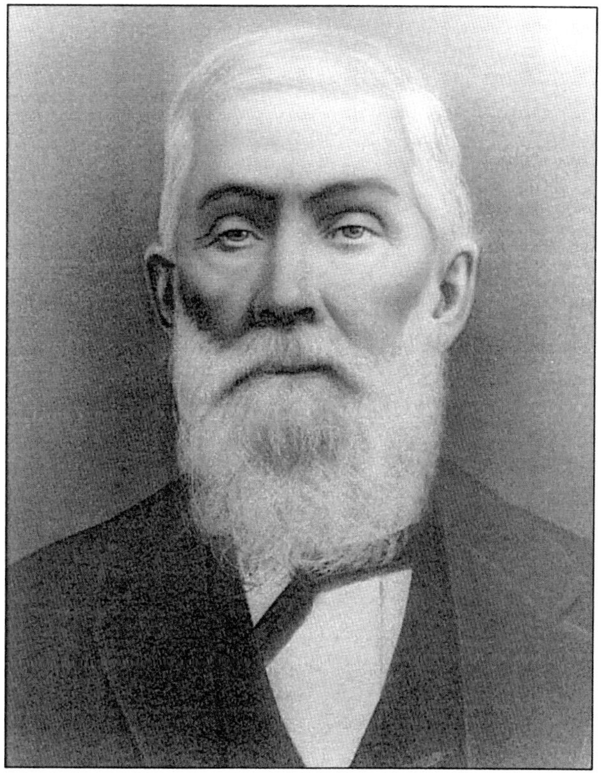

PRINCIPAL CHIEF WILLIAM POTTER ROSS, SERVED 1866 TO 1867 AND 1872 TO 1875. William Potter Ross had served as clerk of the Cherokee Senate and had been instrumental in drafting legislation for former chief John Ross. Ross was named the first editor of the *Cherokee Advocate* newspaper. He became a merchant in later life, then an attorney. (Courtesy of Cherokee National Archives.)

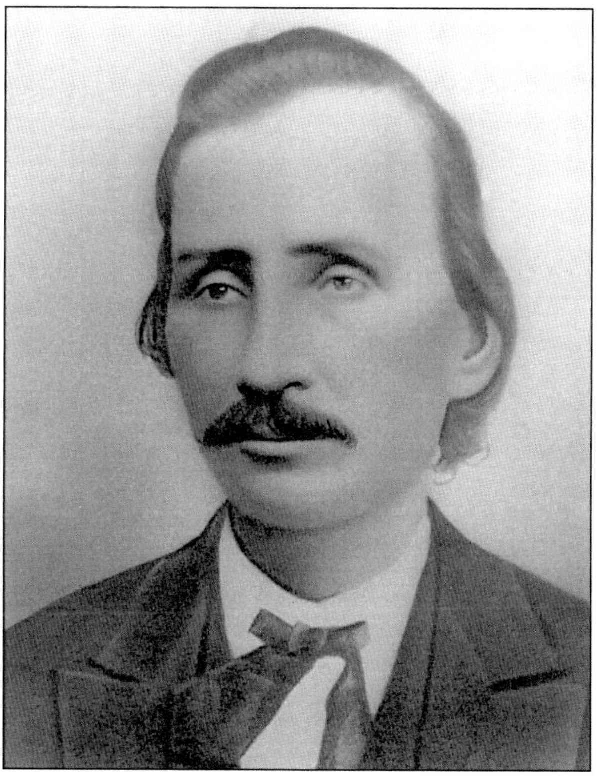

PRINCIPAL CHIEF LEWIS DOWNING, SERVED 1867 TO 1872. The election of 1867 was a heated battle between feuding factions. Fights broke out at the polls, even between women. Downing served as a Confederate chaplain in the Civil War, though he changed over to the Union at the Battle of Pea Ridge. Remembered as one of the noblest of Cherokees, his leadership helped to reunite his people. (Courtesy of Cherokee National Archives.)

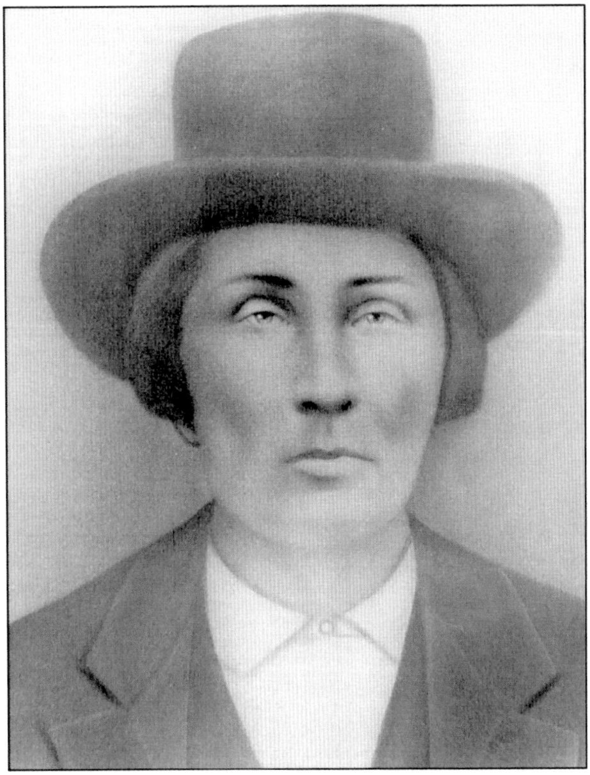

Principal Chief Charles Thompson, Served 1875 to 1879. Shortly after his election, Thompson was ordained as a Baptist minister. Although not a full-blood, he spoke little English and was known as Oochalata. The principal concern during Thompson's term was the intrusion of unwanted whites and the crimes they committed in the Territory. (Courtesy of Cherokee National Archives.)

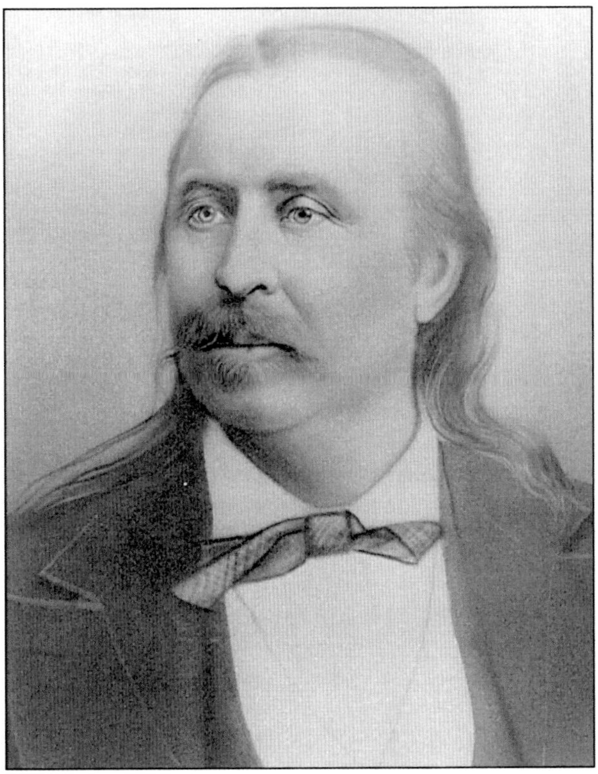

Assistant Principal Chief William Penn Adair, Served 1879 to 1880. Elected assistant to Chief Dennis Bushyhead, Adair was a Cherokee senator before becoming a colonel of the Southern Second Regiment of Mounted Volunteers. Adair was a beloved Cherokee and a popular war hero, having fought at the Battle of Fort Gibson. His name, the 'Colonel' included, was given to Will Rogers at birth. (Courtesy of Cherokee National Archives.)

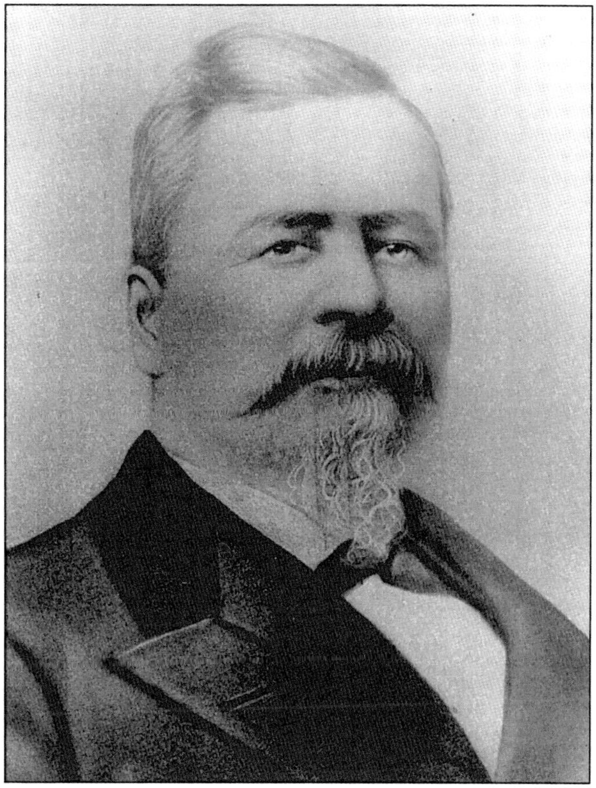

Principal Chief Dennis Wolf Bushyhead, Served 1879 to 1887. The eldest son of Rev. Jesse Bushyhead, Dennis enjoyed a peaceful tenure as chief. In 1849, he joined the gold rush to California and stayed until 1868, avoiding both the Civil War and the factionalism that plagued the nation. He helped with the leasing of the Cherokee Outlet to the Cherokee Strip Livestock Association. (Courtesy of Cherokee National Archives.)

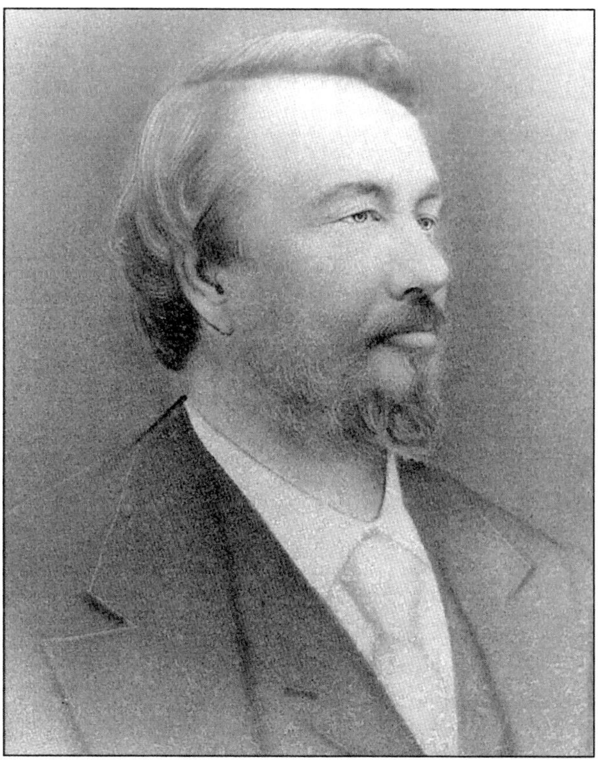

Principal Chief Joel Bryan Mayes, Served 1887 to 1891. Mayes served in the Confederate Army and later as a district judge. Joel was chief justice of the Cherokee Nation Supreme Court when elected as chief. Great changes within the Cherokee Nation occurred during his terms. The federal government's Dawes Act caused the Cherokees a loss of nearly 7 million acres and the first of the white settler land runs began. (Courtesy of Cherokee National Archives.)

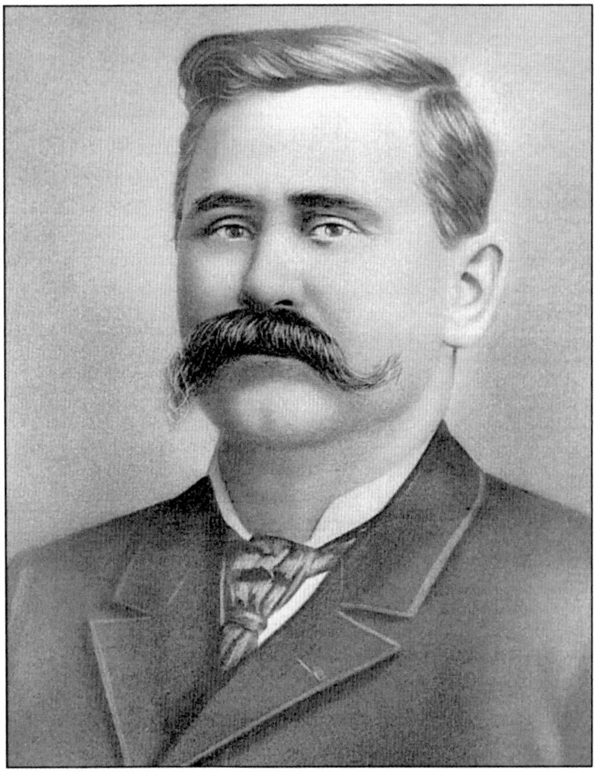

PRINCIPAL CHIEF COL. JOHNSON HARRIS, SERVED 1891 TO 1895. As chief, Harris dealt with the issues of the Cherokee Strip payment and land run, as well as negotiations with the Dawes Commission. There he focused his efforts on keeping the lands communal, opposing allotment. A former teacher and one-quarter Cherokee, Harris lived out his years in Tahlequah. (Courtesy of Cherokee National Archives.)

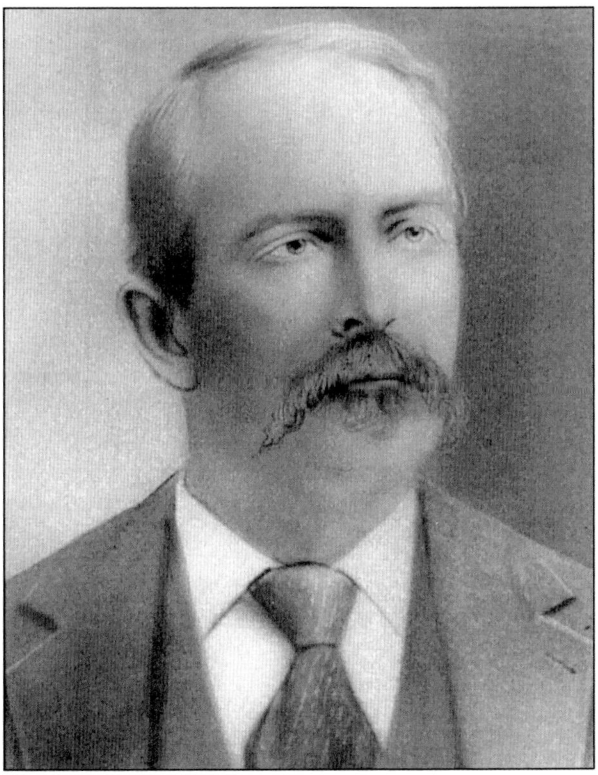

PRINCIPAL CHIEF SAMUEL HOUSTON MAYES, SERVED 1895 TO 1899. At 16, Sam enlisted in Company K with the Confederates. He became sheriff of the Cooweescoowee district and later a senator. Mayes took up the battle with the Dawes Commission, which could not reach agreement with the Cherokees regarding allotment. Nighthawk Keetoowah Redbird Smith urged followers to reject allotment in hopes America would see its injustice. (Courtesy of Cherokee National Archives.)

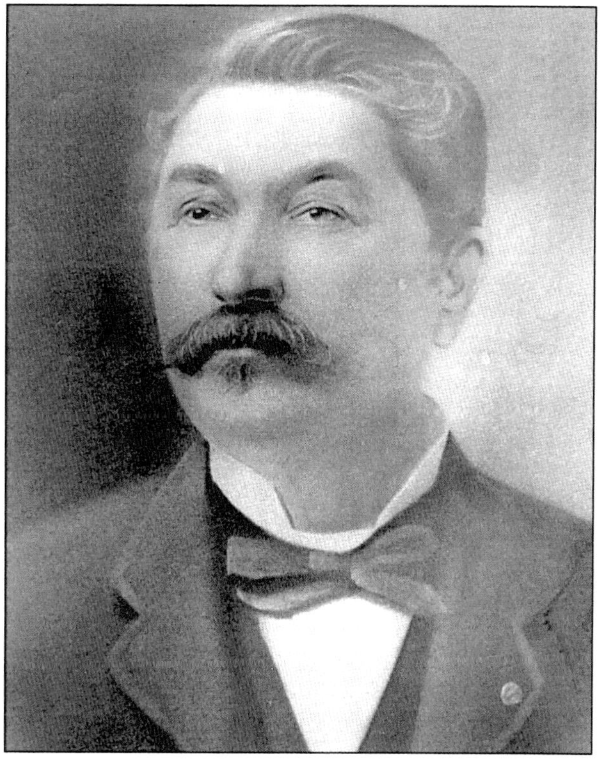

Principal Chief Thomas M. Buffington, Served 1899 to 1903. Elected by council, Buffington faced serious issues. On August 7, 1902, Cherokees finally agreed to accept allotment. Whites seeking land jammed the enrollment centers and had to be weeded out from eligible Cherokees. Buffington dealt with the situation with diplomacy and tact. He later served as the mayor of Vinita, living there until his death in 1938. (Courtesy of Cherokee National Archives.)

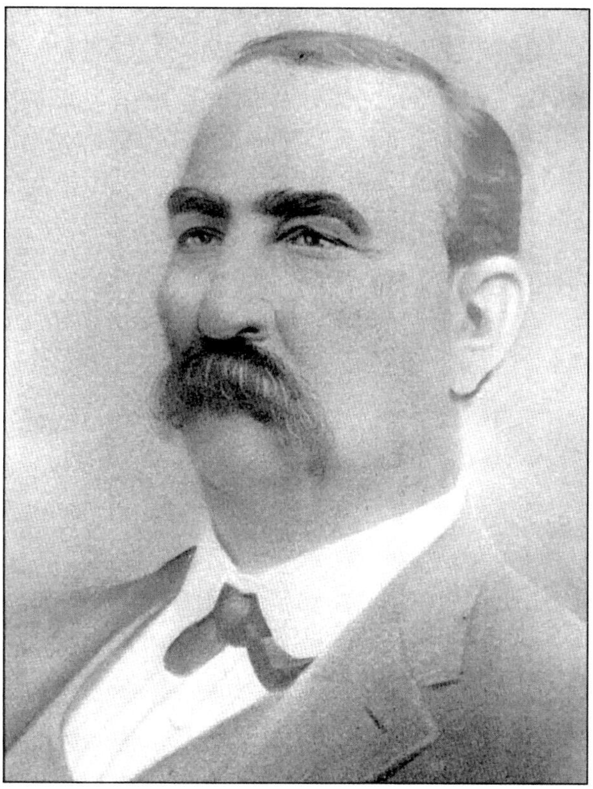

Principal Chief William C. Rogers, Served 1903 to 1917. The grandson of John Rogers, the last chief of the Old Settlers, Rogers was the last elected chief of the Cherokees until 1971. At statehood, he was reappointed as chief by the federal government. Rogers helped to complete land division for the Cherokees by 1914. Rogers passed away while still in office. (Courtesy of Cherokee National Archives.)

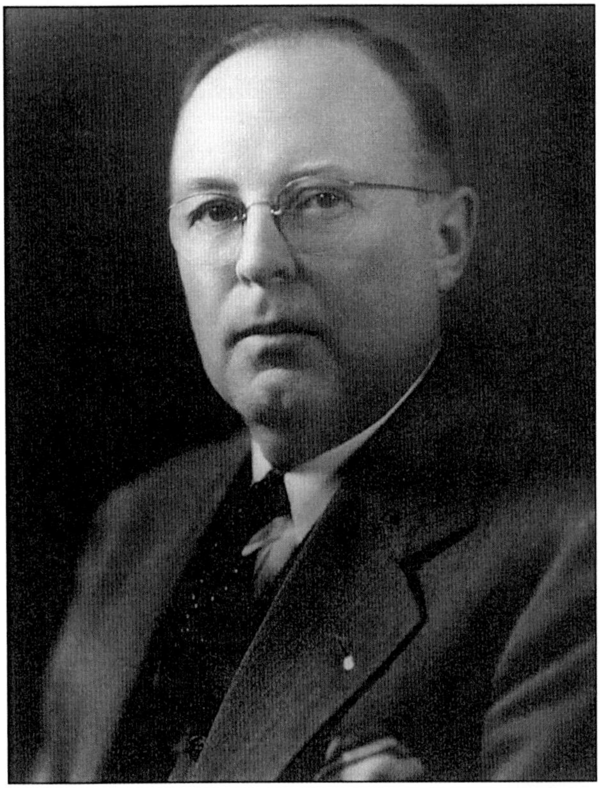

Principal Chief Jesse Bartley Milam, Served 1941 to 1949. An oil man and banker, Milam was the only chief never elected by the Cherokees. He was appointed by President Roosevelt in 1941, serving until his death in 1949. He was the first to lead the tribe since Rogers died in 1917. Milam helped the tribe obtain property and fought for treaty rights. (Courtesy of Cherokee National Archives.)

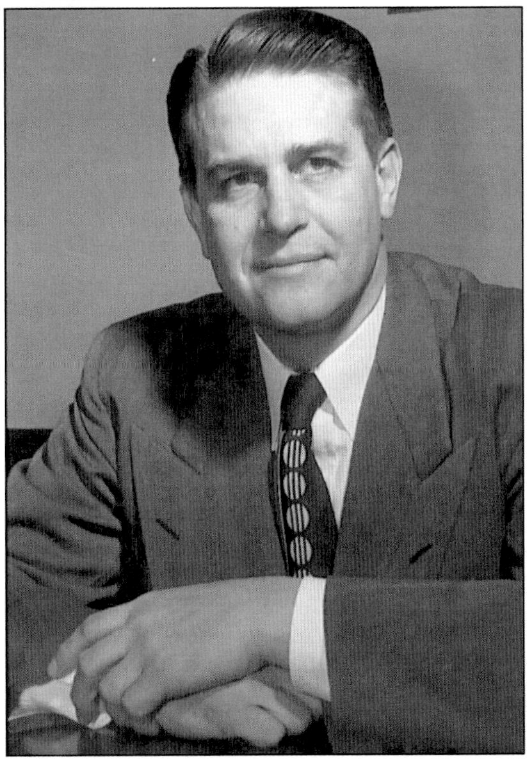

Principal Chief William Wayne Keeler, Served 1949 to 1975. Appointed by President Truman in 1949, Bill Keeler devoted himself to the Cherokees. A most popular leader, Keeler set out to acquire land, office buildings, and businesses like the Restaurant of the Cherokees. In 1971, he arranged the first election for chief since statehood. He ran for the office and won. (Courtesy of Cherokee National Archives.)

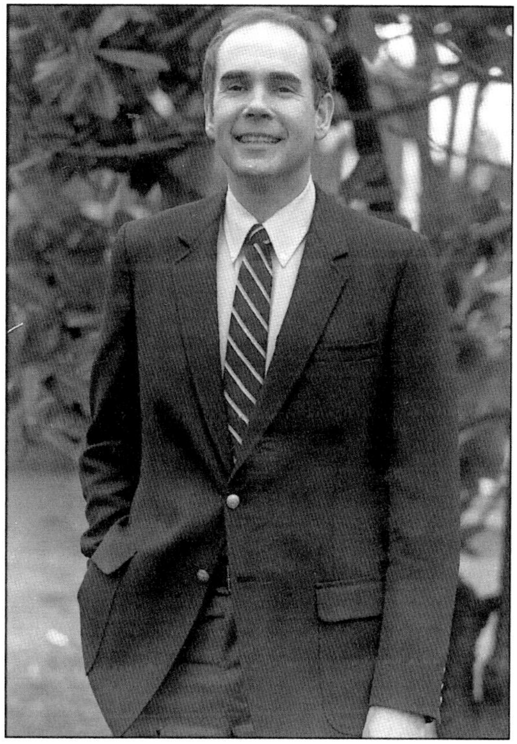

PRINCIPAL CHIEF ROSS O. SWIMMER, SERVED 1975 TO 1985. An astute businessman and bank president, Swimmer led the fight for rights to property taken during allotment. The Cherokees took legal claim to the Arkansas riverbed. The new W.W. Hastings Hospital opened in Tahlequah as did the tribe's 54,000-square-foot office complex. In 1985, the net worth of the Nation was $23 million. (Courtesy of Cherokee National Archives.)

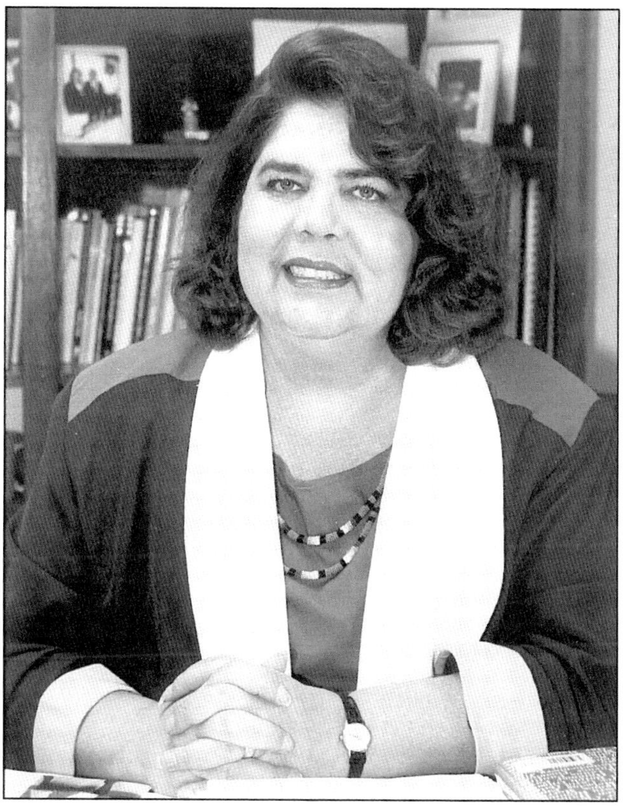

PRINCIPAL CHIEF WILMA P. MANKILLER, SERVED 1985 TO 1995. Mankiller is among the most beloved and accomplished Cherokees to lead the Nation. She swept the 1991 election with over 80 percent of the vote. Her 1990 Self-governance Agreement allowed the tribe to manage its own affairs for the first time since statehood, resulting in continuous improvements for the Nation. (Courtesy of Sammy Still, photographer.)

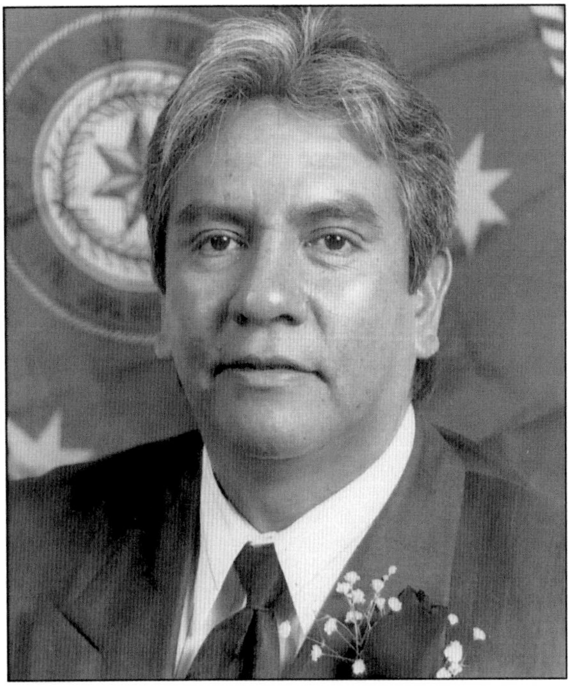

Principal Chief Joe Byrd, Served 1995 to 1999. A full-blood Cherokee speaker, Chief Joe Byrd helped secure important legislation for the tribe. The 1997 Fuel Tax Act boosted the Nation's economy, and 11,000 acres of land was obtained. A new health clinic opened in Muskogee. Unfortunately, the Nation also suffered a division in its leadership that took its toll on all tribal efforts. (Courtesy of Bobby Watkins, photographer.)

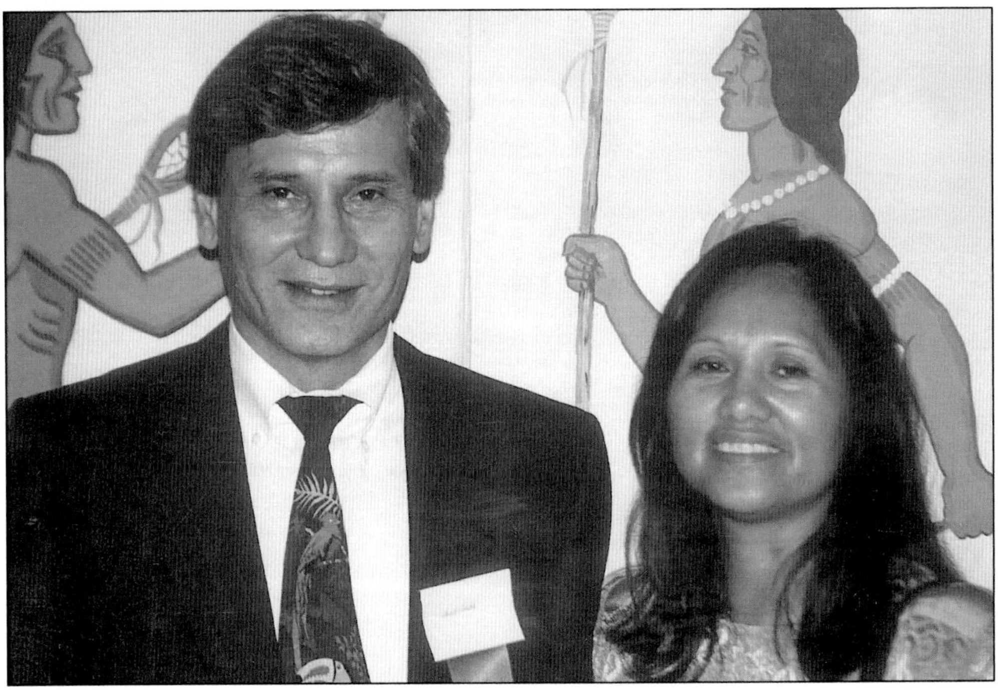

Principal Chief Chad "Corntassel" Smith, Elected 1999. One-half Cherokee and a great-grandson of traditionalist Redbird Smith, Chad Smith was elected chief on July 24, 1999. Smith's campaign platform focused on honest leadership, the people's involvement in government, job opportunities, economic development, improved essential services, and the preservation of culture and tradition. Pictured with Smith is his wife, Bobbie Gail Scott Smith. (Courtesy of Murv Jacob.)

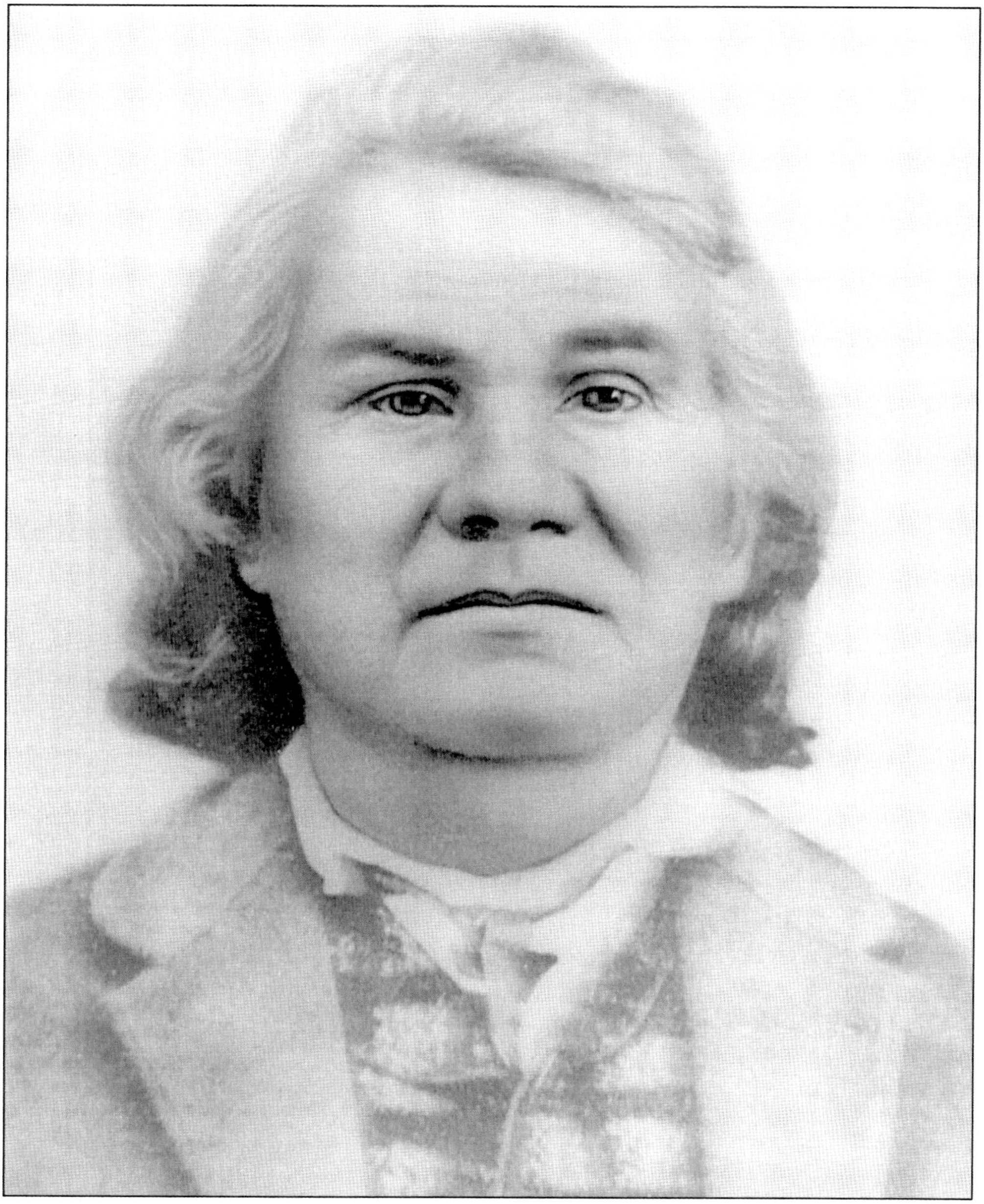

BRIG. GEN. STAND WATIE, c. 1865. Destined to become one of the most colorful figures in Cherokee history, Stand Watie was born December 12, 1806, in Georgia. Watie was involved in the secret treaty that led to the signing of the Treaty of New Echota and, ultimately, the Trail of Tears. When the Ridges and Boudinot were killed, it fell upon Watie to lead the Treaty Party. He did so with a vengeance. Watie is remembered for his valiant service to his beloved South. A defiant enemy of Chief John Ross, Stand Watie personally burned Ross's mansion to the ground during the Civil War. In 1861, Watie was commissioned by General McCullough to command the Cherokee Mounted Rifles. He was made a brigadier general on May 10, 1864, leading his Indian Brigade on raids through the Territory. Stand Watie was the last Civil War general to surrender on January 23, 1865. It was believed that no weapon could kill him. (Courtesy of Cherokee National Archives.)

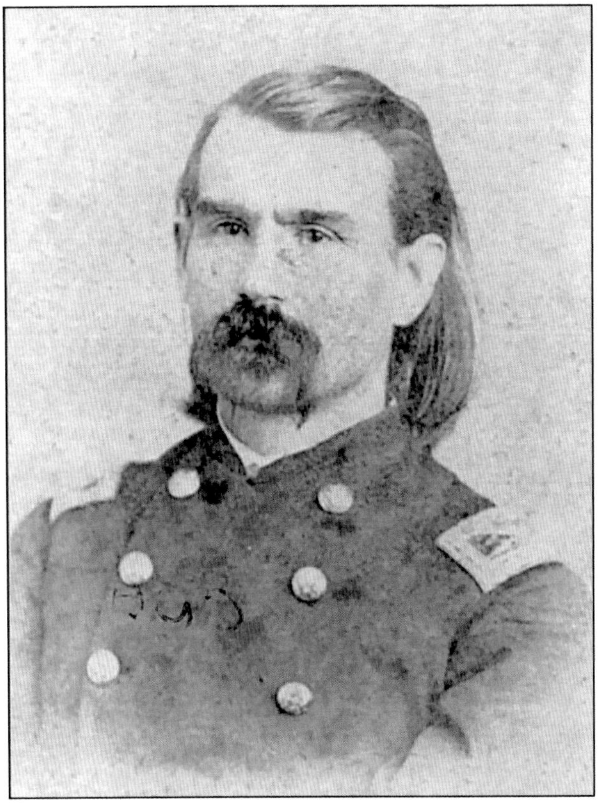

Colonel Cloud, Civil War Officer, January 26, 1864. The Cherokees of Chief Ross's party attempted to remain neutral during the Civil War. But Union forces pulled out of Indian Territory and the Confederates took over. Only after the other four Civilized Tribes signed treaties with the South did Ross follow suit. On October 7, 1861, the Confederate flag was raised over Tahlequah. (Courtesy of Cherokee National Archives.)

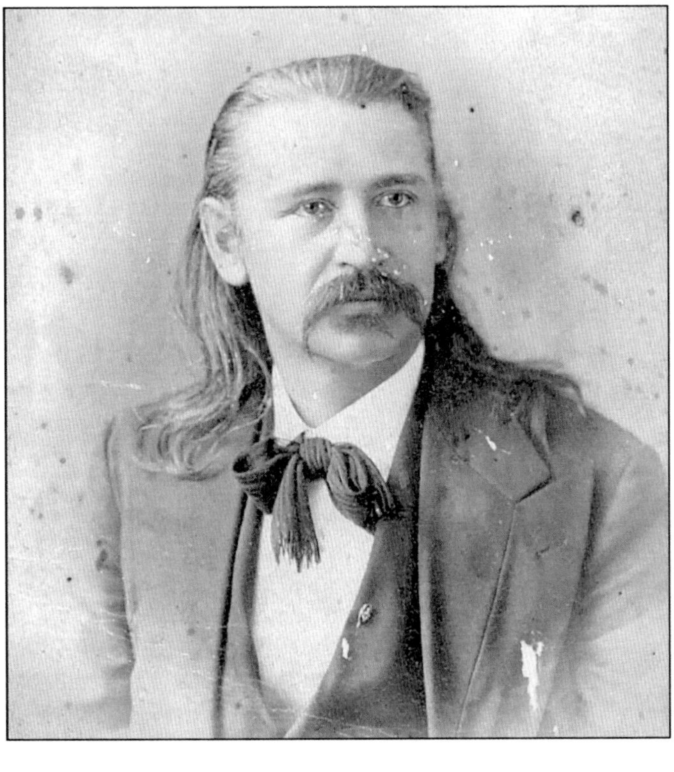

Colonel Elias Cornelius Boudinot, c. 1865. Considered one of the most brilliant Cherokees of history, Boudinot was also among the most hated. The lawyer and orator was a great proponent of opening the lands to white settlement in the 1880s. Boudinot served under Gen. Stand Watie, helping to raise the Cherokee Regiment, and was a delegate to the Congress of Confederate States. (Courtesy of Cherokee National Archives.)

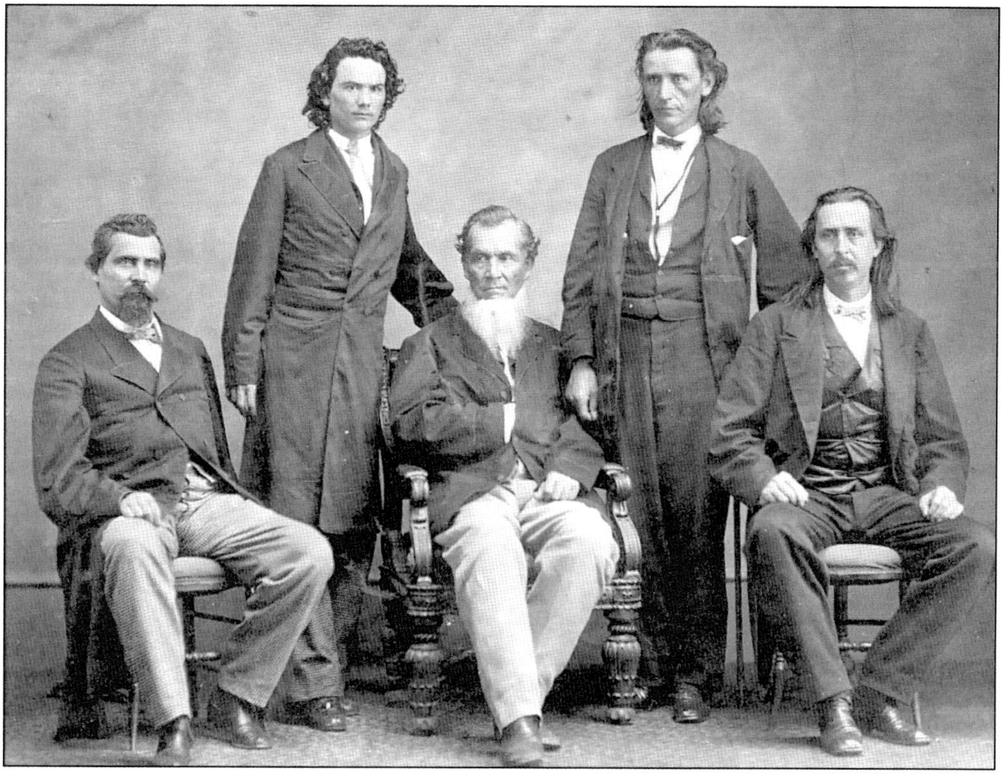

SOUTHERN DELEGATES, C. 1866. Representing the Southern sympathizers of the Cherokee Nation are, from left to right, John Rollin Ridge, Saladin Ridge-Watie, Richard Fields, Elias C. Boudinot, and William Penn Adair. Negotiating in Washington for the Treaty of 1866, they wanted the Cherokee lands divided into two separate nations. The situation mirrored the unrest and factionalism of their constituents. (Courtesy of Cherokee National Archives.)

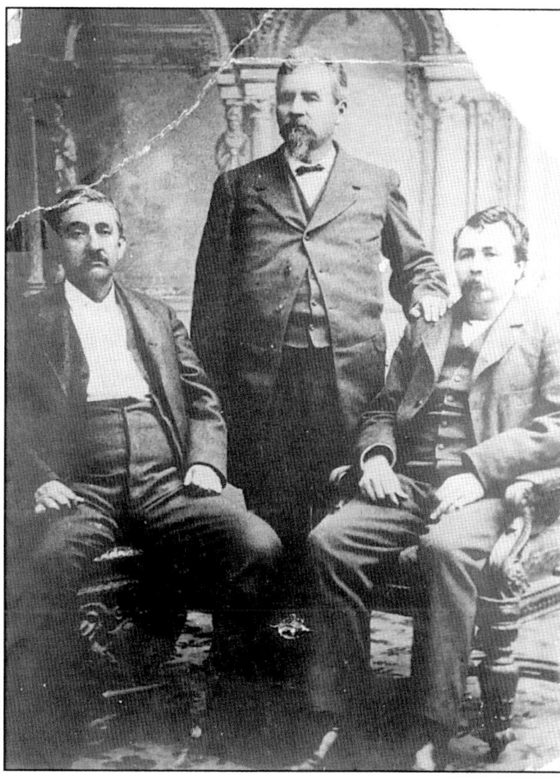

NEGOTIATORS FOR THE CHEROKEE OUTLET, C. 1889. Pictured here are John Gunter Schrimsher, Dennis Wolf Bushyhead, and Hoolie Bell, all influential Cherokee leaders. The men were members of a delegation working on the particulars of the sale of the Cherokee Outlet. (Courtesy of Will Rogers Memorial.)

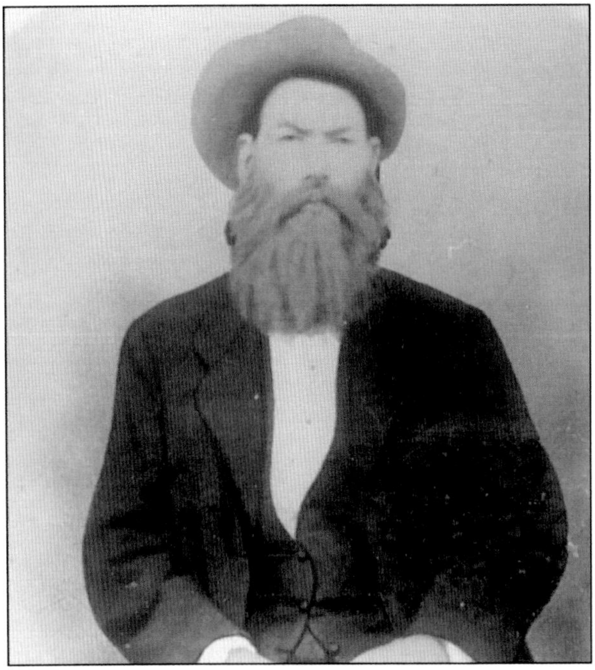

Supreme Court Justice, c. 1892. John Wright Alberty was named Supreme Court justice in 1892. The Cherokee Constitution, drawn up in 1839, provided for a judiciary system consisting of a Supreme Court, circuit courts, and four justices of the peace in each of eight districts. (Courtesy of Cherokee National Archives.)

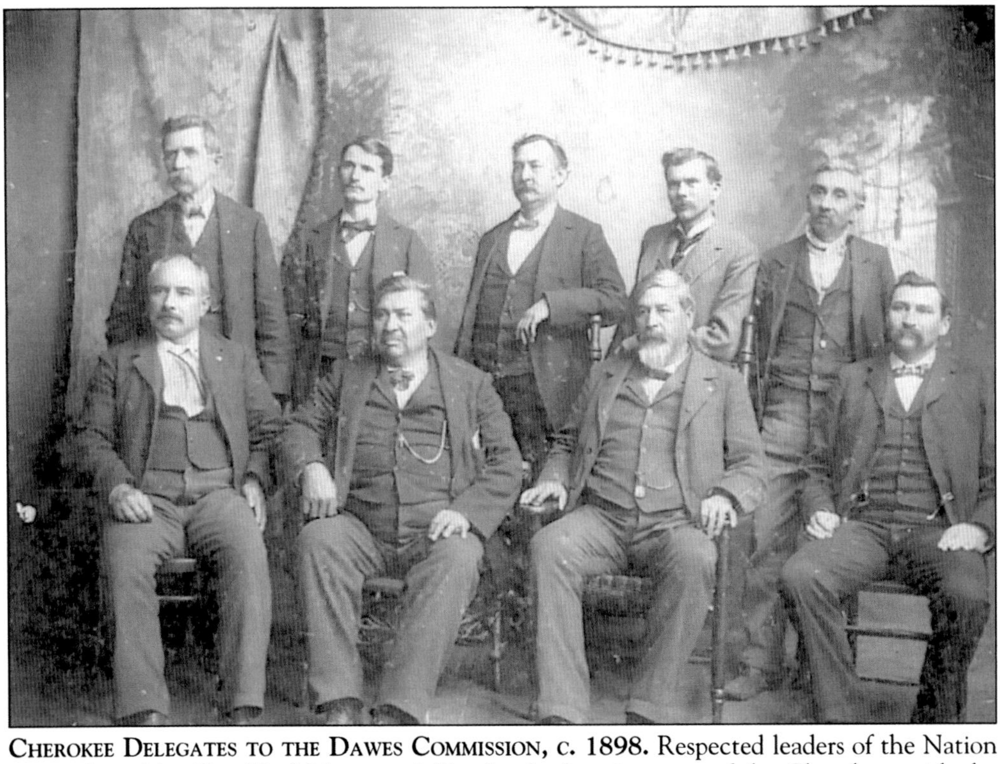

Cherokee Delegates to the Dawes Commission, c. 1898. Respected leaders of the Nation were selected by Chief Joel Mayes to lobby for the best interests of the Cherokees with the Dawes Commission. From left to right are (seated) Dave Lowery, Soggy Sanders, Robert Bruce Ross, and Percy Wyly; (standing) Clement Rogers, W.W. Hastings, George Benge, William Thompson, and Dave Faulkner. (Courtesy of Cherokee National Archives.)

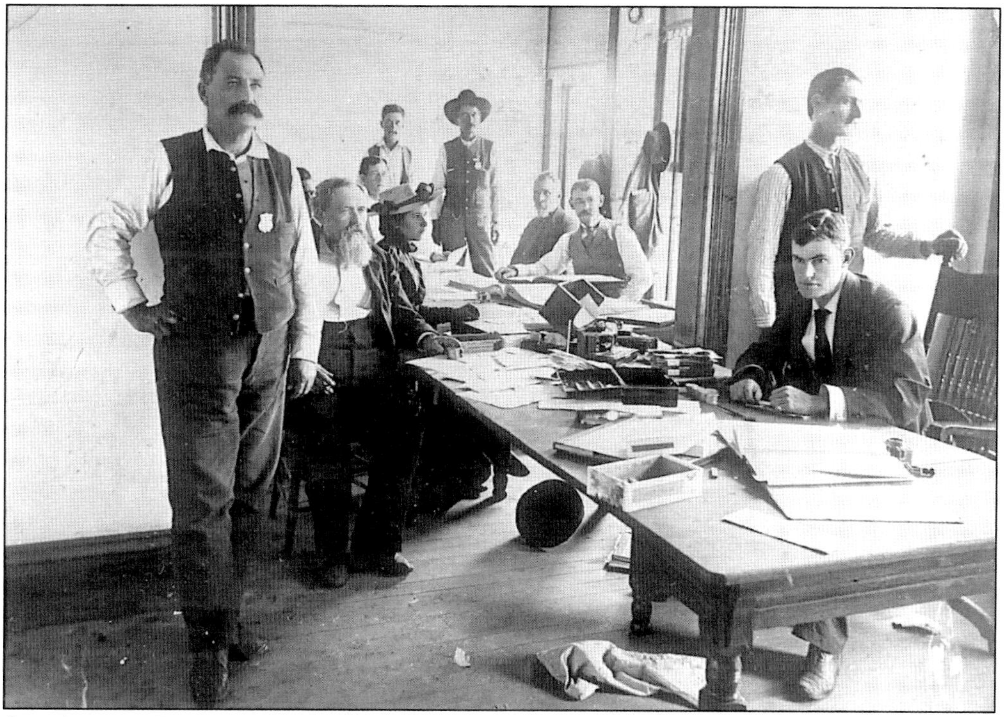

OLD SETTLER PAYMENT, JUNE 8, 1896. In the early 1800s, the Old Settlers were living in Arkansas. When land there opened to whites, the Cherokees were given land to the west, including the Cherokee Outlet and part of Indian Territory. The Treaty of 1828 provided for the move and ownership rights. In 1896, the Old Settlers received payment for lost land. (Courtesy of Rogers State College.)

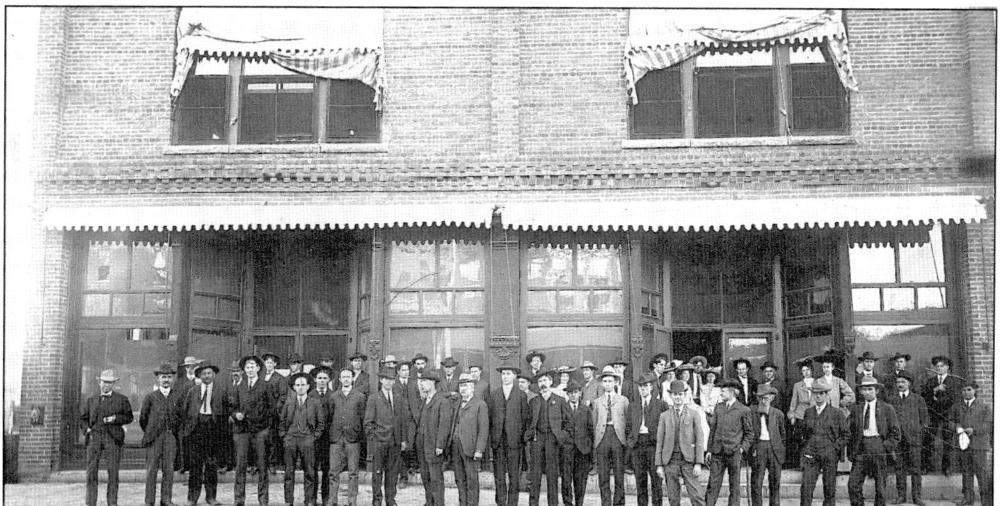

DELEGATES BEFORE THE DAWES COMMISSION OFFICE, C. 1899. The Dawes Act and the resultant Dawes Commission changed forever the face of the old Cherokee Nation. For the first time in their history, Cherokee individuals would actually own property. Cherokee land had been held in common for centuries, belonging to no one person. (Courtesy of Cherokee National Archives.)

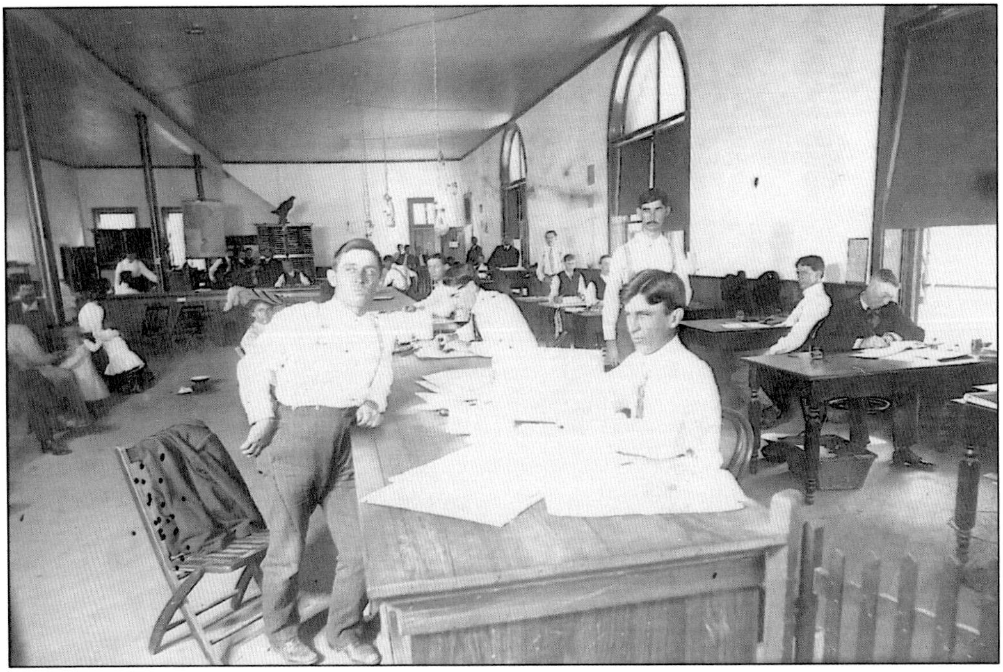

Inside the Dawes Commission Office, c. 1902. When the U.S. secretary of the interior decreed that an agreement with the Cherokee Nation concerning land division was not required, Dawes agents set out to forcibly enroll Cherokees who had previously resisted. A few months later, an agreement was reached, and by September 1902, some 50,000 applications for land had been collected. (Courtesy of Cherokee National Archives.)

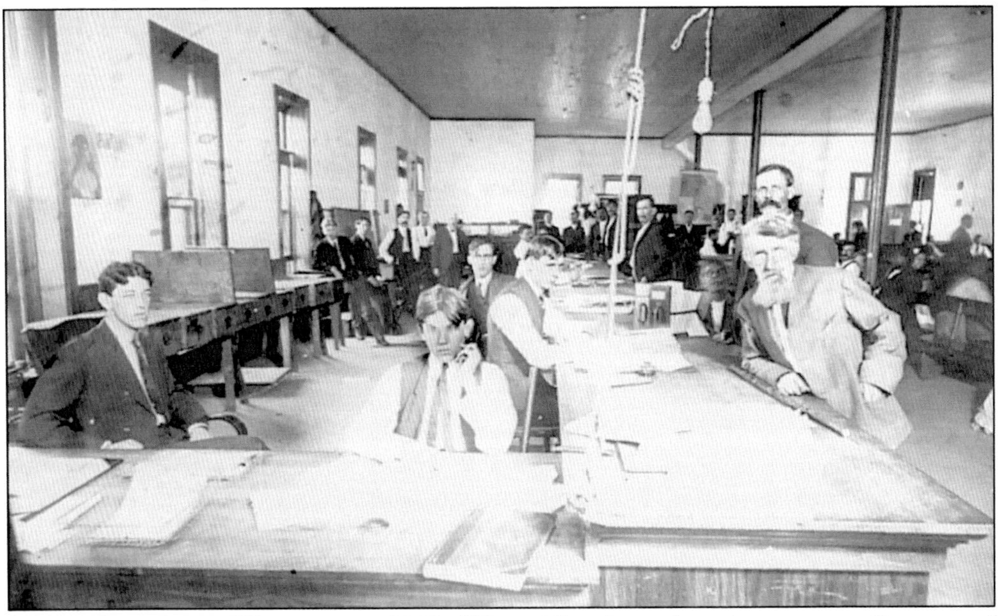

Dawes Commission Workers, c. 1902. When Cherokees elected to accept allotment of their lands, enrollment centers were jammed with white applicants claiming to be Cherokee. Discerning between these and the legitimate claimants was a difficult task for Dawes Commission officials. (Courtesy of Cherokee National Archives.)

Six

FAME

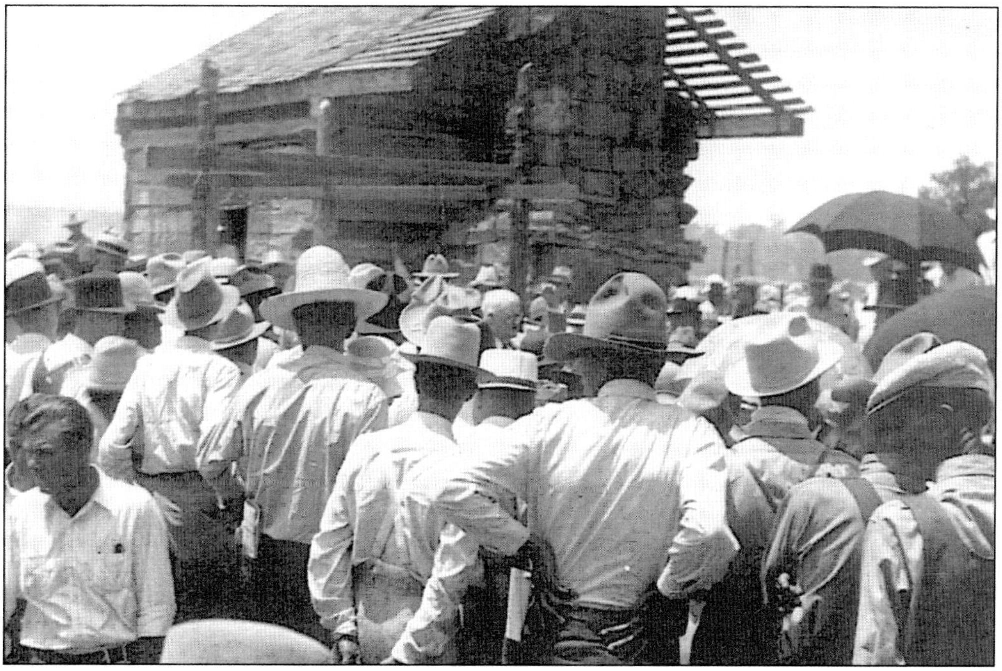

DEDICATION OF SEQUOYAH'S HOME, C. 1936. The cabin pictured here was built in 1829 by George Guess, better known as Sequoyah, one of the most famous Cherokees who ever lived. The cabin stands at Skin Bayou in present-day Sequoyah County. In this photograph, the cabin is being dedicated as a memorial to Sequoyah. A much larger building has since been constructed over and around the original cabin. The site, with its beautiful acreage, is a major visitor attraction in Sequoyah County. George Guess left his eastern home around 1820 when the Old Settlers began to migrate west. Working with Rev. Jesse Bushyhead and George Lowery, Sequoyah helped bring together the feuding factions of the Nation after the Trail of Tears. For all his statesmanship, Sequoyah is better known as the inventor of the Cherokee alphabet, or syllabary, that made the Cherokees literate in their own language. (Courtesy of Cherokee Studies Institute.)

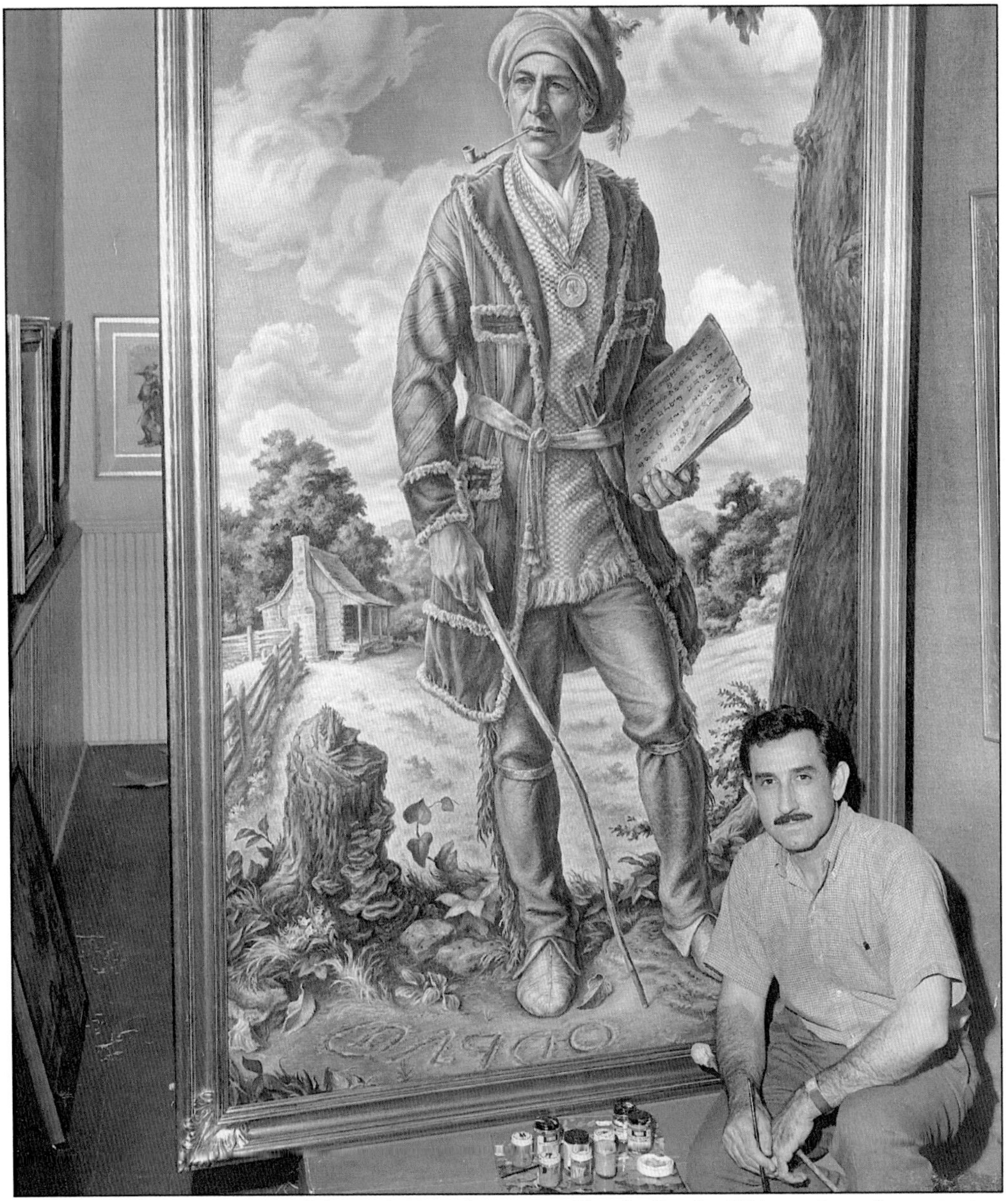

Painting of Sequoyah. Celebrated Cherokee artist Charles Banks Wilson shows his painting of Sequoyah, one of the most popular Sequoyah images in existence. Sequoyah is shown wearing the medal given to him by the Cherokee Nation to honor his work with the syllabary. It took only 12 years for Sequoyah to perfect the symbols. Each one of the 85 characters represents a syllable of Cherokee speech. For speakers of the language, it was a simple matter learning to read and write with the syllabary. Within six months of its introduction, the Cherokee Nation was literate, an astounding accomplishment for the tribe. Within five years, newspapers and books were printed in Cherokee. Sequoyah was the first person in history to invent an alphabet for a previously unwritten language. The great Sequoia trees of California were named for him. His sculpture stands in Statuary Hall in Washington, D.C. In later years, Sequoyah traveled far to look for lost Cherokees. It is believed he is buried in Mexico. (Courtesy of Charles Banks Wilson.)

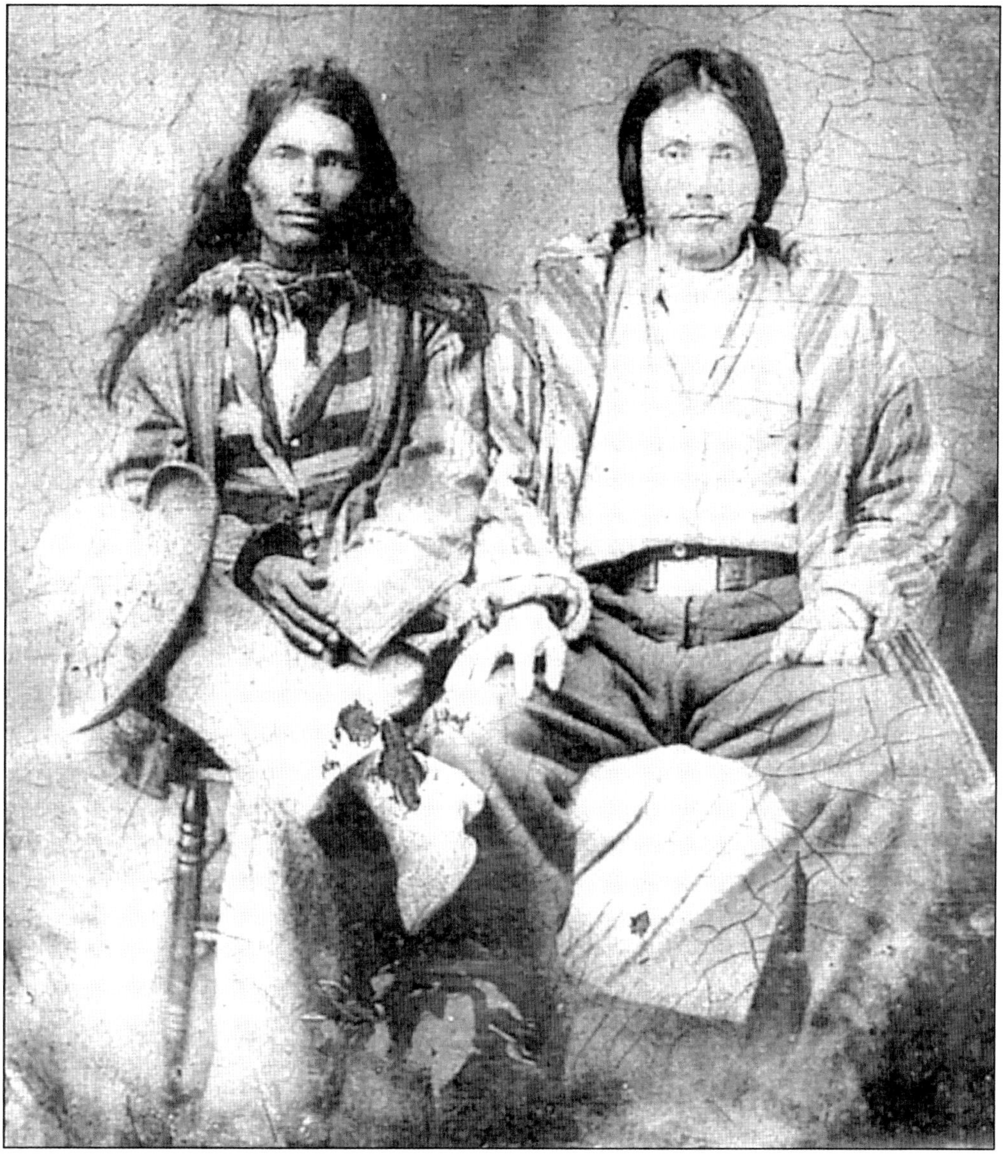

NED CHRISTIE, C. 1872. Born in 1852, Christie (left) was called "Nede" by family and friends and was known to be a good fiddle player. Christie is remembered as a patriot of the Cherokee Nation. He served as an executive councilor under Principal Chief Dennis W. Bushyhead. In 1885, U.S. Marshal Dan Maples was found shot to death and the finger of blame pointed to Ned Christie. Many argue that Ned was framed for the shooting because he was an outspoken critic of the changes taking place in the Cherokee Nation. Christie wanted to protect the traditional lifestyle of the tribe, protesting the railroad and white settlement. Guilty or not, Christie became a hunted outlaw. For years, Ned eluded the U.S. Marshals sent by "hanging judge" Isaac Parker to bring him in. He built a virtual fortress that bullets could not penetrate. Finally resorting to dynamite, the marshals shot Ned Christie as he ran from his stronghold into the woods. (Courtesy of Roy Hamilton.)

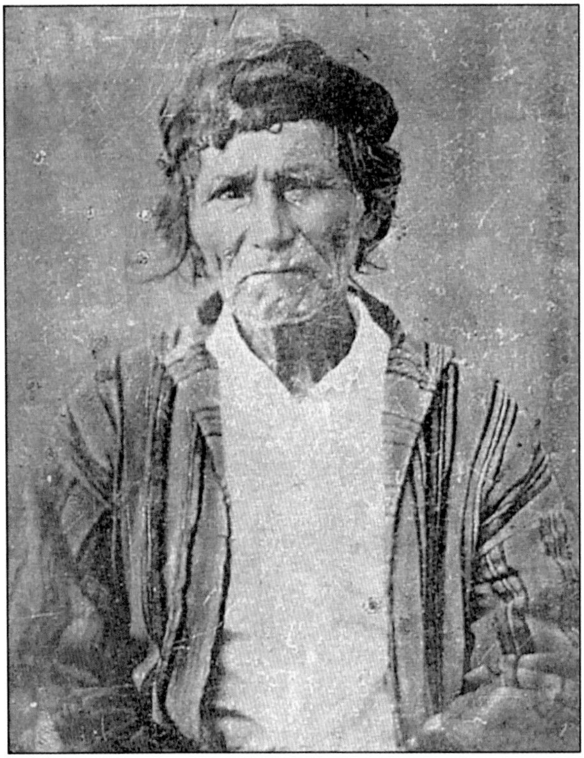

LACIE, GRANDFATHER OF NED CHRISTIE, C. 1865. Wearing a traditional Cherokee hunting jacket is Christie's grandfather. Ned Christie left behind a host of relatives whose descendants still live and work within the Cherokee Nation. Near the community of Wauhillau, Ned Christie's burial place and the ruins of his fort can be found. (Courtesy of Roy Hamilton.)

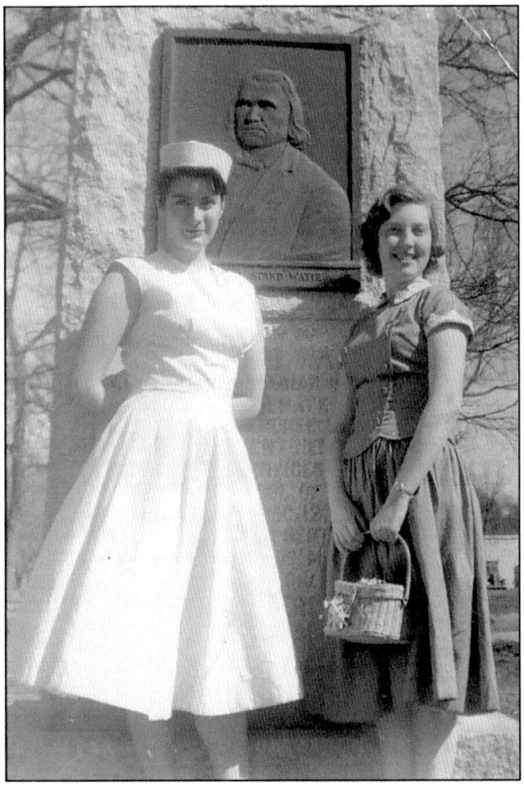

TAHLEQUAH TOURISTS, C. 1950. Two young ladies get their picture taken with Brig. Gen. Stand Watie on the Capitol Square in Tahlequah. Watie was one of the best-known and most passionate figures of the Civil War years. At one point he was even elected chief by Southern sympathizers while John Ross held the office. (Courtesy of Ralph and Loretta Dunham.)

Rogers with Roommate John Payne, c. 1897. Clement Vann Rogers, Will's father, sent him to at least six schools near their home in the Cooweescoowee district. The last one was Kemper Military Academy. He stayed there long enough to make lasting friends but soon ran away, returning to the ranch. (Courtesy of Will Rogers Memorial.)

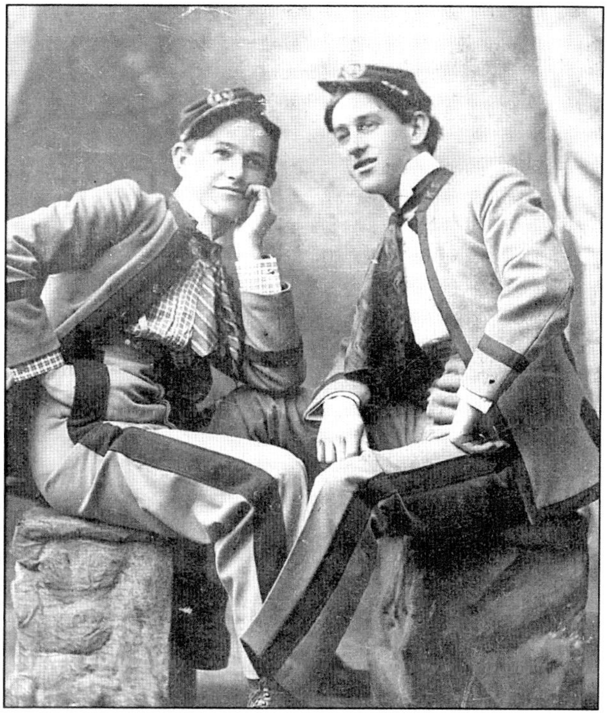

A Royal Flush?, c. 1896. Poker probably seemed a lot more enjoyable than school to young Will Rogers (left). Will enjoyed a carefree childhood in Indian Territory, learning rope tricks and riding horses on his father's ranch. (Courtesy of Will Rogers Memorial.)

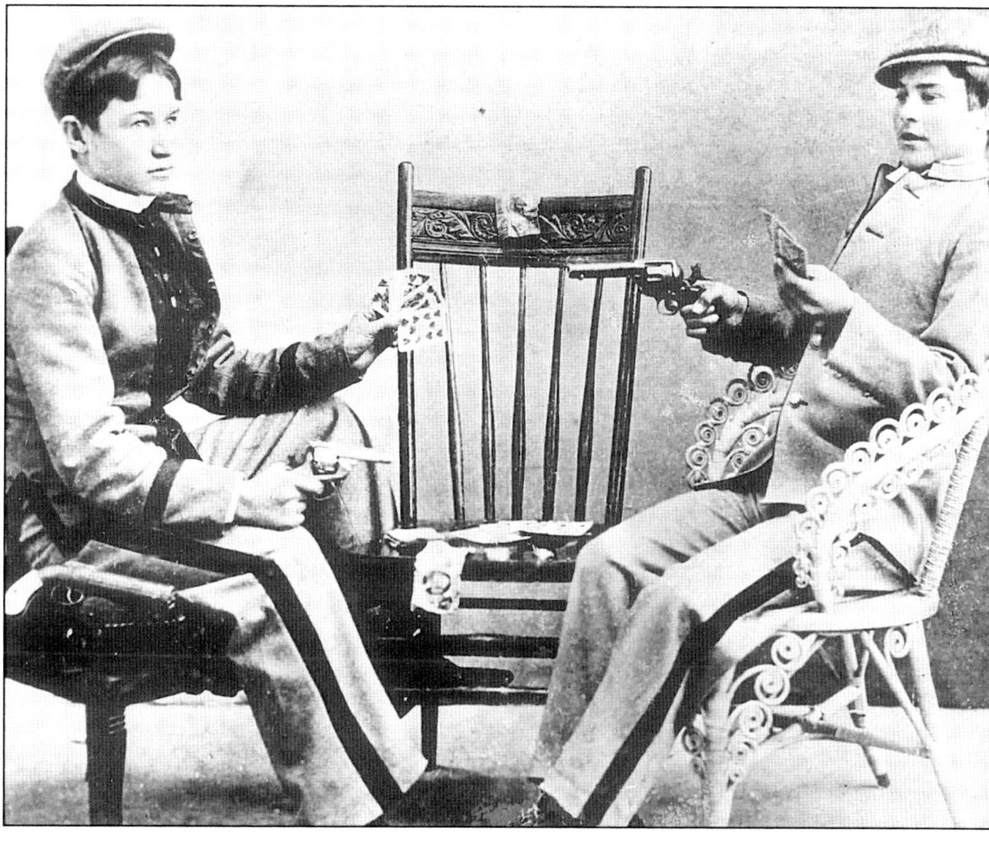

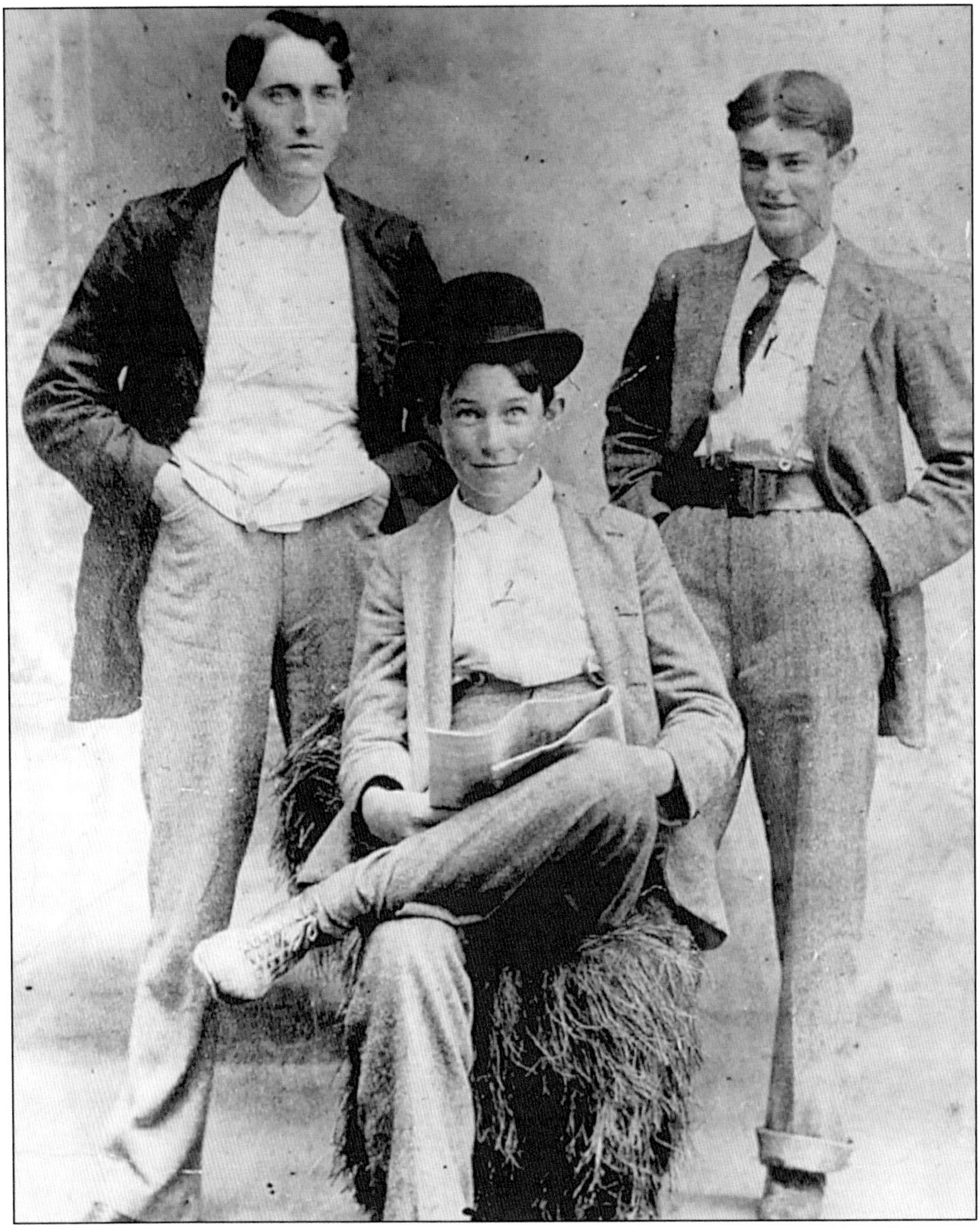

At Scarret College in Missouri, c. 1896. Seated on a hay bale is 17-year-old Will Rogers with friends John Phillips (left) and Gordon Lindsey. There happened to be a Grecian goddess statue gracing a fountain at Scarret College. But she was left short one arm after the day fun-loving Will Rogers roped it and pulled it off. Will's full name was Colonel William Penn Adair Rogers. Adair's wife named him that at his birth on November 4, 1879. Will was born in the Cooweescoowee district of the Cherokee Nation near present-day Oologah. Will was 7/32 Cherokee and the youngest son of Clement Vann Rogers. It was from his Cherokee mother, Mary America Schrimsher Rogers, that he inherited his humor and wit. Of the Paint Clan, Rogers was proud of his Cherokee blood and once stated, "My ancestors didn't come over on the Mayflower, but they met 'em at the boat!" (Courtesy of Will Rogers Memorial.)

IN KEMPER MILITARY ACADEMY UNIFORM, c. 1898. Rogers poses with a rifle on a visit home to the ranch. With, at most, a tenth-grade education, Rogers was an avid reader of all written materials. As such, he became quite well educated and qualified to be a writer himself. Will penned six books, numerous magazine articles, and over 4,000 newspaper columns. (Courtesy of Will Rogers Memorial.)

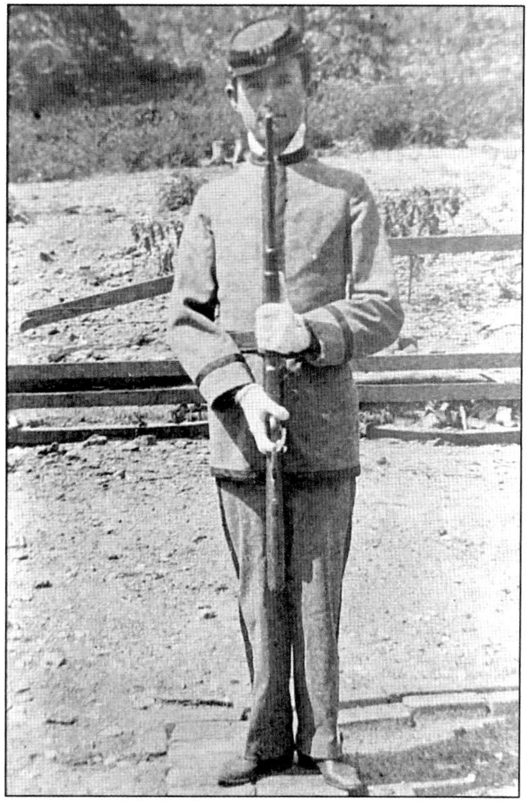

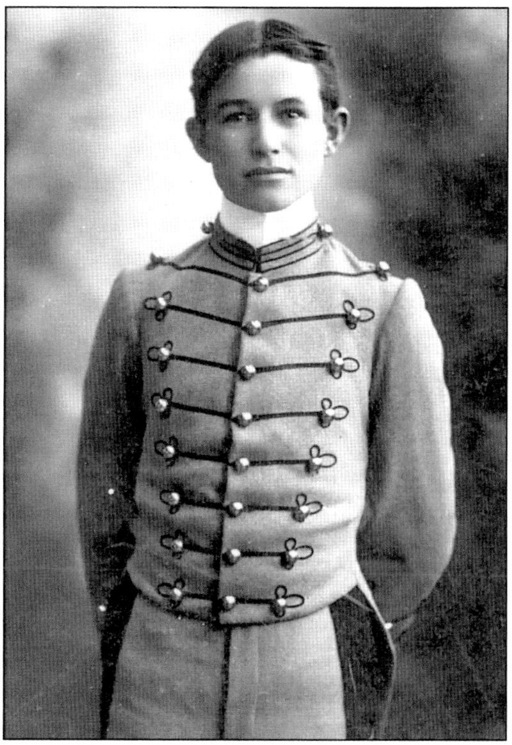

A THOUGHTFUL WILL ROGERS, c. 1897. Since he is wearing a school uniform, Will is likely thinking of a way out of both it and the school. As he told his friend Spi Trent, "I can't keep myself inside a schoolroom . . . I reckon my body stays put, but I personally am out in green pastures." (Courtesy of Will Rogers Memorial.)

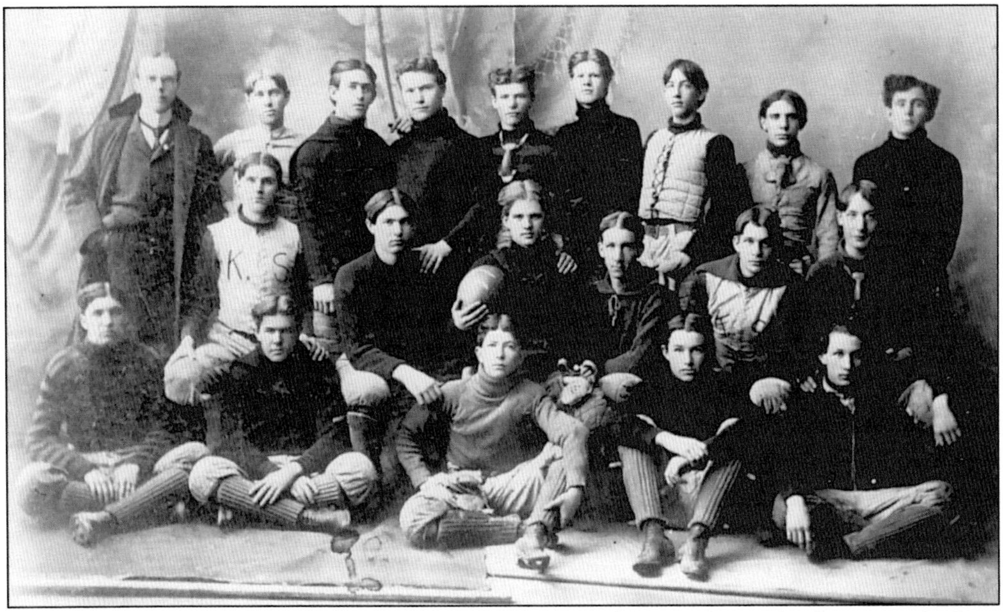

Kemper Football Team, c. 1898. Will Rogers sits second from right on the front row, looking much a part of the group but dreaming of adventure and home. He had grown up with cattle and horses and longed to be out on the range. (Courtesy of Will Rogers Memorial.)

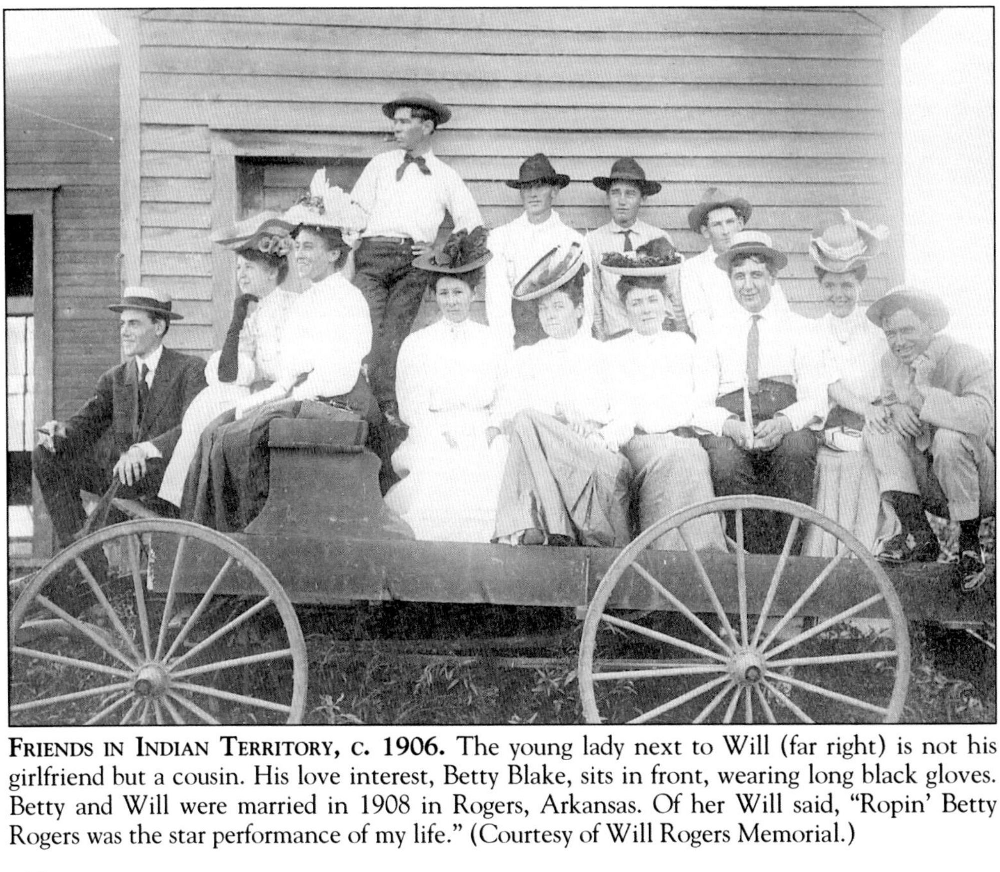

Friends in Indian Territory, c. 1906. The young lady next to Will (far right) is not his girlfriend but a cousin. His love interest, Betty Blake, sits in front, wearing long black gloves. Betty and Will were married in 1908 in Rogers, Arkansas. Of her Will said, "Ropin' Betty Rogers was the star performance of my life." (Courtesy of Will Rogers Memorial.)

MARY MCCLELLAN, C. 1905. This beautiful young woman was one of a multitude of friends who were entertained by Rogers on his visits home to Indian Territory. Will particularly liked having as many of his friends and relatives as possible in the audiences of his vaudeville performances. (Courtesy of Will Rogers Memorial.)

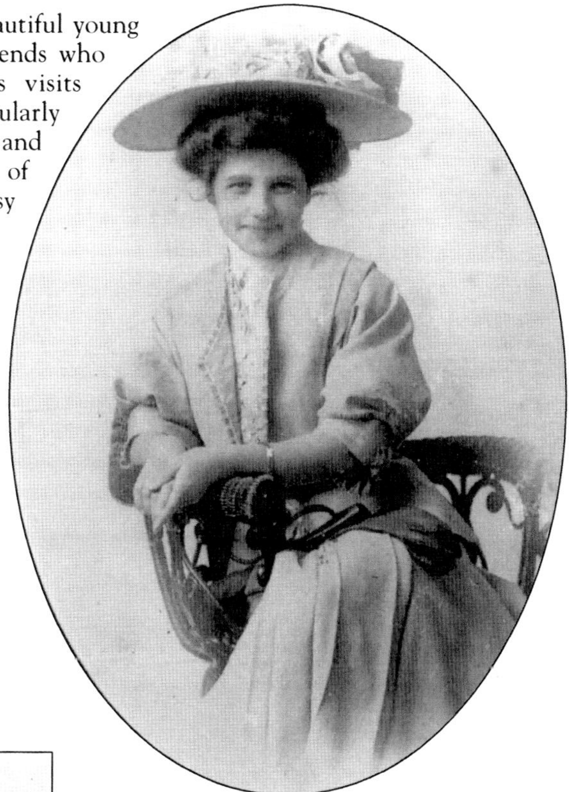

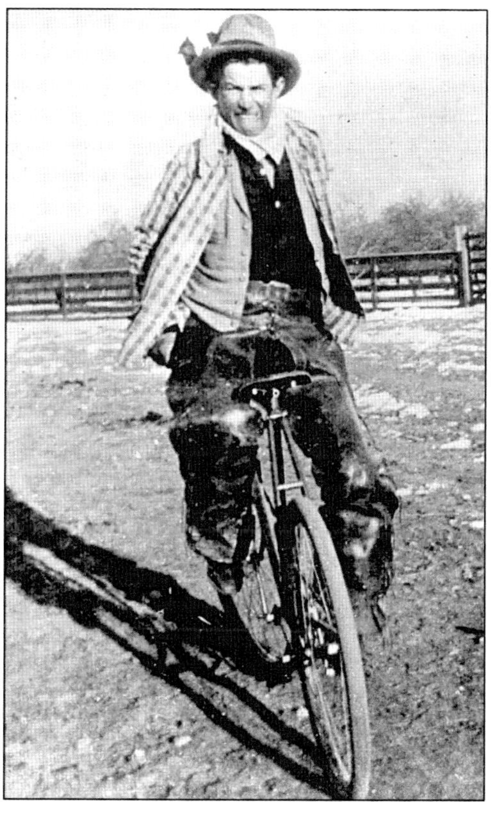

BACKWARD TRICK RIDING, EARLY 1900S. Out of school and back on the ranch, Will Rogers soon developed a bad case of wanderlust, traveling first to California and then to South America and Africa on the search for adventure. Letters home to his sisters were often printed in the *Claremore Progress* newspaper. (Courtesy of Will Rogers Memorial.)

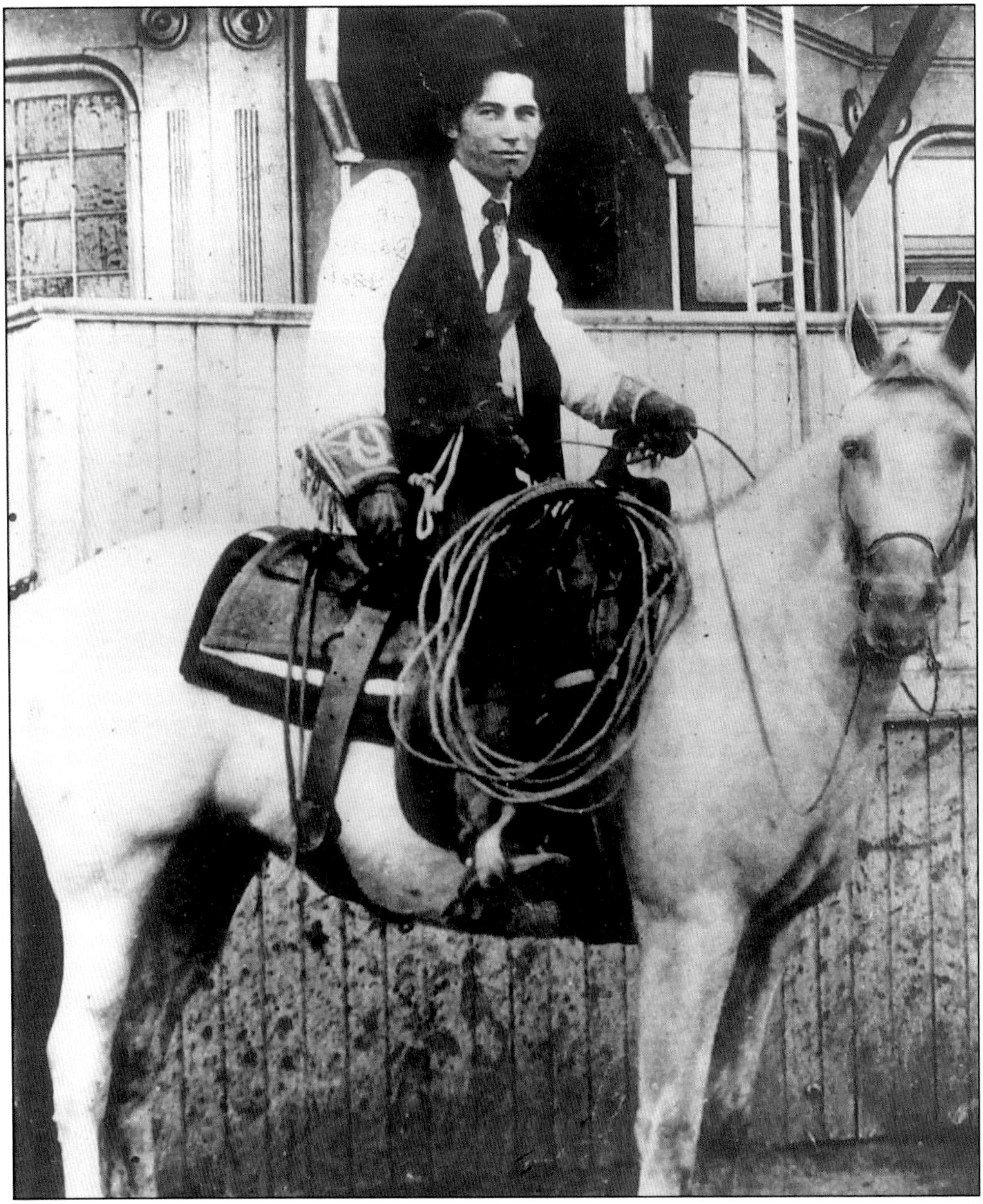

A Rising Star, early 1900s. Returning from his travels abroad, Will Rogers joined Col. Zak Mulhall's Wild West Show at the St. Louis World Fair. There he shared the stage with Geronimo, the famous Indian chief. When he appeared at Madison Square Garden, Rogers stunned the audience when he managed to rope a running horse on stage. This was also his first time to speak directly to the audience during an act. Their laughter at his manner of speech made him feel depressed, but another actor convinced him he was genuinely funny and urged him to continue getting laughs. After that the jokes and one-liners came pouring out. In the early teens, Rogers joined Zeigfield Follies, becoming a star attraction. When dignitaries were in the audience, he made a habit of bringing them on stage, to everyone's delight. He also poked fun at them, a practice first tried on Pres. Woodrow Wilson. Both Wilson and the audience were charmed. (Courtesy of Will Rogers Memorial.)

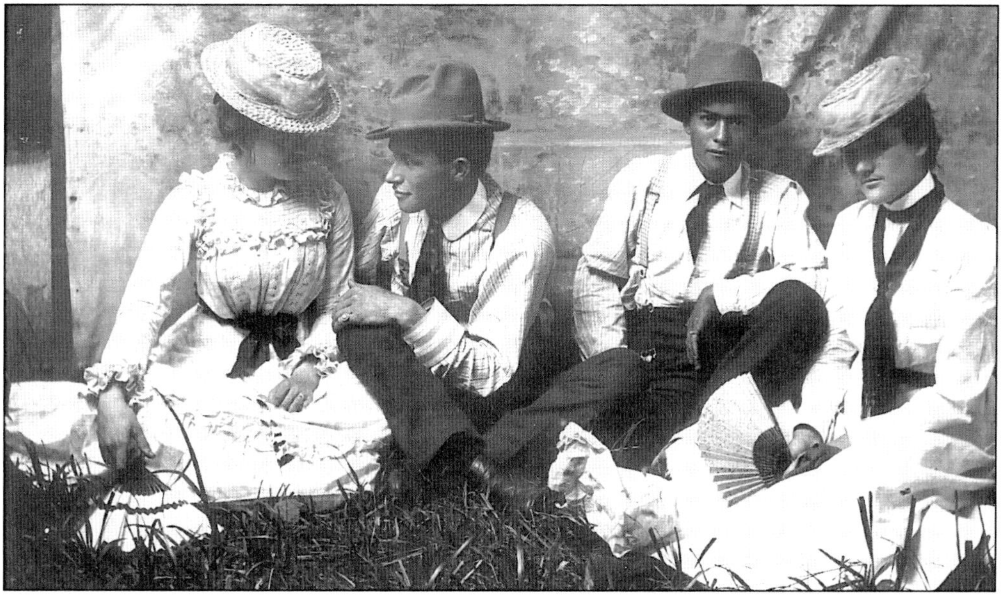

WILL AND CLOSE FRIENDS, EARLY 1900s. Relaxing on the Rogers ranch near Claremore are, from left to right, Emma Scott, Will Rogers, Spi Trent, and Rosanna Harnage. Rogers also had alliances with celebrities like Henry Ford, who gave Rogers the first Model A he produced. Other good friends included Charles Lindbergh, Mickey Rooney, Joel McCrae, Spencer Tracy, and Charlie Chaplin, to name a few. (Courtesy of Will Rogers Memorial.)

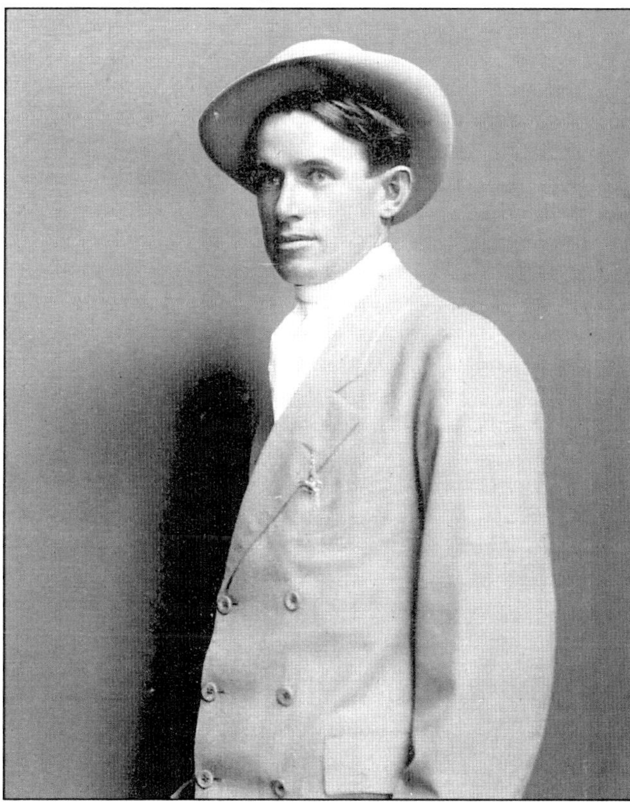

FUTURE MOVIE STAR, C. 1910. Will Rogers starred in silent films and, in 1929, entered the world of the "talkies." His most popular movies were *They Had to See Paris*, *Too Busy to Work*, *A Connecticut Yankee*, *Judge Priest*, *Life Begins at Forty*, and *Steamboat 'Round the Bend*. (Courtesy of Will Rogers Memorial.)

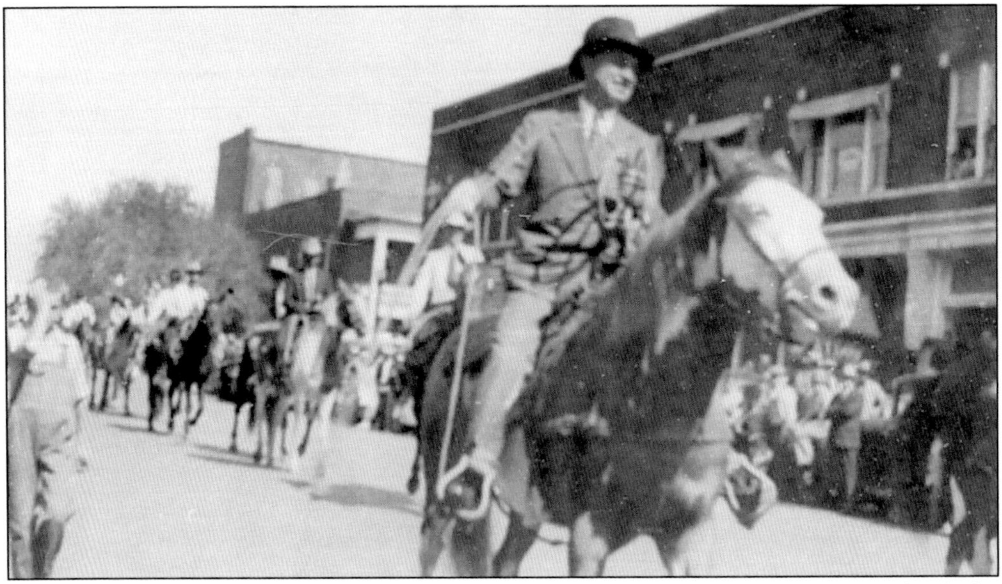

OLD SETTLERS DAY, c. 1934. Holding his lariat and riding a beautiful pony, Rogers leads the Old Settlers Day parade in Vinita, Oklahoma. That day Will recommended they hold a rodeo to promote the celebration, promising to attend the next year. Although he did not live to see it, Vinita's Will Rogers Rodeo became an annual event. (Courtesy of Will Rogers Memorial.)

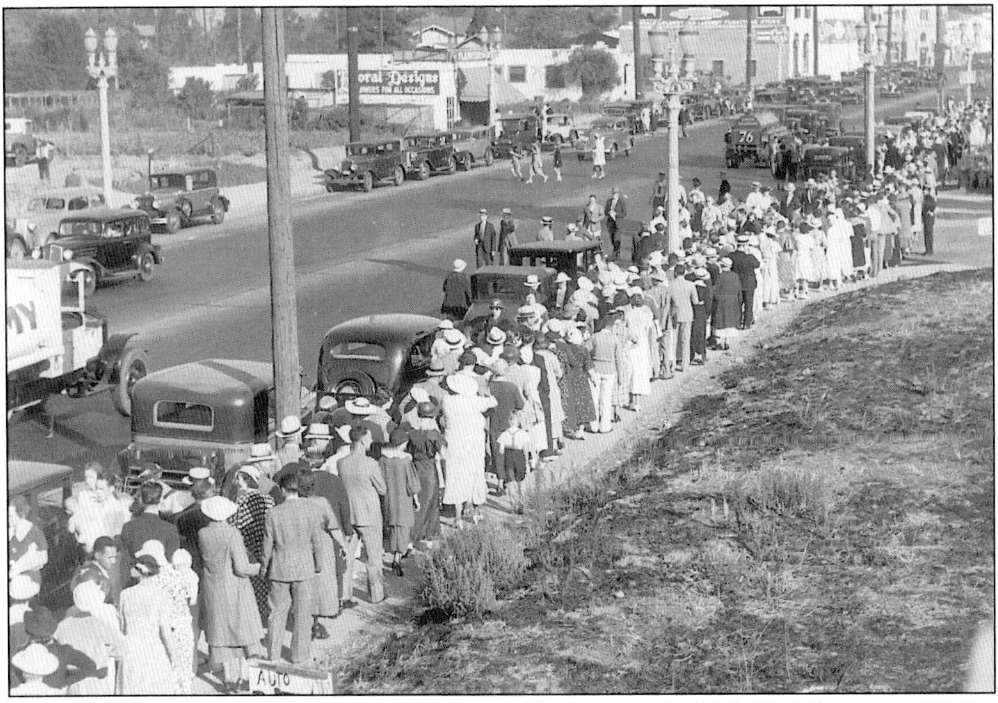

CALIFORNIA PAYS ITS RESPECTS, AUGUST 1935. On August 15, 1935, Will Rogers and Wiley Post were killed when their plane went down at Point Barrow, Alaska. Shocked fans in Los Angeles crowded the walkways to the memorial park where Will's body lay in state. The Red Cross set up first aid stations to help with the crowd of over 50,000. (Courtesy of Will Rogers Memorial.)

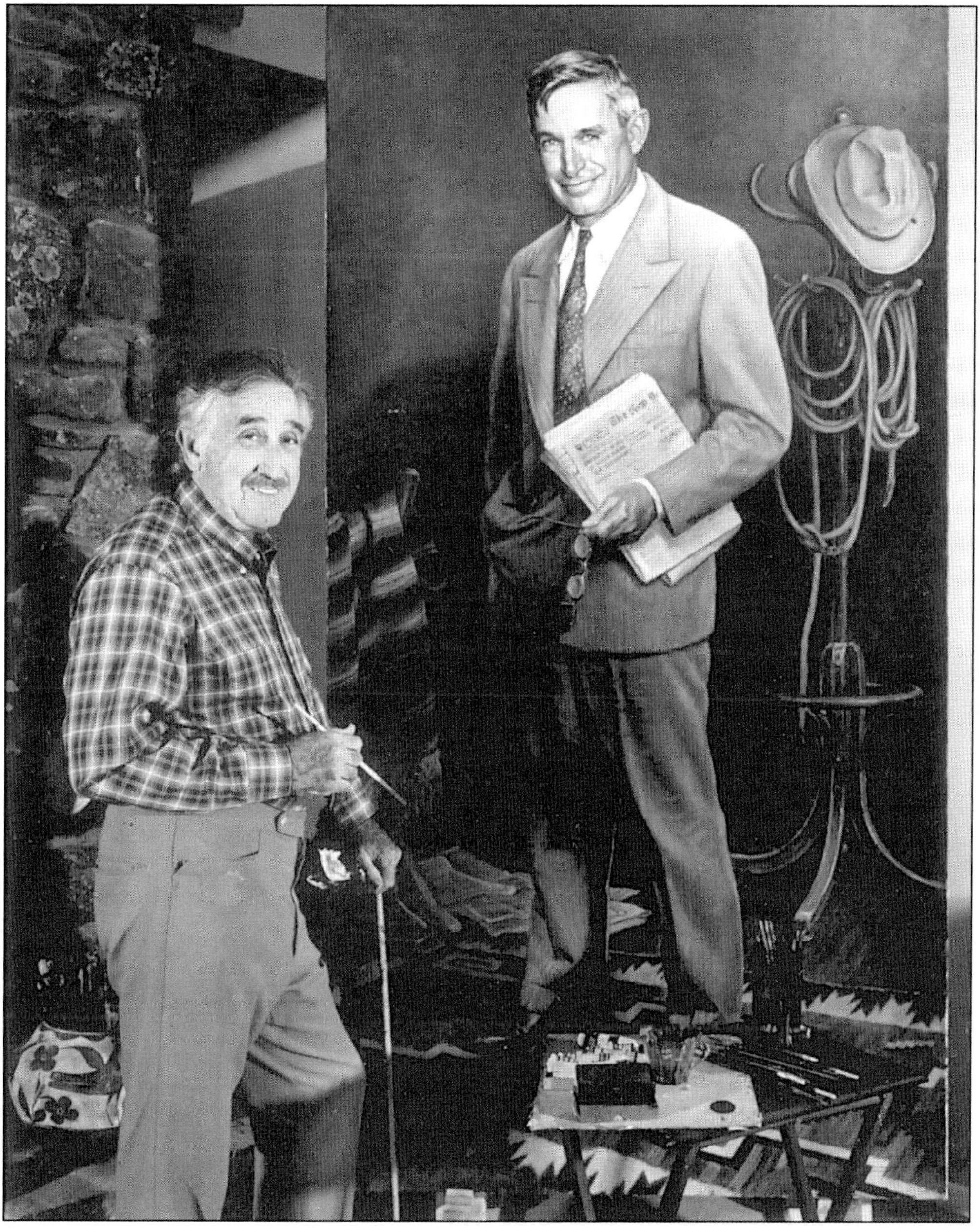

America's Favorite Son. Cherokee artist Charles Banks Wilson created this portrait of the legendary Will Rogers, one of dozens housed in Claremore's Will Rogers Memorial. After Will's accident, the entire country was in mourning. His passing was compared to the loss of Abraham Lincoln. In the words of Damos Runyan, "Will Rogers was undoubtedly America's most complete document. His place in this country is unique, amazing. In thought and manner of appearance and in his daily life, he was probably the closest living approach to what we call the true American." Will Rogers spoke of his own epitaph, "I joked about every prominent man of my time, but I never met a man I didn't like. I am so proud of that I can hardly wait to die so it can be carved. And when you come to my grave you will find me sitting there, proudly reading it." (Courtesy of Will Rogers Memorial.)

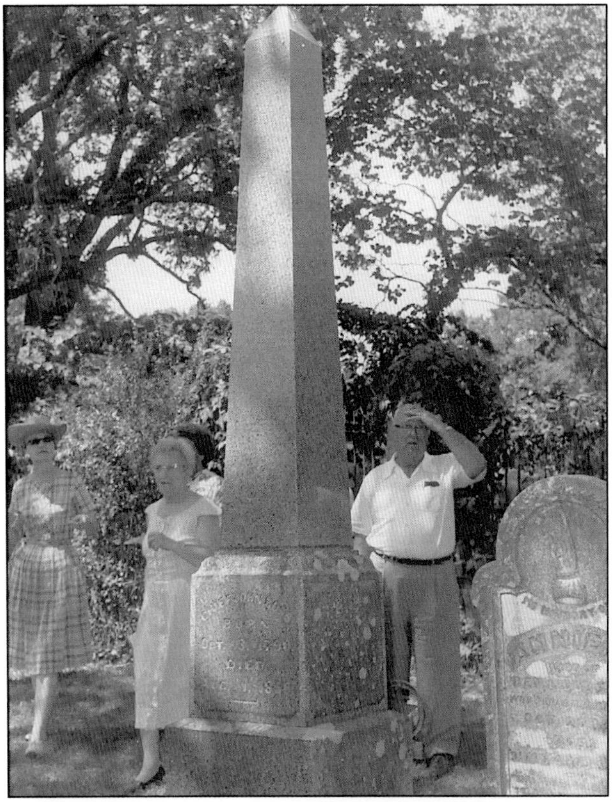

JOHN ROSS MONUMENT. For years, tourists have journeyed to the Ross Cemetery near Park Hill to visit the grave of Principal Chief John Ross, who led the Cherokee Nation through its most difficult yet triumphant years. The great chief's passion until the day he died was keeping the Nation united as one people. (Courtesy of Cherokee National Archives.)

REAR ADMIRAL JOCKO CLARK, c. 1944. Cherokee Adm. Jocko Clark, left, displays the Oklahoma flag to a gathering at Pearl Harbor. One of the highest-ranking and most decorated military leaders of his time, Clark was honored when a Navy ship, the S.S. *Clark*, was named for him. (Courtesy of Cherokee National Archives.)

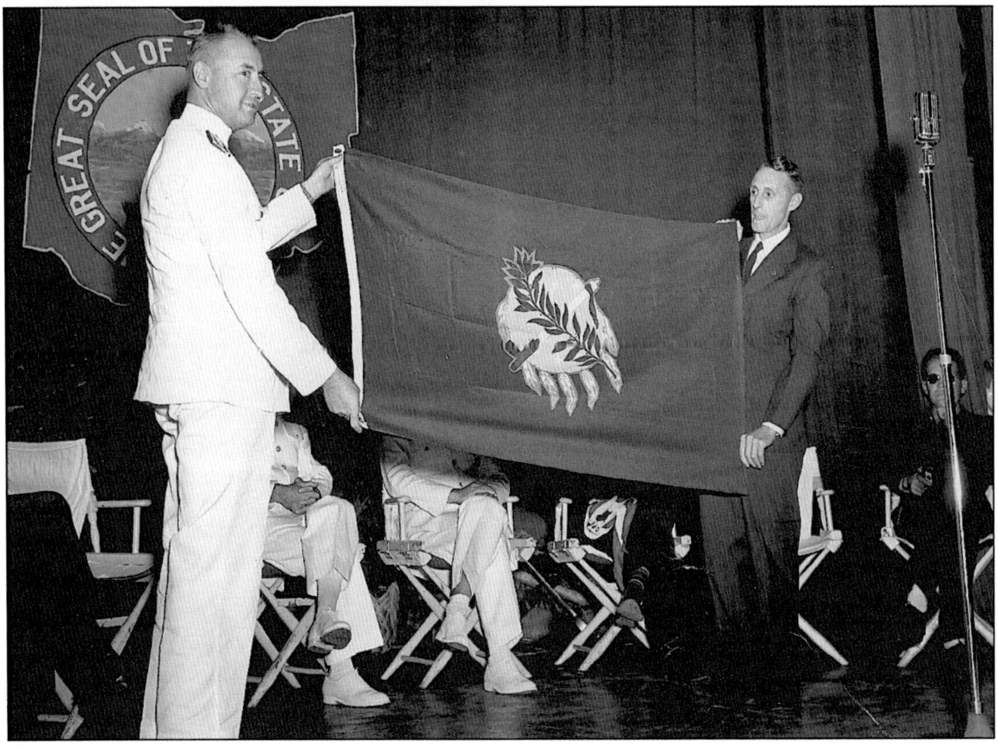

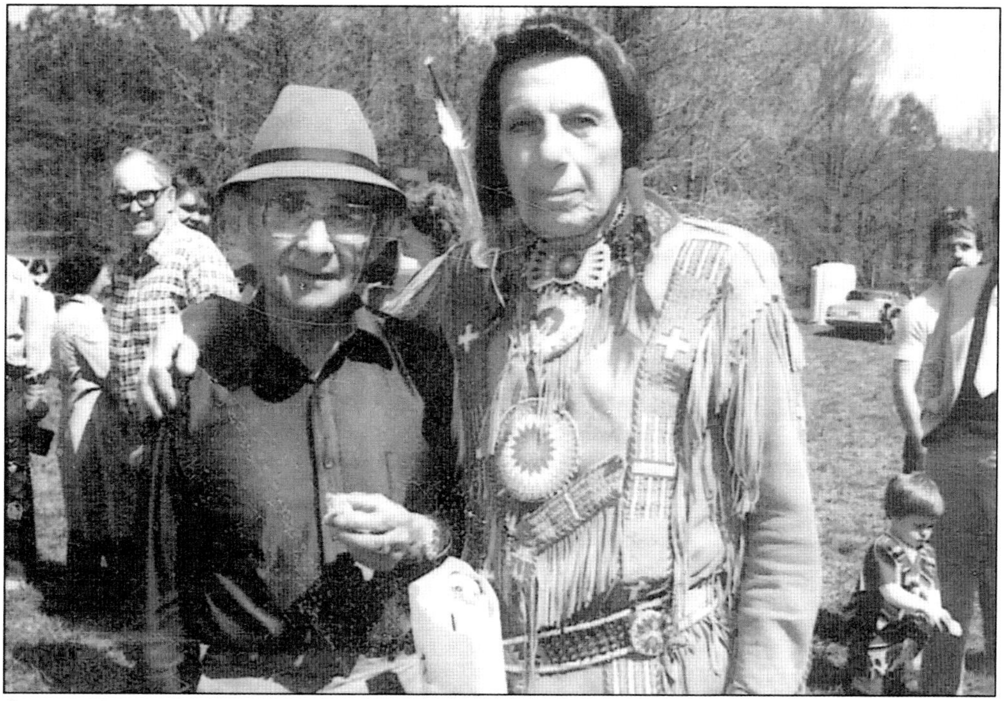

George Cochran and Iron Eyes. Beloved Cherokee artist George Cochran poses with actor Iron Eyes Cody, who earned fame for his portrayals of Native American characters in television and film. Although Cody played the role both on and off camera, he was not of Native American descent. (Courtesy of Brenda Carpenter.)

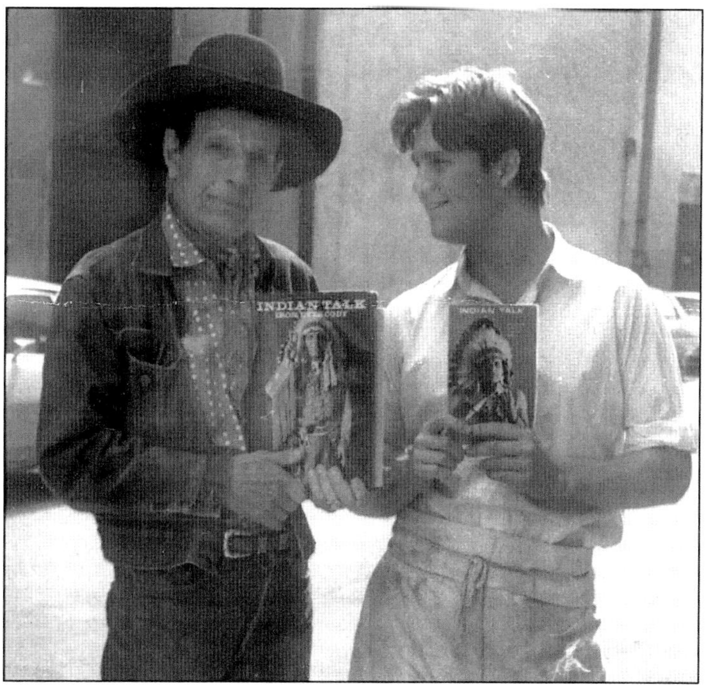

Iron Eyes and Jeff Bridges. Actor Iron Eyes Cody and co-star Jeff Bridges hold copies of Cody's book, *Indian Talk*. The two became friends while working on the MGM movie *Heart of the West* in 1974. (Courtesy of Cherokee National Archives.)

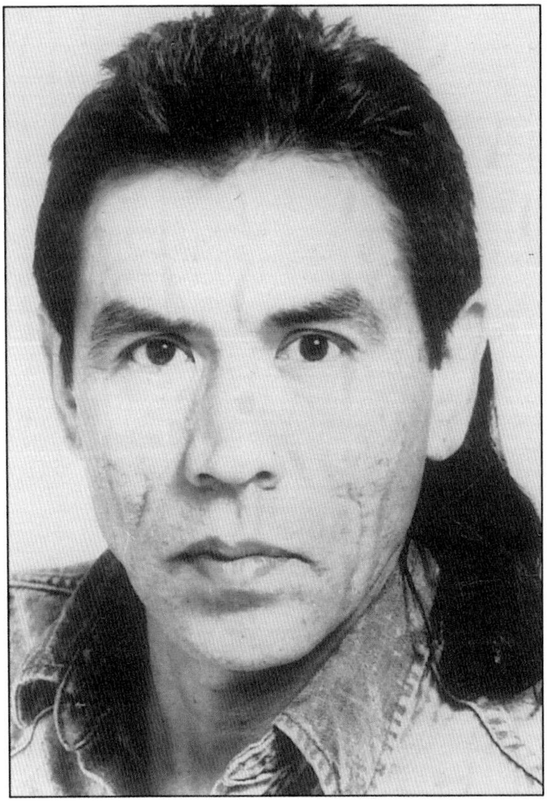

ACTOR WES STUDI. Raised in Nofire Hollow in the Cherokee Nation, Studi spoke his native language from birth. Wes starred in the movie *Geronimo* and stole the show as Magua in *Last of the Mohicans*. The celebrated actor and Cherokee Medal of Honor recipient returns regularly to the Nation and is often involved in tribal activities that promote his native culture. (Courtesy of Cherokee Honor Society.)

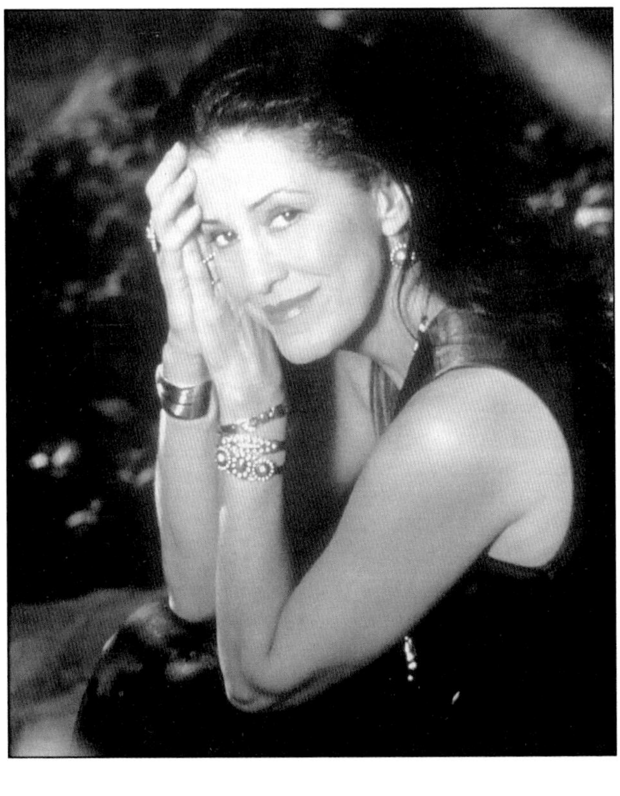

SONGWRITER RITA COOLIDGE. Grammy Award winner and star of rock, pop, and country music, Rita Coolidge speaks proudly of her Native American roots. One-half Cherokee, Rita shares the stage with her sister Priscilla Coolidge and her niece Laura Satterfield. They perform as "Walela," Cherokee for "hummingbird." The Cherokee Honor Society awarded Rita with its Cherokee Medal of Honor for her accomplishments. (Courtesy of Cherokee Honor Society.)

Novelist Robert J. Conley. Showing off his Cherokee sense of humor and wit, young Robert Conley looks like a character from his paperback westerns. Robert's dramatic historical novels, such as *Mountain Windsong* and *Ned Christie's War*, bring his readers into the very heart and soul of the Cherokee experience. This award-winning writer is a respected founding member of the Cherokee Honor Society. (Courtesy of Evelyn Conley.)

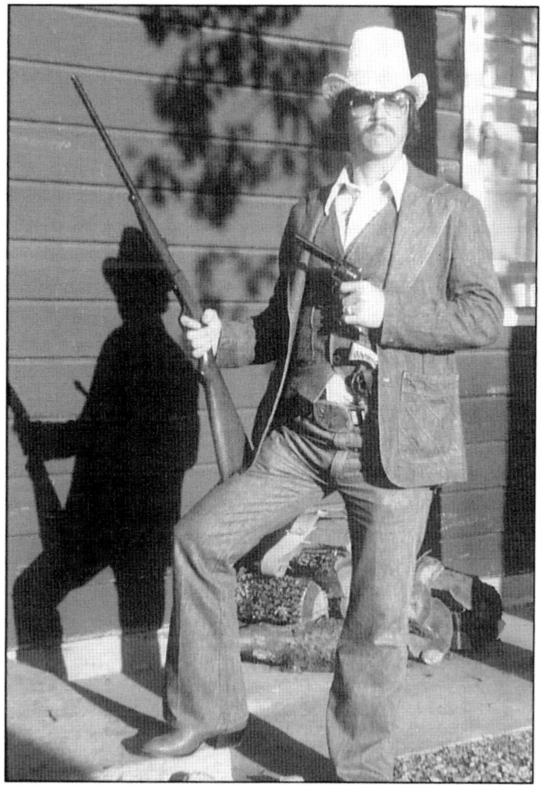

Songwriter John D. Loudermilk. This Cherokee writer of hit songs recorded by artists such as Johnny Cash, Roy Orbison, and the Allman Brothers, is himself a great performer. "Tobacco Road," "Windy and Warm," and "Break My Mind" only begin the list of favorites. John's "Indian Reservation" made "Cherokee" a household word. Awarded the Cherokee Medal of Honor, John lives and works outside Nashville. (Courtesy of Cherokee Honor Society.)

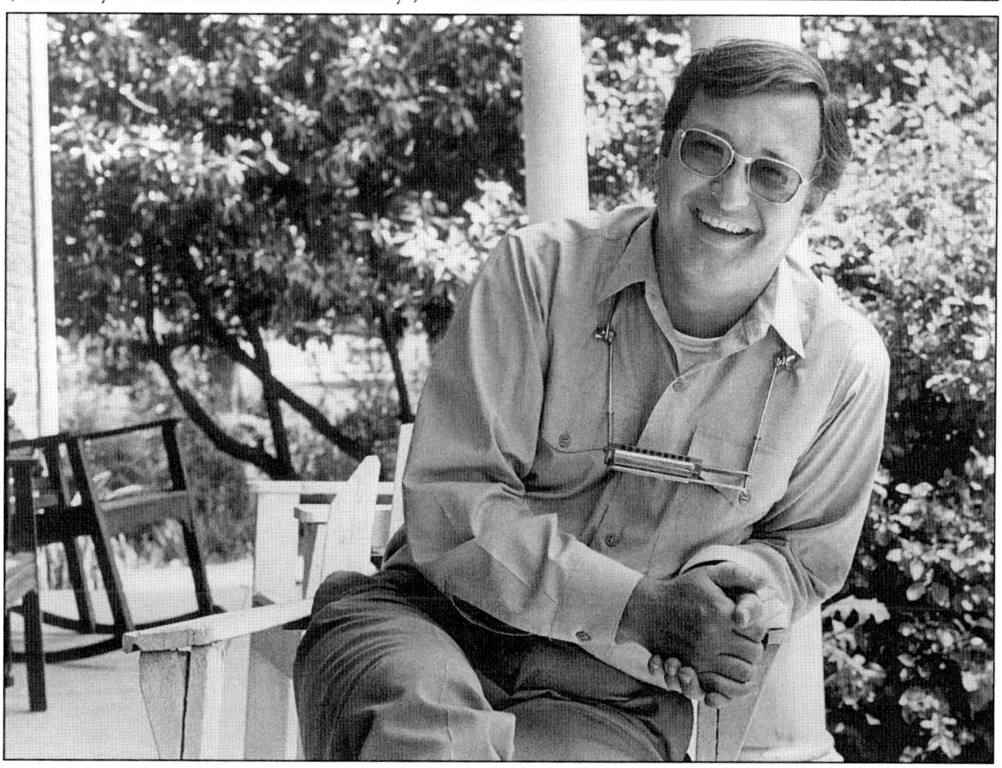

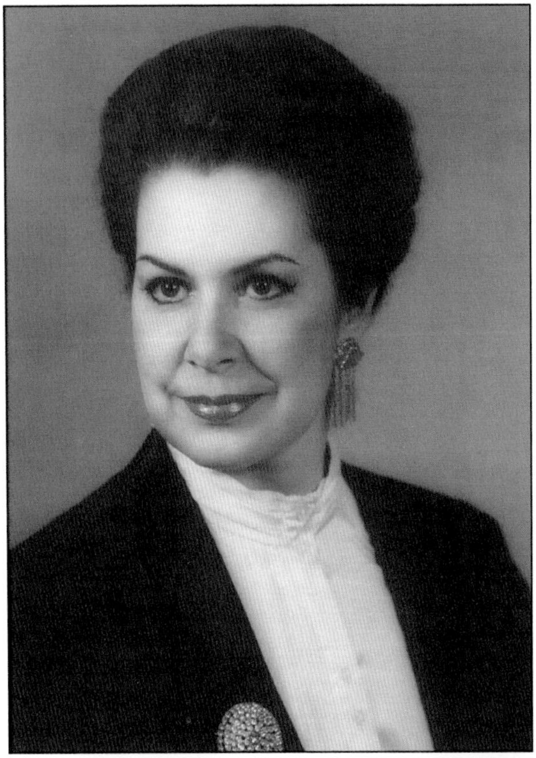

Opera Star Barbara McAlister. When performing solo at Carnegie Hall, in Paris opera houses, or in the Cherokee capital, Barbara's vibrant voice is dramatic and impressive. In addition to her award-winning vocal skills, Barbara speaks fluent Cherokee, Chippewa, and Winnebago and is a respected visual artist. Barbara received the Cherokee Medal of Honor for her dedicated cultural work. (Courtesy of Cherokee Honor Society.)

Impressario Jim Halsey. For 50 years, Halsey managed the careers of greats in the music business, such as the Oak Ridge Boys, Lee Greenwood, Reba McEntire, and Clint Black. A recipient of the Cherokee Medal of Honor, Jim appears here with his wife, famed artist Minisa Crumbo, and Pres. George Bush. Jim arranged the only Native American art show ever held in the Soviet Union. (Courtesy of Cherokee Honor Society.)

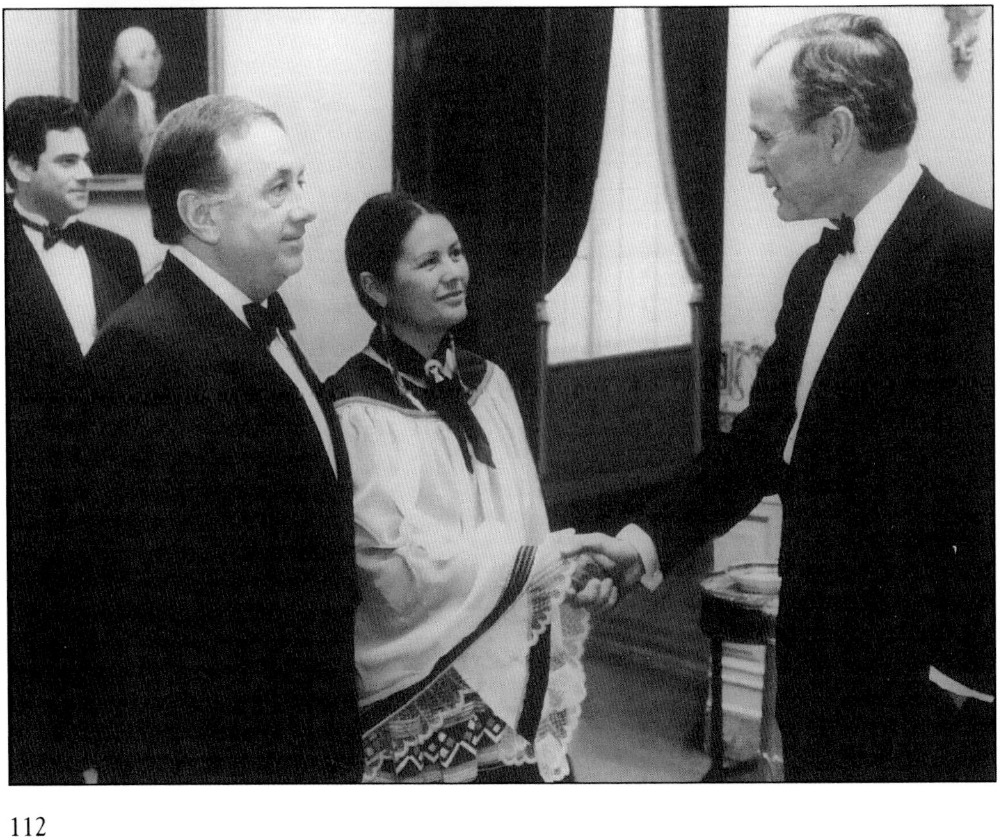

Seven

TRADITION

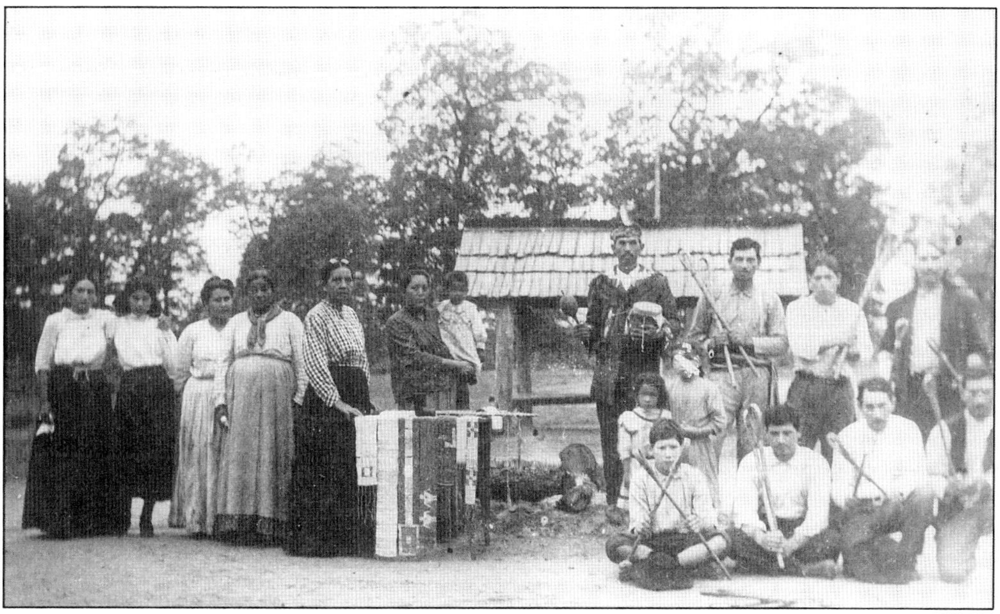

TRADITIONAL CHEROKEES, EARLY 1900S. The ancient and secret religion of the Cherokees was revived in 1859 by Baptist missionary Evan Jones. After the Civil War, Redbird Smith again reorganized the Keetoowah Society. Meetings in those days were held in secret at night, and religious dances and ceremonies took place on sacred days throughout the year. As time passed, outsiders were invited to attend ceremonies that the visitors respected and enjoyed. Pictured here is Redbird Smith's son (with rattle and drum) and a group of Nighthawk Keetoowahs. The men will participate in a game of stickball in accordance with tradition. The women stand near the sacred wampum belts. The belts, woven of clam shell beads, record the ancient history of the Cherokees. Atop the belts is a large smoking pipe for ceremonial use. Descendants of Redbird Smith still guard the precious belts and the original seal of the Keetoowah Society as Nighthawk groups continue to keep the centuries-old religion alive. (Courtesy of Cherokee National Archives.)

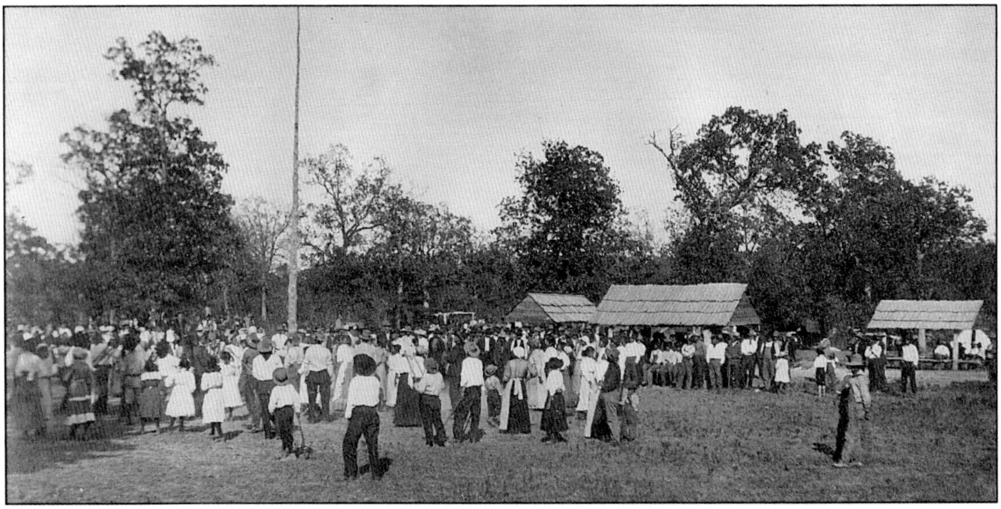

Ceremonial Grounds, early 1900s. A large crowd gathers at the ceremonial grounds near Vian in Indian Territory. This may be the Green Corn festival, when prayers are sent up for a good harvest. The tall pole holds the target for the stickball game. (Courtesy Cherokee National Archives.)

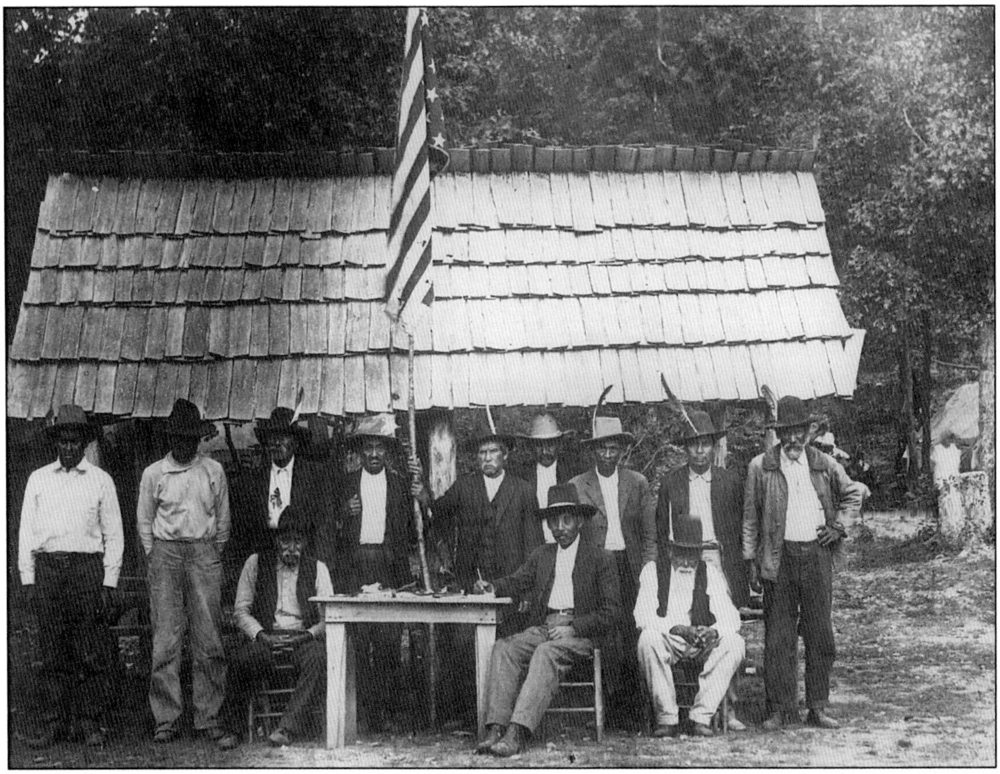

Nighthawk Meeting, early 1900s. Two Keetoowahs steady the American flag at a society business meeting. Each man wears a prominent feather on his hat. Perhaps they follow the advice of Sequoyah. He felt that Cherokees dressed and looked too much like white men. He encouraged them to proudly wear a feather to identify themselves as Cherokees. (Courtesy of Cherokee National Archives.)

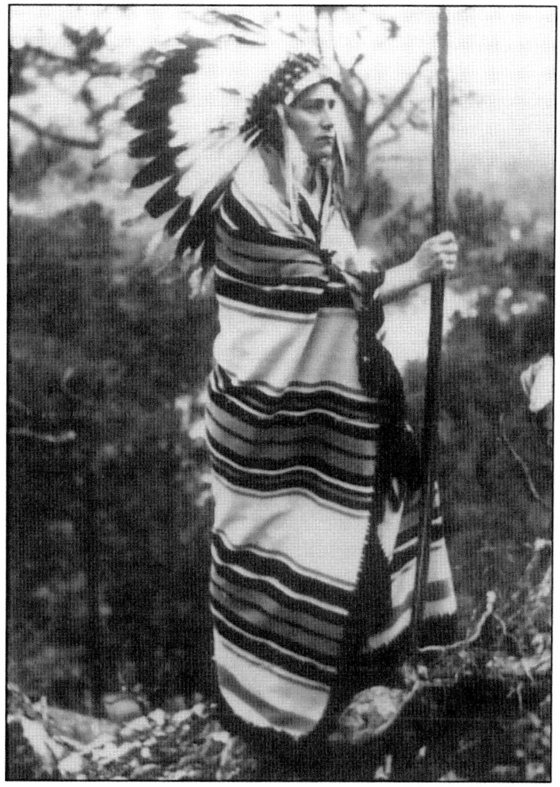

Looking the Part, c. 1919. Robert Lee Sanders, a direct descendant of "Beloved Woman" Nancy Ward, stands on a bluff overlooking the river. He wears the headdress and robe of a plains native and is posing for a picture postcard company. The caption reads, "Cherokee Indian by the Illinois River, Tahlequah, Oklahoma." (Courtesy of Sally Sanders Finch.)

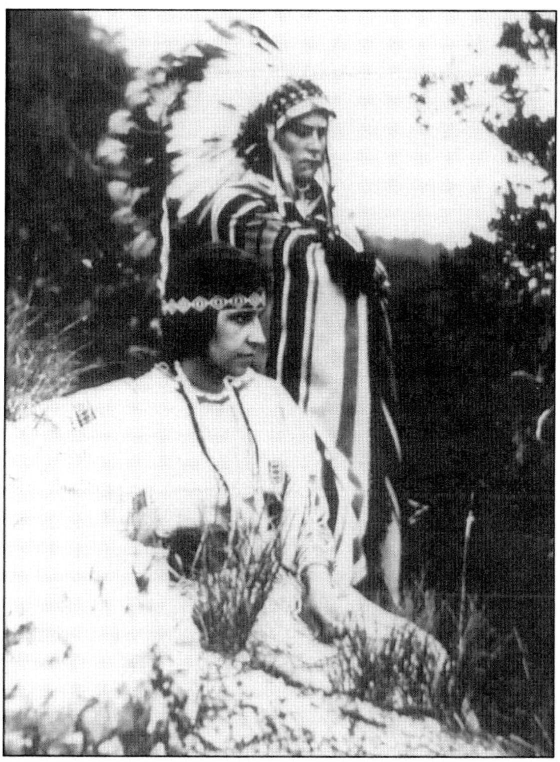

Not Quite Cherokee, c. 1919. Anne Ross joins in on the fun of dressing up like a "real Indian" for the camera. Though she and Robert look authentic, the look is definitely not Cherokee. Even in modern times, visitors arrive in the Cherokee Nation expecting to find the people living in teepees. (Courtesy of Sally Sanders Finch.)

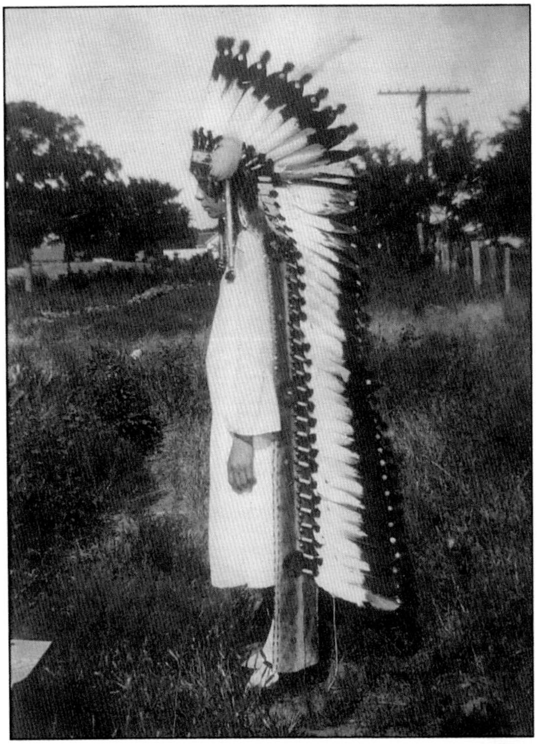

Ida C. Canada, Dancer, c. 1916. Original enrollee Ida C. Canada of the Cherokee Wolf Clan is not making a postcard. Shown here in full headdress, Ida is preparing to dance at a powwow. Though not culturally Cherokee, the tradition is practiced by many other Oklahoma tribes, such as the Kiowas, who honor members of other tribes by inviting them to participate. (Courtesy of Duane Canada.)

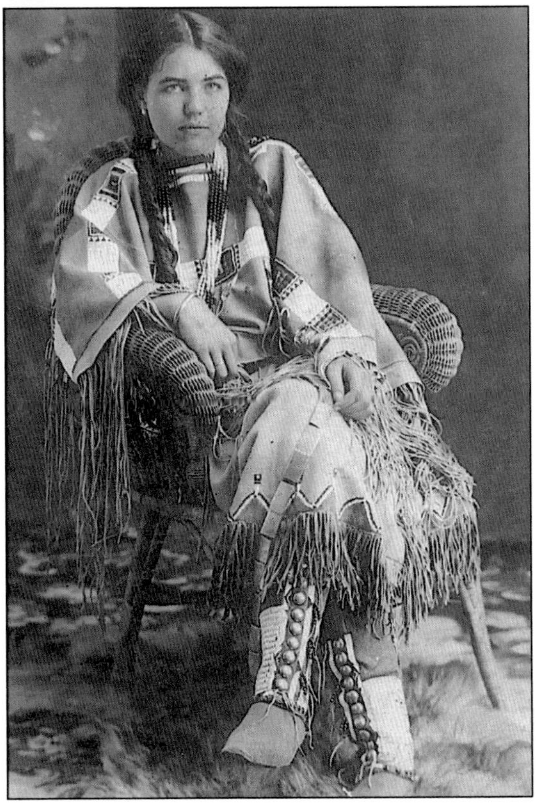

Maudelia Chitwood, early 1900s. This lovely young lady could easily be mistaken for a plains Indian, but she is Cherokee. A member of the Chitwood family, she is the younger sister of Jimalee Burton, a performer known as Ho Chee Nee. (Courtesy of Cherokee National Archives.)

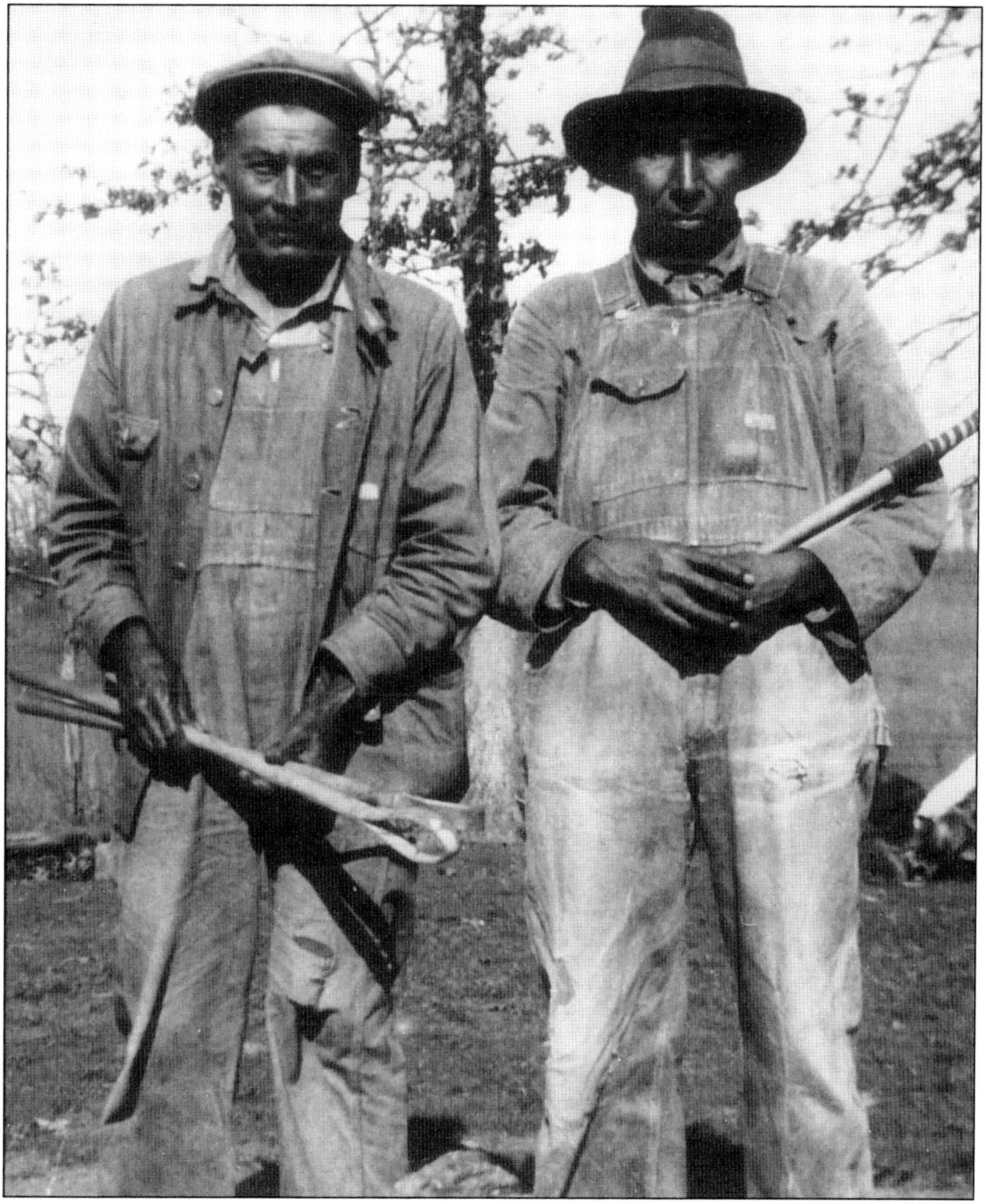

True Cherokee Traditionalists, c. 1925. Full-blood stomp dance leaders Thomas Pigeon (left) and Mr. Mose reflect the true image of Cherokee tradition. In Cherokee culture you will not find feather headdresses, but you will find stickball. The sticks the men carry have been precision made by hand. The skills required to play the game develop over much time and practice, and the game itself is rigorous. But today's game is mild in comparison to the old practice of stickball. Once known as the "little brother of war," stickball games would often be called to settle disputes between neighboring villages. The old playing field had goals at either end, defended by each team. Scores were won by getting the tiny ball to the goal. The problem was getting there. Preparation took days of fasting and prayer, and teams would taunt each other until the actual meeting on the field where the intense spectacle took place. (Courtesy of Betty Holcomb.)

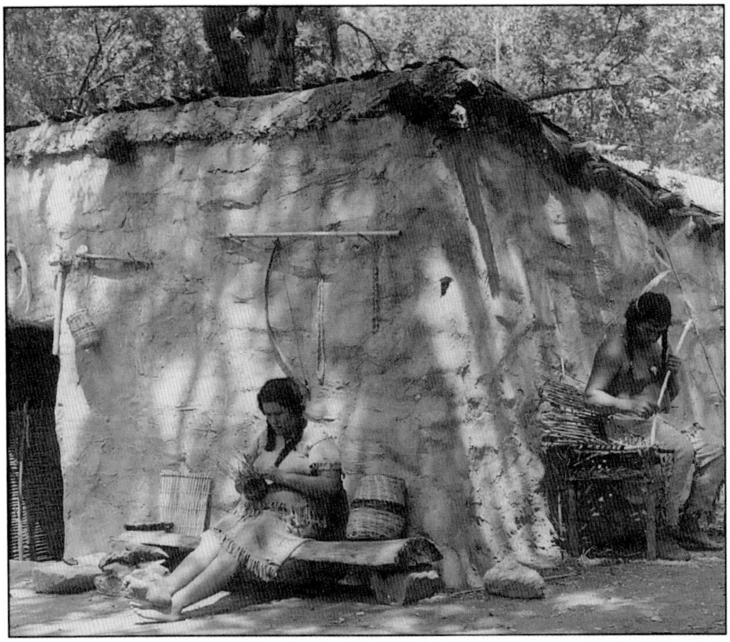

ANCIENT VILLAGE AT TSA-LA-GI. Cherokees demonstrate basket weaving and arrow making at Tahlequah's Ancient Village at Tsa-La-Gi (the Cherokee word for "Cherokee"). The village is a popular attraction where visitors learn about pre-Columbian Cherokee life. Local artisans have staffed the village every summer for more than 30 years. (Courtesy of Cherokee National Archives.)

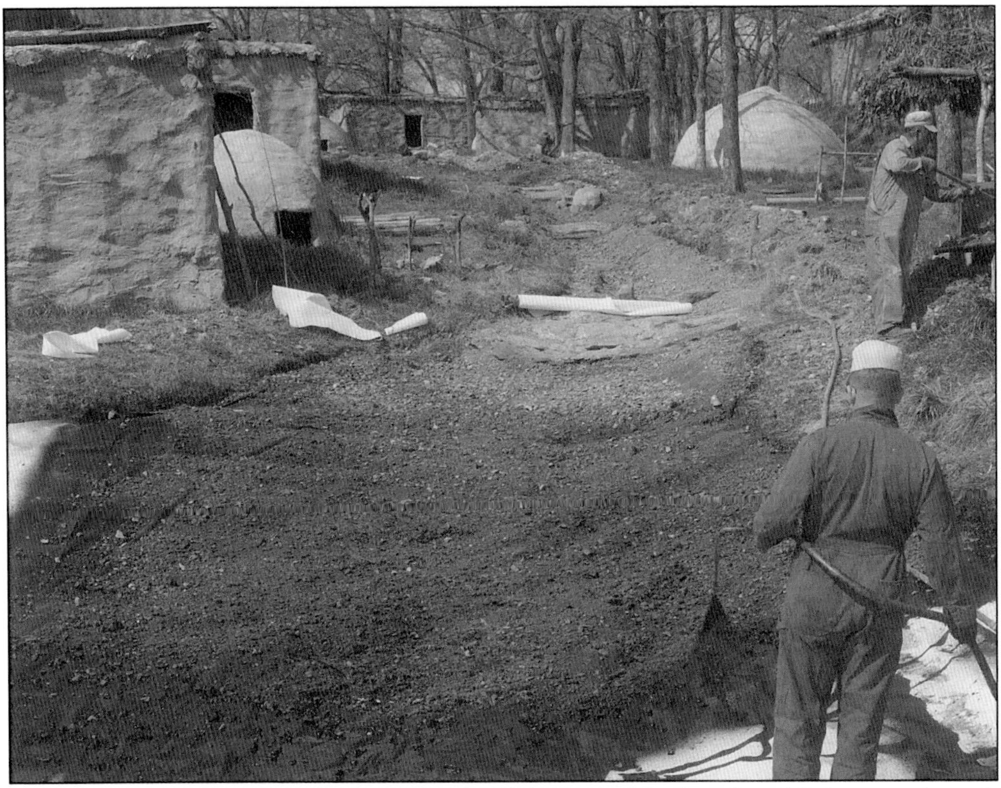

CONSTRUCTION OF THE VILLAGE. Engineers build the natural-looking "creek" that runs through the village at Tsa-La-Gi. In ancient times, walls of the houses were made of woven saplings or river cane covered with a clay mixture. The rounded structure was heated by fire on winter days for a warm sleeping area. (Courtesy of Cherokee National Archives.)

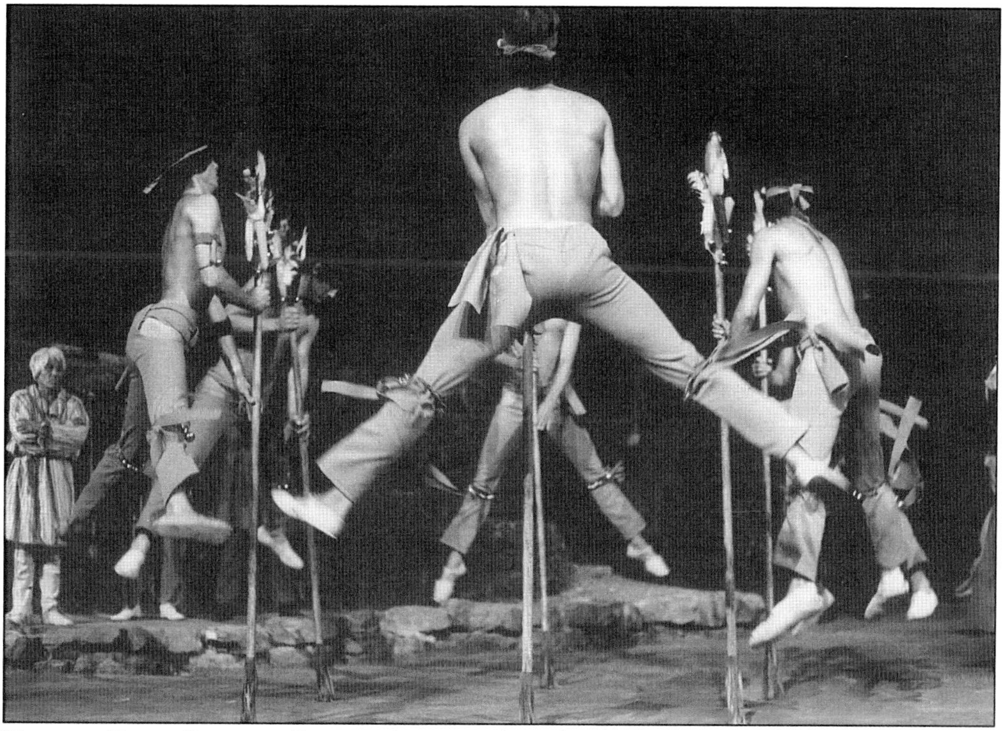

TRAIL OF TEARS OUTDOOR DRAMA. Actors perform the Green Corn Dance on the stage of the Amphitheater at Tsa-La-Gi. This scene reflects the pageantry of the popular Trail of Tears drama, performed for decades in Tahlequah. The production, which traces the Cherokee story from the Trail of Tears to Oklahoma statehood, has brought world-wide attention to the Cherokee Nation. (Courtesy of Cherokee National Archives.)

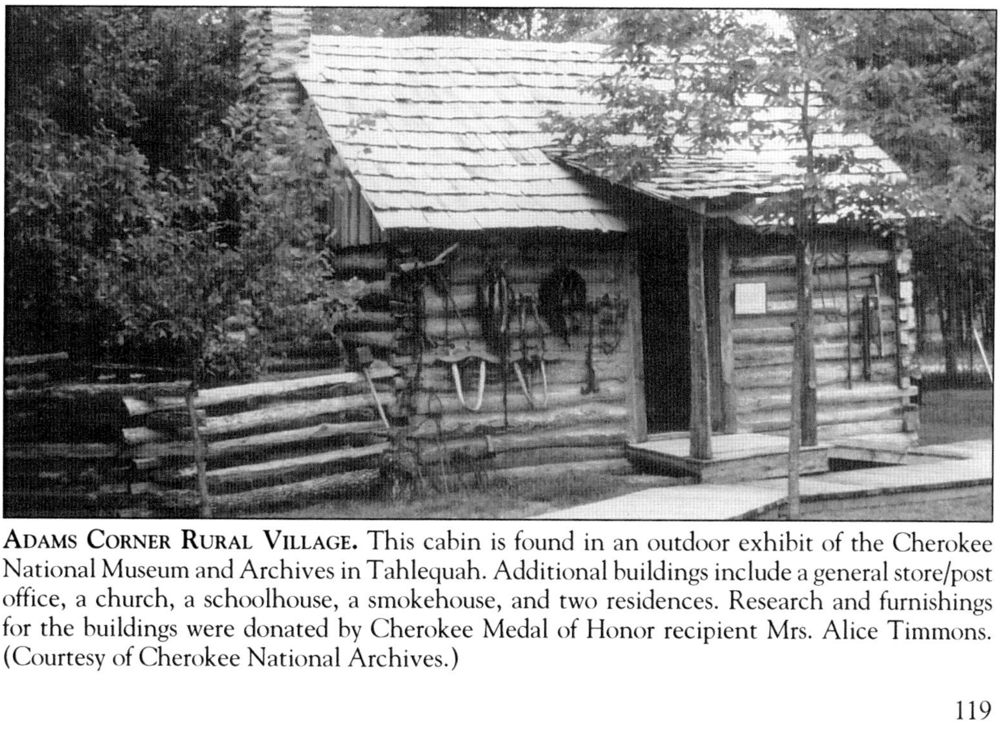

ADAMS CORNER RURAL VILLAGE. This cabin is found in an outdoor exhibit of the Cherokee National Museum and Archives in Tahlequah. Additional buildings include a general store/post office, a church, a schoolhouse, a smokehouse, and two residences. Research and furnishings for the buildings were donated by Cherokee Medal of Honor recipient Mrs. Alice Timmons. (Courtesy of Cherokee National Archives.)

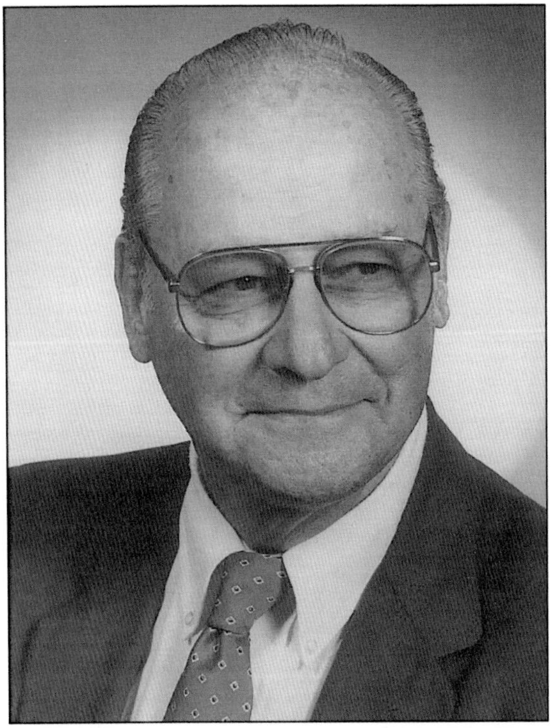

Col. Martin A. Hagerstrand. Marty Hagerstrand founded the Cherokee National Historical Society and conceived of and built Tahlequah's beautiful Cherokee Heritage Center, home to the Trail of Tears Drama, the Cherokee National Museum, and the Ancient Village at Tsa-La-Gi. Awarded the Cherokee Medal of Honor, Marty continued his work of uplifting Oklahomans until he was 87 years old. (Courtesy of Cherokee Honor Society.)

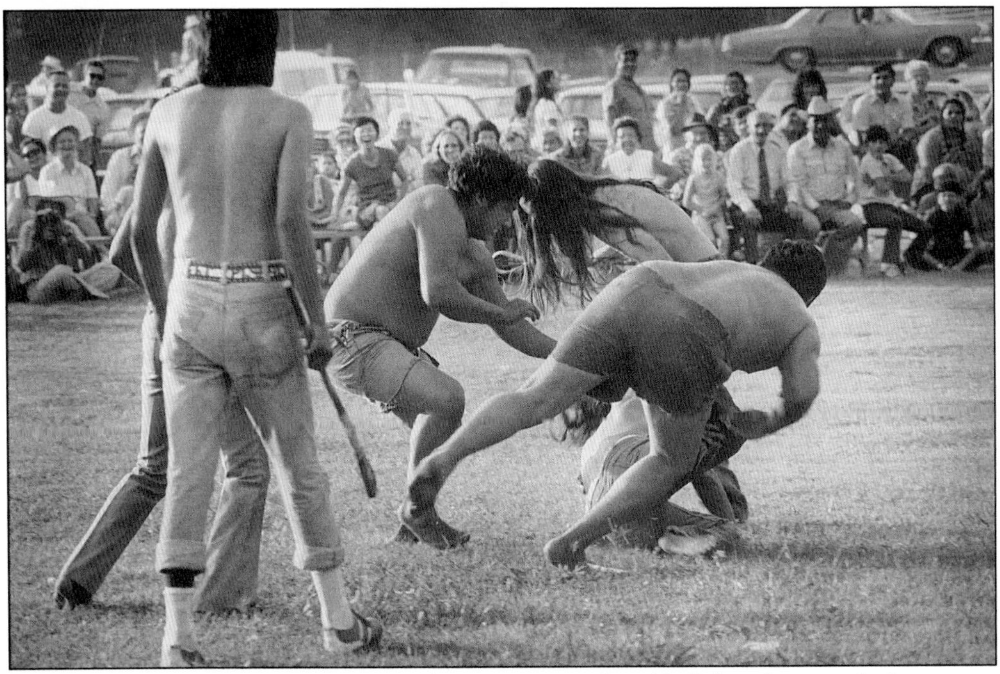

East Meets West in Tahlequah. A historic game of stickball has the crowd cheering as players from the Eastern Band of Cherokees go against locals from the Cherokee Nation. The match, the first ever held between the two groups, was won by the Eastern Band. The game was organized by Chad Smith, great-grandson of Redbird Smith, a skilled stickball player. (Courtesy of Cherokee National Archives.)

Cecil Dick, the Father of Cherokee Painting. Around his neck, Cecil wears the prized Sequoyah Medal, a distinction shared with Sequoyah himself. Cecil Dick's career as a painter of authentic Cherokee artwork and murals spanned 50 years. Cecil researched and painted the culture and history of his southeastern ancestors, teaching and encouraging other artists to follow suit. (Courtesy of Cherokee National Archives.)

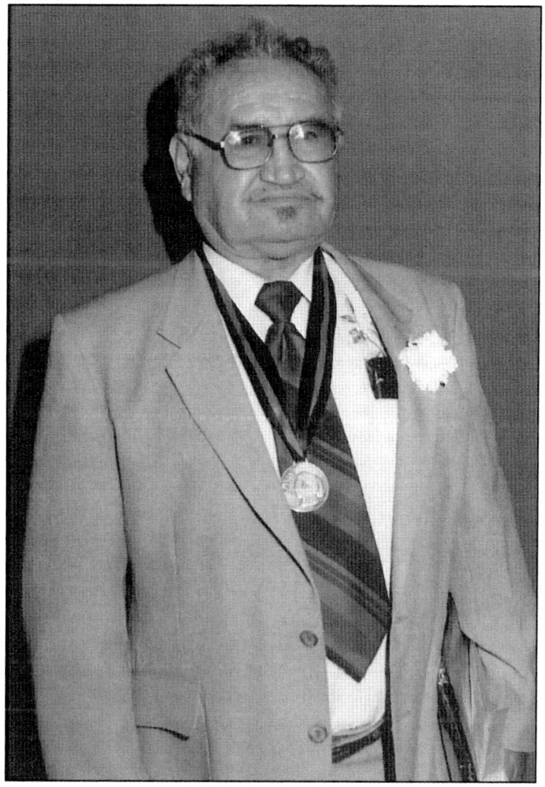

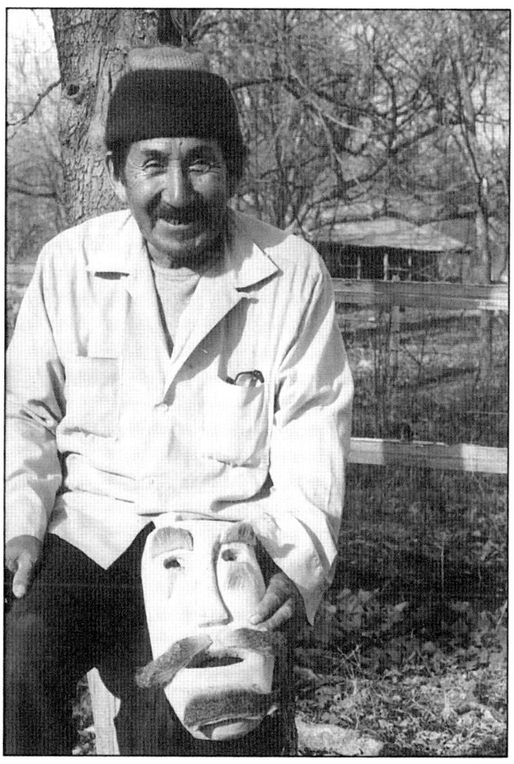

Traditionalist Sam Mellowbug. Sam Mellowbug, a woodcarver and traditional Cherokee doctor, lived at Rocky Ford in the Cherokee Nation. Teachings were passed to Sam from his great-great-grandmother. At the age of seven and able to read and write Cherokee, she kept a diary of her journey along the Trail of Tears that is still owned by the family. (Courtesy of Murv Jacob.)

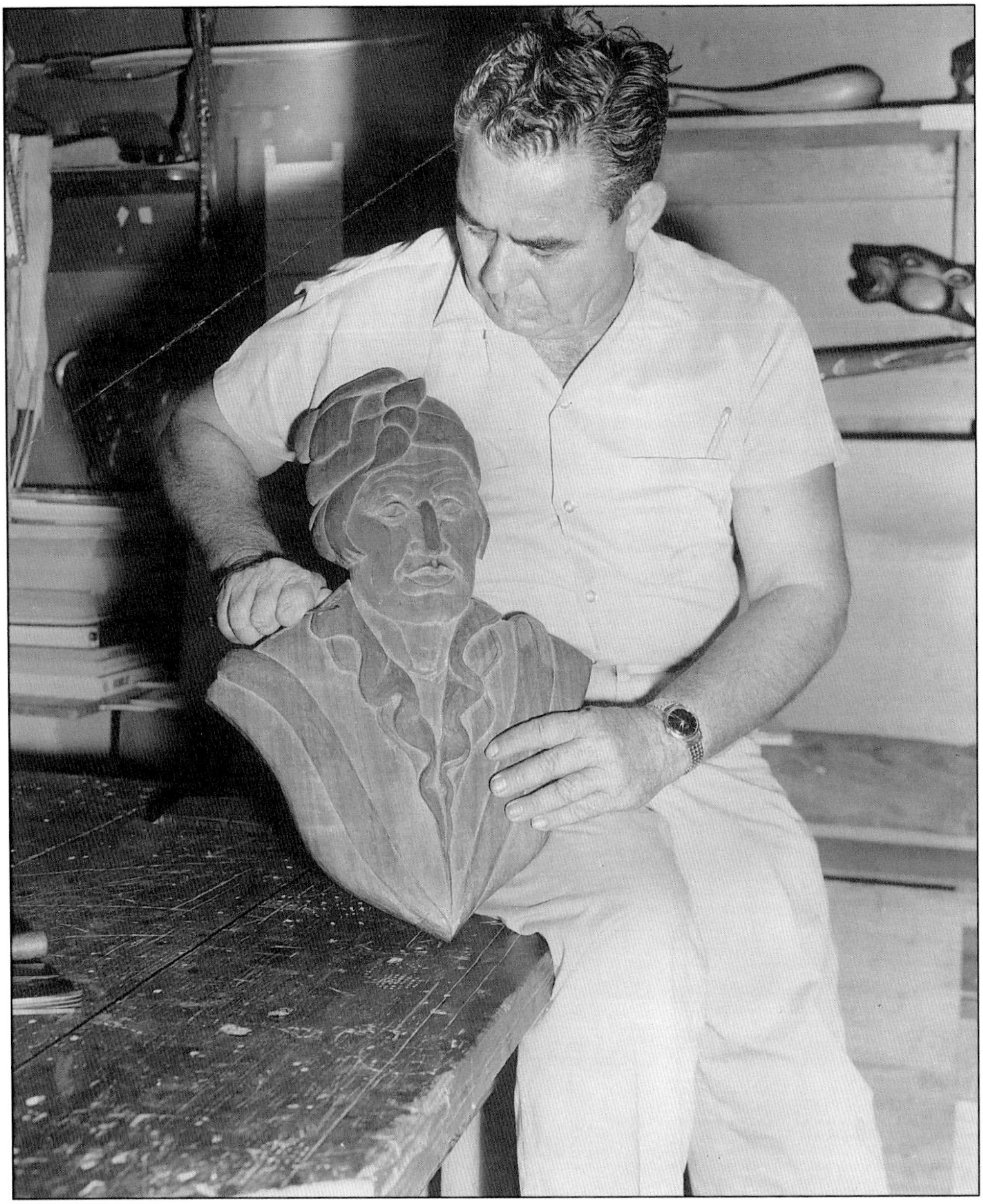

WOODCARVER WILLARD STONE. Internationally acclaimed Cherokee woodcarver Willard Stone was the foremost carver to ever live in Oklahoma. He is pictured here working on an image of Spring Frog, the famous Cherokee leader. Willard studied art at Bacone College along with fellow artist Cecil Dick. Willard and Cecil remained fast friends throughout Stone's life. His sons, Jason Stone and Dwight Stone, learned from the master and carry on his skills. Jason is a full-time woodcarver who lives and works at Willard's home in Locust Grove. His mother operates the Willard Stone Museum there. Willard Stone's most famous piece is entitled "Exodus," his tribute to the Cherokee Trail of Tears. The walnut sculpture is proudly displayed at the Cherokee National Museum in Tahlequah. "Exodus" has become a treasured symbol of the endurance, courage, and strength of the Cherokee people. (Courtesy of Cherokee National Archives.)

STORYTELLER GAYLE ROSS. One of America's best-known storytellers, Gayle Ross learned the old stories and legends from her Cherokee grandmother. Gayle has also written several illustrated books of Cherokee stories. A direct descendant of Principal Chief John Ross, Gayle is an outspoken advocate of Cherokee tradition and culture, as well as a wellspring of knowledge. Gayle is a founding member of the Cherokee Honor Society. (Courtesy of Gayle Ross.)

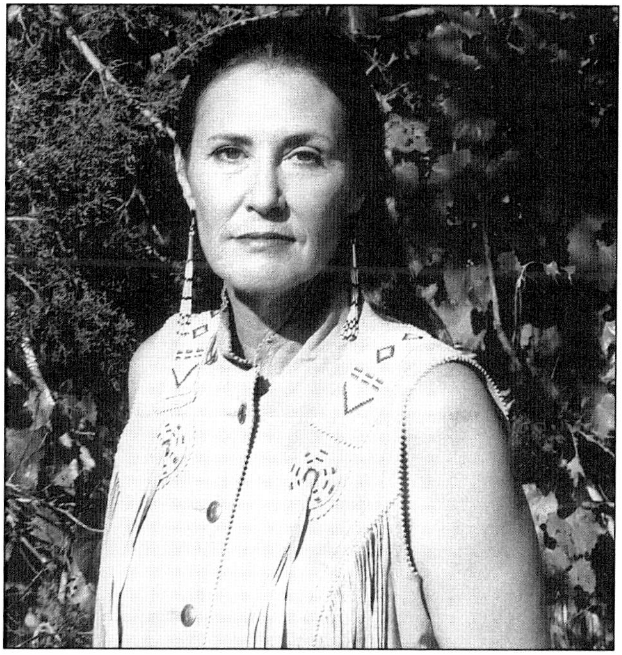

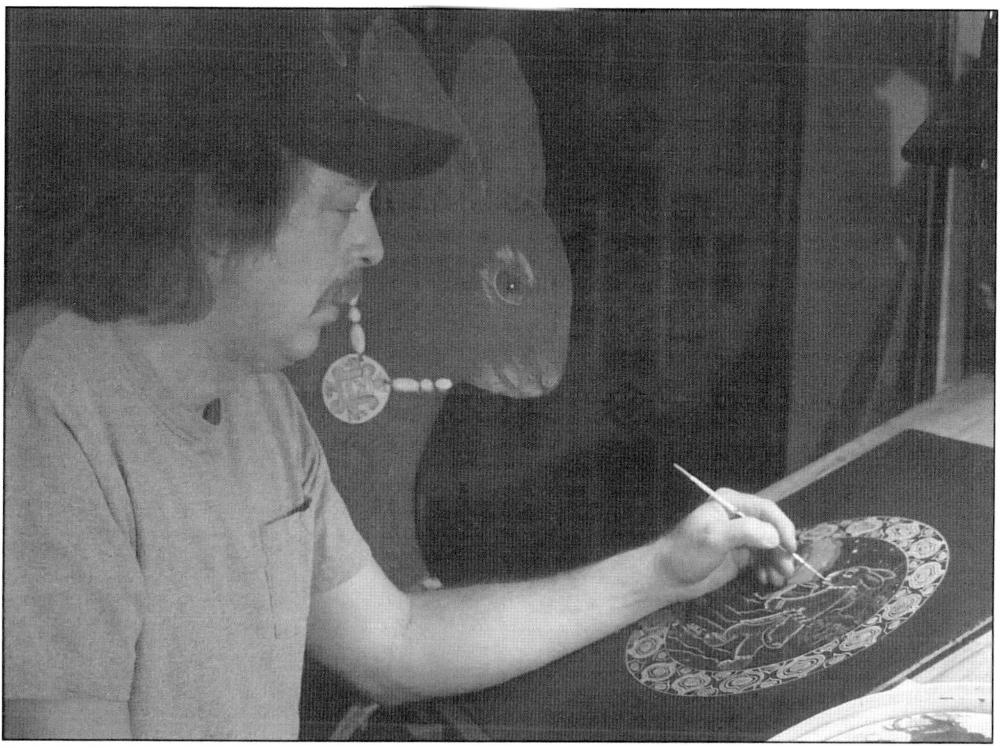

PAINTER/ILLUSTRATOR MURV JACOB. A transplanted Kansan now living in Tahlequah, Jacob has illustrated over 50 book and video projects. He is noted for his brightly colored, intricately detailed paintings of the ancient Cherokees and their legendary characters. Murv is shown here working with Rabbit, the Cherokee Trickster, who appears in many of his paintings. Murv is a founding member of the Cherokee Honor Society. (Courtesy of Cherokee Honor Society.)

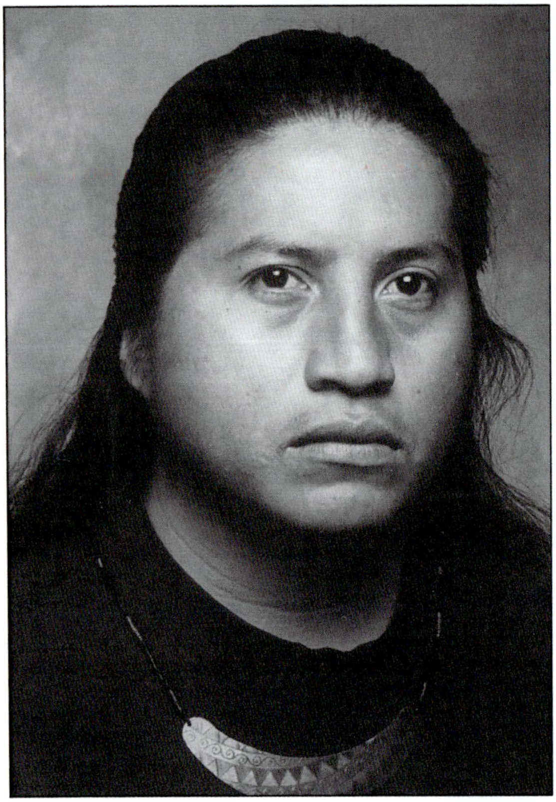

TRADITIONALIST TOMMY WILDCAT. This talented Tahlequah stomp dance leader and singer is of Cherokee, Creek, and Natchez ancestry. Tommy learned the ancient songs of these tribes from his father, one of the last Natchez speakers. In turn, Tommy taught the old dances to many. A founding member of the Cherokee Honor Society, Tommy Wildcat travels extensively, sharing the culture and tradition of his people. (Courtesy of Cherokee Honor Society.)

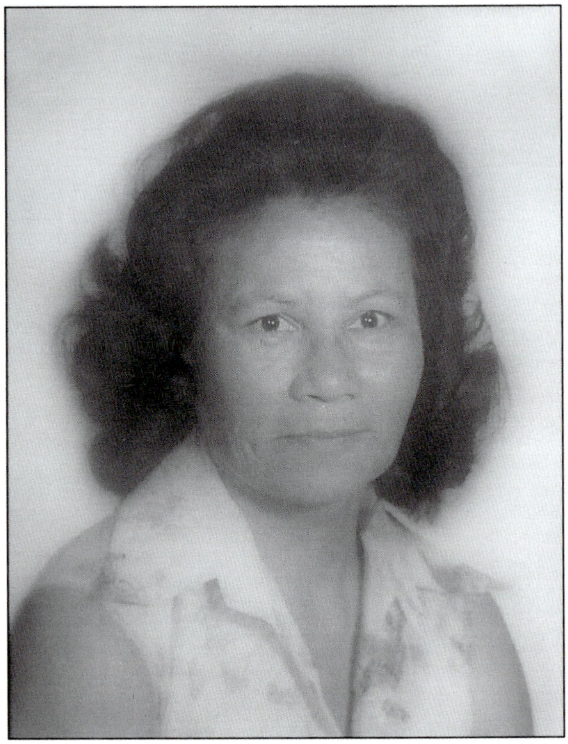

TRADITIONALIST BETTY SMITH. Cherokee National Treasure Betty Smith of Hulbert received the honor for her expertise in traditional cooking. She is an expert at preparing specialties like kanuche, a rich hickory nut-based soup, and wild grape dumplings. In addition, Betty is an accomplished potter, an actress, a former council member, a historian, and a beloved and respected Cherokee mother. Skilled artisans who work to preserve Cherokee culture and tradition are eligible to be named as living National Treasures by the tribe. (Courtesy of Cherokee National Archives.)

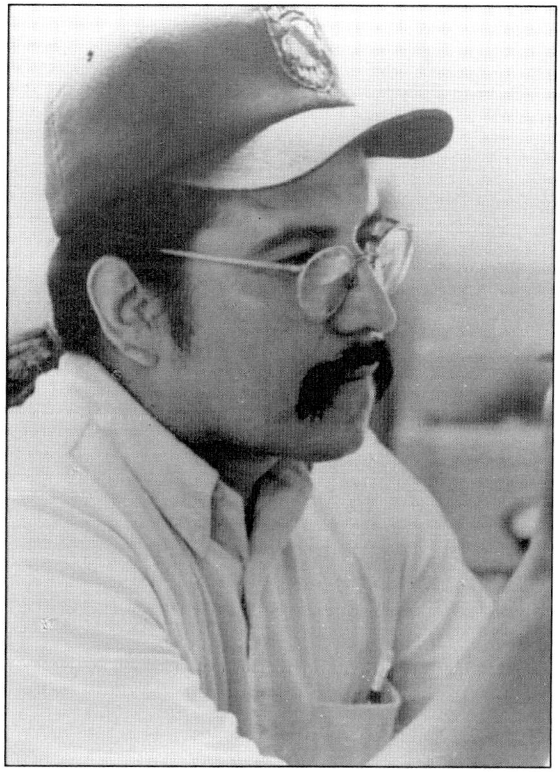

Ceramist Bill Glass Jr. Among his many awards, Bill Glass Jr. of Locust Grove received the Cherokee Medal of Honor for his work as a contemporary ceramist. Although he uses modern tools and methods, his subject matter is ancient. Bill's work is a beautiful testament to the rich cultural achievements of his southeastern ancestors. (Courtesy of Cherokee Honor Society.)

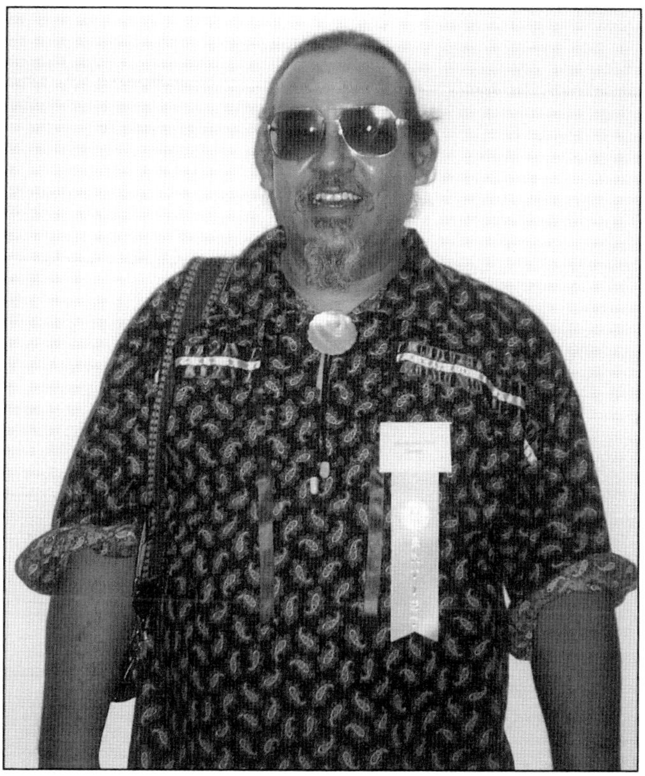

Shell Carver Knokovtee Scott. One of only three professional shell carvers, Knokovtee is preserving this ancient art form. From Rose, Oklahoma, he often uses pink mussel shell, native to the Cherokee Nation. The carvings feature designs of the southeastern mound culture. Knokovtee is Cherokee and Creek. His name in the Creek language means, "Clenched Fist." Knokovtee is a knowledgeable historian and a Cherokee National Treasure. (Courtesy of Cherokee Honor Society.)

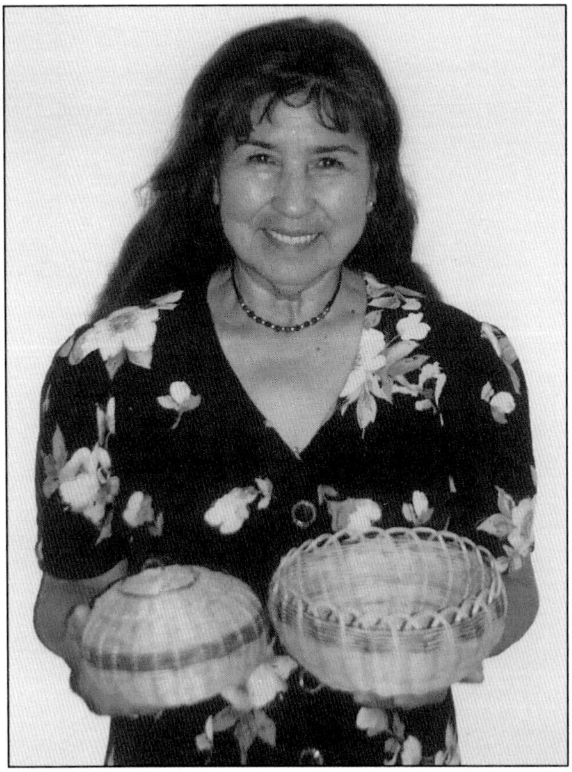

Basket Weaver Lena Blackbird. This lovely Tahlequah lady was named a Cherokee National Treasure for her skill in the ancient art of basket weaving. Lena has worked summers at the Ancient Village at Tsa-La-Gi for years, demonstrating her work and teaching the principles to young Cherokees. Her beautiful double-walled honeysuckle baskets are prized by collectors. (Courtesy of Cherokee Honor Society.)

Gig Maker Totum Hair. A traditional Cherokee blacksmith from the Wickliffe community, Totum Hair was named a Cherokee National Treasure for his exceptional ability to make fishing gigs. Totum is one of Oklahoma's finest fishermen and his hand-forged gigs are sought after by collectors. He is pictured holding two samples. (Courtesy of Cherokee Honor Society.)

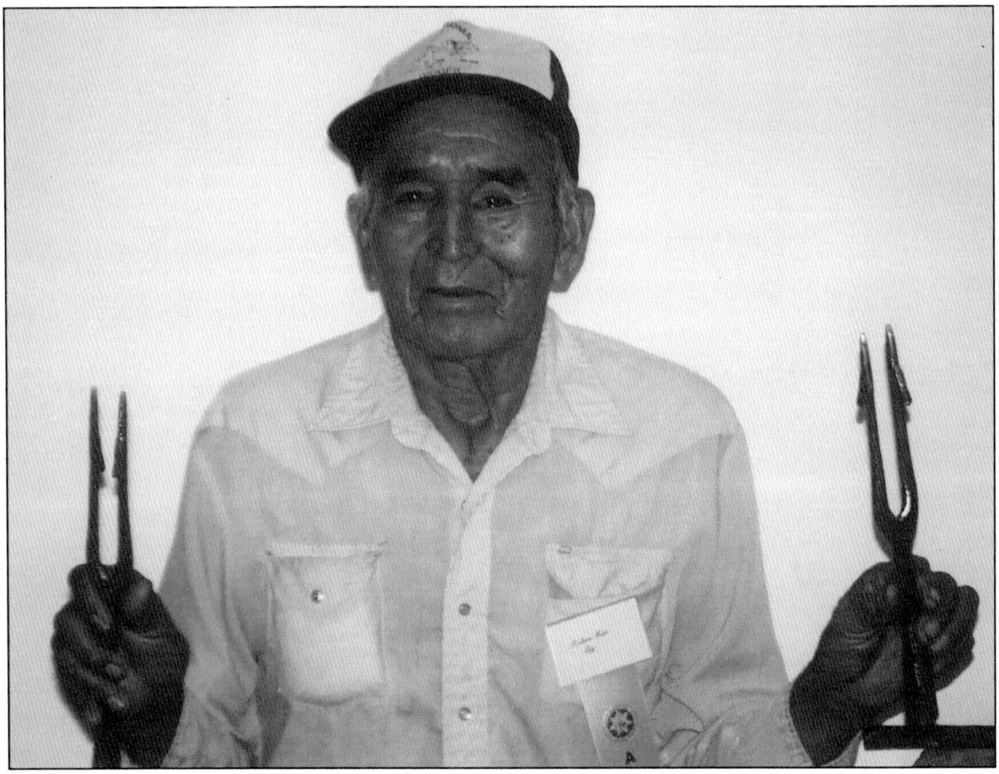

Bowmaker Noel "Tim" Grayson. Holding a handmade arrow and bow is one of the youngest of the living National Treasures of the Cherokee Nation. A Tahlequah native, Grayson has worked among his elders most of his life, learning how to select materials and create fine goods. (Courtesy of Cherokee Honor Society.)

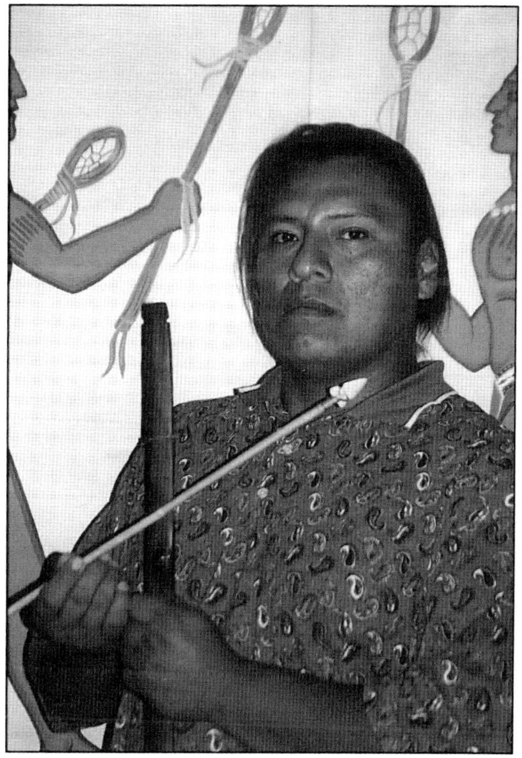

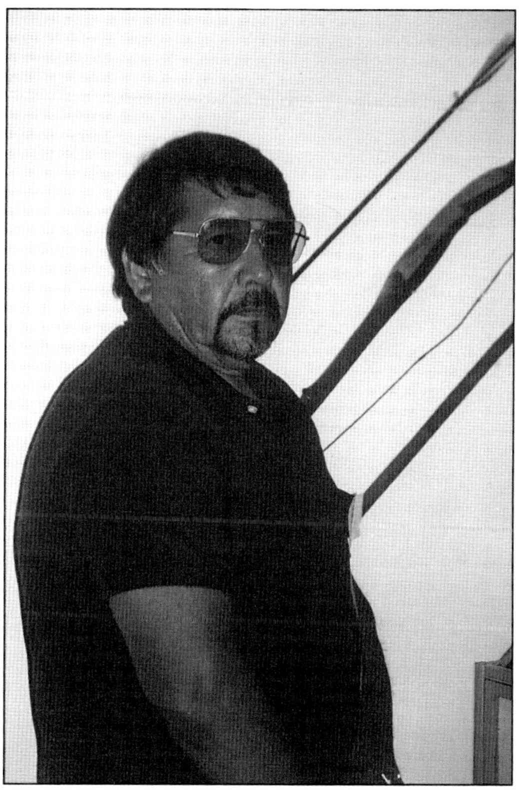

Traditionalist Hastings Shade. For years, Hastings Shade has traveled through the Cherokee Nation teaching Cherokee language and culture. Hastings is also a published writer and one of the few designers of the stone marbles used in the ancient Cherokee marble game. A Cherokee National Treasure from near the Hulbert community, Hastings Shade was elected deputy chief on July 24, 1999. (Courtesy of Cherokee Honor Society.)

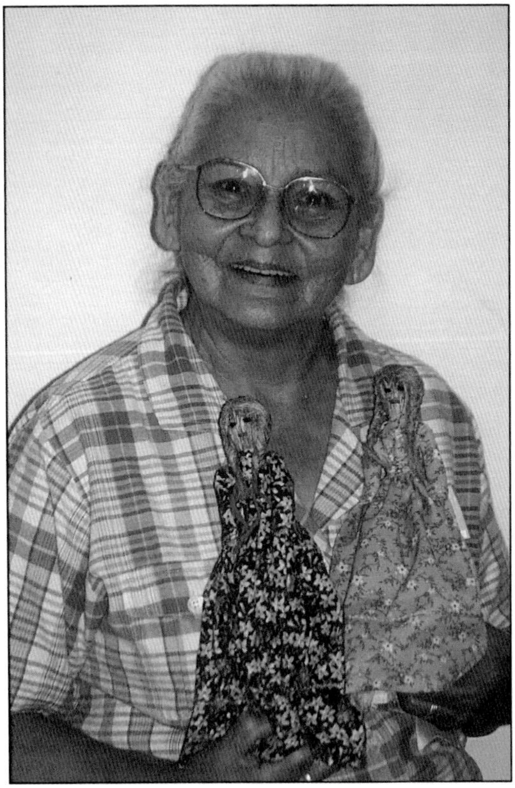

Doll Maker Lorene Drywater. Holding two beautiful buffalo grass dolls, with their tiny Cherokee tear dresses, is the equally beautiful Lorene Drywater. Lorene has revived and mastered this ancient art. Her efforts were rewarded when she was named a National Treasure by the Cherokee Nation. (Courtesy of Cherokee Honor Society.)

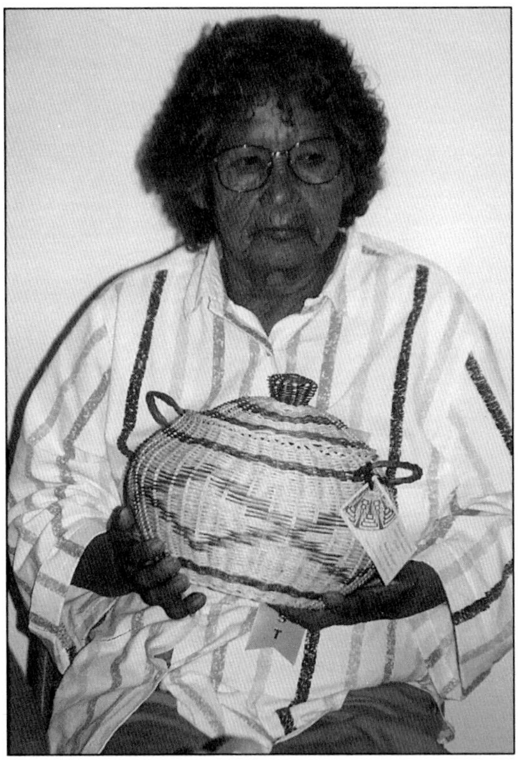

Basket Weaver Mary Foreman. Cherokee National Treasure Mary Foreman of Oaks is the undisputed master basket maker of the Cherokees. Her big, solid baskets are made from honeysuckle and buckbrush, gathered and prepared by hand. Her dyes come from natural sources like walnut, bloodroot, and poke berries. Mary's legacy is her unique contribution to the history and heritage of her beloved Cherokee Nation. (Courtesy of Cherokee Honor Society.)